Early Praise for *Pragmatic Unit Testing in Java with JUnit, Third Edition*

Jeff makes an interesting and readable presentation of the basics of unit testing. It's not just mechanics—you also get the benefit of his guidance in creating comprehensive and meaningful tests.

➤ **Bill Wake**
Consultant, XP123 LLC

I found *Pragmatic Unit Testing in Java with JUnit, Third Edition*, a fantastic read; even as an experienced Java developer, I was learning new tricks. If you would like to learn about TDD and how Unit Testing actively encourages clean code, read on. I think this will help developers up their game and increase their value.

➤ **James Bowen**
Senior Software Engineer, Commonwealth Bank of Australia

Pragmatic Unit Testing in Java with JUnit, Third Edition, is an essential guide for both novice and experienced developers. Jeff Langr provides clear, practical insights that make mastering unit testing and improving code quality accessible and enjoyable. A must-read for anyone serious about software craftsmanship.

➤ **Ahmed Misbah**
Chief Software Architect, Orange Innovation Egypt

The new material in this edition makes it a worthwhile read, especially the parts that focus on how tests support refactoring and TDD. Jeff goes beyond the mechanics of testing with a lot of great advice on elements of form and style. This book will help you take your testing practice up a few notches.

➤ **Junilu Lacar**
Executive Director, Dojo Coach

I'm embarrassed that I haven't read Jeff's book in the past. What he's gathered here is a practical path through what I feel to be the important bits of unit testing without beating you over the head with dogma. This most especially strikes me in the new section on generative AI—where Jeff hits you straight up with the reality of its limitations and through detailed examples offers a glimpse into practical ways you can use it today to strengthen your own abilities. I will be recommending this book wholeheartedly to all my coachees who work with Java!

➤ **Stacey Vetzal**
    Principal Agile Technical Excellence Coach, Royal Bank of Canada

As a young, entry-level programmer, *Pragmatic Unit Testing in Java with JUnit, Third Edition*, offered a simple approach to understanding Unit Testing and Test Driven Development, whilst making me chuckle throughout the read.

➤ **Clarice Levison**
    Computer technology student

The book stands out as a comprehensive guide that addresses the what, why, and how of unit testing with JUnit and beyond in great depth and breadth. It is an invaluable resource for individual developers and teams, novices, and veterans alike—a must-read for anyone working with the Java platform.

➤ **Wenyu Shi**
    Sr. Application Systems Developer, Columbia University

I am frequently advising on clean code matters and have a library of go-to resources—this book is my advice for anyone who wants to improve their unit testing.

➤ **Sebastian Larsson**
    Competence Team Lead, Knowit

I've been using JUnit since before it had a version number. I still learned something. Readability, the number one problem I see in code, Jeff tackles head-on.

➤ **Mark Levison**
    Certified Scrum Trainer and Agile Coach of 20 years experience

Pragmatic Unit Testing in Java with JUnit, Third Edition

Jeff Langr

The Pragmatic Bookshelf

Dallas, Texas

See our complete catalog of hands-on, practical,
and Pragmatic content for software developers:
https://pragprog.com

Sales, volume licensing, and support:
support@pragprog.com

Derivative works, AI training and testing,
international translations, and other rights:
rights@pragprog.com

The team that produced this book includes:

Publisher: Dave Thomas
COO: Janet Furlow
Executive Editor: Susannah Davidson
Development Editor: Kelly Talbot
Copy Editor: Karen Galle
Indexing: Potomac Indexing, LLC
Layout: Gilson Graphics

ISBN-13: 979-8-88865-103-2
Book version: P1.0—November 2024

Contents

Part II — Mastering JUnit with "E"s

Part IV — Bigger Topics Around Unit Testing

Foreword

If you'd told me 21 years ago that today I'd be writing the foreword for the third edition of our then fresh-off-the-press *Unit Testing in Java* book, I'd have laughed. Unit testing was a pretty obscure activity back then, practiced mostly by agile folk and other zealots. Our book was written with hope but also with no expectation that testing might become common.

Testing has had something of a wild ride between then and now. For maybe the first ten years, it grew to be first an accepted practice and later a mandated one. Teams who had never previously written automated tests found that they had a newfound confidence, both during initial development and, as importantly, when they later made changes. Testing was good.

Sometime during the start of the second decade, though, there seemed to be something of a sea change. Testing went from being a jolly good practice to being something of a religion. If you weren't on board with all the latest testing ideas, you were shunned. If you said out loud that you didn't always write tests, you became a pariah.

Now, though, things seem to be a little more rational.

Every single practice we follow as developers is contextual; there are no universal rules that every developer must follow. Testing is just one of these practices. Creating and maintaining tests is a good thing, except when it isn't. Tests can make it easier to refactor code until you find yourself spending an order of magnitude more time updating the tests than you did moving a function from module A to module B. Test coverage is a ridiculous metric to impose, but it's also a useful litmus test. Quite often, the code that isn't covered is the code that's hard to test, so that's code that needs refactoring anyway.

So, a pragmatic developer (like you) has to make informed decisions about testing, just as you do about all of your work. This is the book that gives you the knowledge and confidence to make those choices.

The More Things Change...

This book is almost unrecognizable from the first edition. Java has become more sophisticated, testing tools are more advanced, and, most importantly, our ideas about testing are more informed and refined.

Jeff has done an outstanding job of capturing all of this, producing a book that is both definitive and pragmatic.

Read it, and then choose wisely.

Dave Thomas
Programmer
Dallas, TX

Acknowledgments

A warm thank you to Jeff Bay, John Borys, James Bowen, Yves Dorfsman, Lars Eckart, Danny Faught, Michael Feathers, Nick Goede, Junilu Lacar, Tim Langr, Sebastian Larsson, Clarice Levison, Mark Levison, Ahmed Misbah, Cameron Presley, Wenyu Shi, Alexander Tarlinder, Dave Thomas, Merlijn Tishauser, Bill Wake, Stacey Vetzal, and all others who provided feedback. Your help is greatly appreciated!

Many thanks to my editor, Kelly Talbot, who provided gentle but stellar feedback and guidance throughout this third edition overhaul and helped me figure out some thorny organizational issues.

If you helped shape a prior edition with your feedback, thank you once again. And if you *wrote* a prior edition and aren't me—hello Dave Thomas and Andy Hunt—thanks for creating what's turned out to be an enduring book!

Finally, if you *bought* a prior edition of this book, thank you, and I still love you! Hopefully, you've been "test infected"[1] ever since. If so, you probably don't need another introductory book, but welcome back anyway. You'll definitely find a few new nuggets that pay for the low price of admission.

---

1. https://www1.udel.edu/CIS/474/pconrad/06S/topics/java/junit/gettingStarted/Test.Infected.Article.pdf

Preface

Andy Hunt and Dave Thomas wrote and published the first edition of this book in 2003, about five years after JUnit was introduced. Yet, if you told a 2003 Java developer to write tests to verify their own code, they'd likely have said, "Not a chance. I'm a programmer, not a tester."

Many developers since then have found value in unit testing. Rather than spend copious time manually testing their solutions and re-manually testing them with each change, these programmers write small tests (in Java) that verify small behaviors in the system. They run these tests through a tool (usually JUnit) and immediately discover if their logic is faulty.

A decade later, unit testing had become an expected developer skill and a common interview topic. At the request of Andy and Dave, I overhauled *Pragmatic Unit Testing in Java with JUnit* with additional topics and up-to-date code. I delivered the second edition in 2015.

By 2015, unit testing was a mandate from many managers and team leads who sought increased quality in their systems. Unfortunately, many of these mandates came with well-meaning but misguided metric goals, particularly around code coverage. Today, many teams are expected to meet code coverage goals (see Improving Unit Testing Skills Using Code Coverage, on page 71) of 80 percent, for example.

However, shops mandating coverage goals usually see a poor return on their unit testing investment. Many developers game the metric because they don't know how to fully leverage unit testing. They write just enough "tests" to meet the metric target. These tests provide very little value; they only minimally gate defects, they don't help document system behaviors, and they afford little safety for improving the design via refactoring.

For too many developers, the taste for unit testing has soured as a result.

We're another decade on, and unit testing has survived and even thrived in some shops, embraced by people who've learned to practice it properly. Its most dedicated practitioners continually write tests to guide the development of code in a practice known as test-driven development (TDD). They achieve near-comprehensive code coverage in the form of fast unit tests. These tests gate most logic defects, document *all* unit behaviors, and provide the utmost confidence to continually clean the code.

No other testing form can help you effectively manage and document the thousands of unit behaviors embodied in your system. Well-written unit tests provide feedback within seconds after each tiny change you make.

This third edition of *Pragmatic Unit Testing in Java with JUnit* represents the staying power of a technique that remains relevant decades after its first formal use. This book has been overhauled—simplified, rewritten, and reorganized to make learning more accessible. Virtually all code examples have been reworked to use Java 21. Many code examples have been reworked to simplify or expand on key concepts, and numerous examples have been added. It extends coverage on JUnit itself and includes a new discussion on testing code generated by an LLM.

Unit testing remains relevant in the age of AI. Until AI tooling can verify the code it writes (it cannot in 2024), you must vet that code with unit tests. Amusingly, AI can help you write those unit tests. Learn how in a new final chapter, Chapter 13, Keeping AI Honest with Unit Tests, on page 245.

Why Unit Testing

You are *unit testing* when you (a programmer) write test code to verify *units* of code. A unit is a small bit of code that exhibits some useful behavior in your system. A unit doesn't usually represent complete end-to-end behavior; it usually supports some small facet of functionality.

The unit tests you write will manipulate your units—small bits of code—directly. As such, you'll code them in Java. You'll run these tests through JUnit, a tool that marks your tests as passing or failing.

Here are a few *whens* and *whys* for writing/running unit tests:

- You finished coding a feature and want to ensure it works as expected.

- You want to document a change so that you and others later understand the choices you coded into the system.

- You changed the code and want to know if you broke anything.

- You want to understand the current behavior of the system.

Most importantly, good unit tests increase your confidence to ship your production system. You still need *integration* and/or *acceptance* tests, which verify end-to-end behavior. This book focuses only on unit tests.

After reading this book, you'll be able to produce lots of unit tests in no time. Take care—it's easy to create lots of costly-to-maintain tests that provide little value. Heed the advice in this book to ensure your investment in unit testing continues to pay off.

Who This Book Is For

This book is an information-loaded introductory book for programmers (comfortable with Java programming) new to unit testing. You'll learn just about everything you need to dive into testing your production systems.

What You Need

To follow along and code the examples shown in this book, you'll need the following three pieces of software:

- *Java*: The examples in this book use Java 21. You can find numerous sources for downloading Oracle and alternative implementations.

- *An IDE*: The examples in this book were built using IntelliJ IDEA (which is available as both a free "community" edition as well as a licensed product), but you can use Eclipse, NetBeans, VSCode, vim, Emacs, or pretty much any editor.

- *JUnit*: JUnit is usually a dependency that your build tool (Gradle or Maven, mostly) will retrieve.

JUnit has been the de facto Java unit testing standard for 25 years, though other tools exist. This book's examples use JUnit 5 (also known as JUnit Jupiter), which supports Java version 8 or higher.

JUnit is shipped with most major IDEs, including IntelliJ IDEA, Eclipse, and NetBeans. For VSCode users, JUnit support is included with its Extension Pack for Java plugin.

If your team uses another unit testing tool, the vast majority of this book still applies to your world. Most of this book focuses on unit testing concepts and best practices, not a specific tool. Unit testing tools are fairly simple tools. As such, you'll still be able to readily understand the tests within this book and adapt them to tests that use your tool.

Refer to the individual product sites for details on how to download, install, and configure the development tools.

How This Book Is Organized

This book is divided into four main parts:

- *Unit Testing Foundations*: Learn JUnit basics by writing tests for a small example and then for a number of common code situations. Learn about testing code with challenging dependencies using test doubles. Dig into code coverage, testing multithreaded code, and integration testing topics.

- *Mastering JUnit with "E"s*: *E*xamine outcomes by using JUnit's many assertion forms, *E*stablish organization in your tests using lifecycle methods, nested classes, and parameterized tests, and *E*xecute appropriate subsets of tests with tags and other mechanisms.

- *Increasing ROI—Unit Testing and Design*: Focus on the relevance of design to unit testing and vice versa. Learn to refactor in the small, in the large, and in your tests.

- *Bigger Topics Around Unit Testing*: Advance your unit testing practice by learning the discipline of TDD. Discover useful considerations for adopting unit testing within your project. Wrap up your journey by understanding how unit testing remains relevant in the era of AI.

Your best path to success: code the examples as you read!

Code and Online Resources

You'll find gobs of Java code throughout the book, most of which is included in the source distribution and downloadable from the official book page.[1]

Code snippets that can be found as part of the distribution appear with the path and filename immediately above the chunk of code like this:

```
utj3-units/02/src/test/java/units/SomeStringUtils.java
@Test
void uppercasesSingleLetter() {
    assertEquals("A", capitalize("a"));
}
```

That snippet of code appears in the SomeStringUtils.java file in the source distribution, in the directory utj3-units/02/src/test/java/units. If you're reading this as an ebook, click the filename header to navigate to the code.

---

1. https://pragprog.com/titles/utj3/pragmatic-unit-testing-in-java-with-junit-third-edition/

You can also find the code at GitHub.[2] The repository name appears as the first part of a listing's file name. The above code snippet resides in the utj3-units repository. The branches in GitHub are named v1, v2, v3, and so on so that snippet would come from branch v2.

Most chapters refer to only one repository. A few chapters reference more than one repository, and some repositories are used across multiple chapters.

Each repository includes a build.gradle file as well as a working Gradle wrapper. From the root of each repository, you can execute the command ./gradlew build to compile the project and execute its tests.

Many of the code listings are annotated with arrows pointing to one or more lines to emphasize what you should focus on—added/changed lines or otherwise interesting bits of code. If an arrow points to a method signature, it means to either focus on the signature itself or on the entire method (you'll be able to figure out which from the context).

The opposite of emphasizing is de-emphasizing. I do this using ellipses. In the following snippet, other things in the code may be interesting or relevant, but the body of someMethod most certainly is not relevant:

```
void someMethod() {
    // ...
}
```

The code snippets you'll see are automatically extracted from source code, meaning that the repository code should match what's in the book. However, your IDE's settings may create formatting and other minor differences (for example, how import statements are represented).

To reduce a bit of clutter, most of the code listings omit package statements.

Visit the book's official Pragmatic Bookshelf page for more resources.[3]

Test-Driven Development (TDD)

I practice TDD, but this isn't a book on it. Chapter 11, Advancing with Test-Driven Development (TDD), on page 211 will show you how it works and how it can help. With TDD, you code unit tests first, in other words, before each bit of production code you need to write. In this book, you'll write tests for code that already exists.

---

2.   https://github.com/jlangr
3.   https://pragprog.com/titles/utj3/pragmatic-unit-testing-in-java-with-junit-third-edition/

Over a couple of decades of practicing TDD, I gathered many insights that have made my unit testing efforts easier and more valuable. You'll learn these insights throughout *Pragmatic Unit Testing in Java with JUnit*. They'll apply whether you write tests before or after you write code.

Coding Style

This book's code exhibits my preferred programming style and formatting for Java, tempered also with a need to keep code listings brief. Many of you *will* be offended by my elimination of "safety braces" around single-line conditional blocks:

```java
if (condition) doSomething();
```

- It gets rid of a line in the code listing.

- In most cases, the if body fits onto a single line, as demonstrated.

- I find it reads better as a singular concept.

- If you ever need a second statement in the conditional body, you'll likely remember to add the safety braces.

- If you forget...that's why you write unit tests.

If you're unswayed, feel free to add braces. Try without, though—you might like it.

Jeff Langr
jeff@langrsoft.com
July 2024

Part I

Unit Testing Foundations

Your intro to unit testing starts with a number of simple examples, moves into dependency challenges, and wraps up with an overview of bigger concepts related to unit testing.

CHAPTER 1

Building Your First JUnit Test

In this chapter, we'll write a unit test by working through a small example. You'll set up your project, add a test class, and see what a test method looks like. Most importantly, you'll get JUnit to run your new, passing test.

Reasons to Write a Unit Test

Joe has just completed work on a small feature change, adding several dozen lines to the system. He's fairly confident in his change, but it's been a while since he's tried things out in the deployed system. Joe runs the build script, which packages and deploys the change to the local web server. He pulls up the application in his browser, navigates to the appropriate screen, enters a bit of data, clicks submit, and...stack trace!

Joe stares at the screen for a moment, then the code. Aha! Joe notes that he forgot to initialize a field. He makes the fix, runs the build script again, cranks up the application, enters data, clicks submit, and...hmm, that's not the right amount. Oops. This time, it takes a bit longer to decipher the problem. Joe fires up his debugger and after a few minutes discovers an off-by-one error in indexing an array. He once again repeats the cycle of fix, deploy, navigate the GUI, enter data, and verify results.

Happily, Joe's third fix attempt has been the charm. But he spent about fifteen minutes working through the three cycles of code/manual test/fix.

Lucia works differently. Each time she writes a small bit of code, she adds a *unit test* that verifies the small change she added to the system. She then runs all her unit tests, including the new one just written. They run in seconds, so she doesn't wait long to find out whether or not she can move on.

Because Lucia runs her tests with each small change, she only moves on when all the tests pass. If her tests fail, she knows she's created a problem and stops immediately to fix it. The problems she creates are a lot easier to fix since she's added only a few lines of code since she last saw all the tests pass. She avoids piling lots of new code atop her mistakes before discovering a problem.

Lucia's tests are part of the system and included in the project's GitHub repository. They continue to pay off each time she or anyone else changes code, alerting the team when someone breaks existing behavior.

Lucia's tests also save Joe and everyone else on the team significant amounts of comprehension time on their system. "How does the system handle the case where the end date isn't provided?" asks Madhu, the product owner. Joe's response, more often than not, is, "I don't know; let me take a look at the code." Sometimes, Joe can answer the question in a minute or two, but frequently, he ends up digging about for a half hour or more.

Lucia looks at her unit tests and finds one that matches Madhu's case. She has an answer within a minute or so.

You'll follow in Lucia's footsteps and learn how to write small, focused unit tests. You'll start by learning basic JUnit concepts.

Learning JUnit Basics: Your First Testing Challenge

For your first example, you'll work with a small class named CreditHistory. Its goal is to return the mean (average) for a number of credit rating objects.

In this book, you'll probe the many reasons for choosing to write unit tests. For now, you'll start with a simple but critical reason: you want to continue adding behaviors to CreditHistory and want to know the moment you break any previously coded behaviors.

Initially, you will see screenshots to help guide you through getting started with JUnit. After this chapter, you will see very few screenshots, and you won't need them.

The screenshots demonstrate using JUnit in IntelliJ IDEA. If you're using another integrated development environment (IDE), the good news is that your JUnit test code will look the same whether you use IDEA, Eclipse, VSCode, or something else. How you set up your project to use JUnit *will* differ. The way the JUnit looks and feels will differ from IDE to IDE, though it will, in general, operate the same and produce the same information.

Here's the code you need to test:

utj3-credit-history/01/src/main/java/credit/CreditHistory.java
```
import java.time.LocalDate;
import java.time.Month;
import java.util.*;

public class CreditHistory {
   private final List<CreditRating> ratings = new ArrayList<>();

   public void add(CreditRating rating) {
      ratings.add(rating);
   }

   public int arithmeticMean() {
      var total = ratings.stream().mapToInt(CreditRating::rating).sum();
      return total / ratings.size();
   }
}
```

The CreditHistory class collects CreditRating objects through its add method. Its current primary goal is to provide you with an average (arithmeticMean) of the scores contained in the credit rating objects.

You implement CreditRating with a Java record declaring a single rating field.

utj3-credit-history/01/src/main/java/credit/CreditRating.java
```
public record CreditRating(int rating) {}
```

Your first exercise is small, and you could easily enter it from scratch. Typing in the code yourself should help you grow your coding skills faster. Still, you can also choose to download the source for this and all other exercises from https://pragprog.com/titles/utj3/pragmatic-unit-testing-in-java-with-junit-third-edition/.

Where to Put the Tests

Your project is laid out per the Apache Software Foundation's standard directory layout:[1]

```
utj3-credit-history
  src/
    main/
      java/
        credit/
          CreditHistory.java
          CreditRating.java
    test/
      java/
        credit/
```

---

1. https://maven.apache.org/guides/introduction/introduction-to-the-standard-directory-layout.html

Your two production source files for this project are stored in the directory src/main/java in the package named credit. (IntelliJ IDEA refers to the directory src/main/java as a *Sources Root*.)

You're ready to write a test that describes the behavior in CreditHistory. You'll be putting the test in the same package as the production source—credit—but in the *Test Sources Root* directory src/test/java.

Your IDE probably provides you with many ways to create a new test class. In IDEA, you'll create it by following these steps in the Project explorer:

1. Select the package src/test/java/credit from the Project or Packages explorer.

2. Right-click to bring up the context menu.

3. Select New ▶ Java Class. You will see the New Java Class popup, which defaults its selection to creating a new class.

4. Type the classname ACreditHistory ("a credit history"); press enter. IDEA's inspections may be unhappy about your test naming convention. You can reconfigure the inspection,[2] or you can go with the old-school name CreditHistoryTest.

Running Tests: Testing Nothing at All

When you press enter from the New ▶ Java Class menu item, IDEA provides you with an empty class declaration for ACreditHistory. Your first job is to squeeze a test method into it:

```
utj3-credit-history/01/src/test/java/credit/ACreditHistory.java
class ACreditHistory {
➤    @org.junit.jupiter.api.Test
➤    void whatever() {
➤    }
}
```

To be a bit more specific: Within the body of ACreditHistory, type in the three lines that start with the @org.junit.jupiter.api.Test annotation.

 Lines marked with arrows in code listings represent added lines, changed lines, or otherwise interesting bits of code.

Type? Yes. It's better to type code and tests in yourself while learning, rather than copy/paste them, unless typing isn't at all your thing. It'll feel more like

---

2. https://langrsoft.com/2024/04/28/your-new-test-naming-convention/

real development, which should help you learn more. It also won't take as long as you think. Your IDE offers numerous time-saving shortcuts, such as intellisense, live templates, and context-sensitive "quick fix."

Your test is an empty method annotated with the type @org.junit.jupiter.api.Test. When you tell JUnit to run one or more tests, it will locate all methods annotated with @Test and run them. It'll ignore all other methods.

You can run your empty test, which, for now, you've given a placeholder name of whatever. As usual, you have many options for executing tests. You'll start by being mousey. Click the little green arrow that appears to the left of the class declaration, as shown in the following figure. (Chances are good your IDE has a similar icon.)

Clicking the green arrow pops up a context menu where you can select the option to run all tests in ACreditHistory, as shown in this figure:

Clicking Run 'ACreditHistory' runs the whatever test. It's passing, as the figure on page 8 reveals.

If your test isn't getting executed, make sure it follows these three guidelines:

- it is annotated with @org.junit.jupiter.api.Test
- it has a void return
- it has no parameters

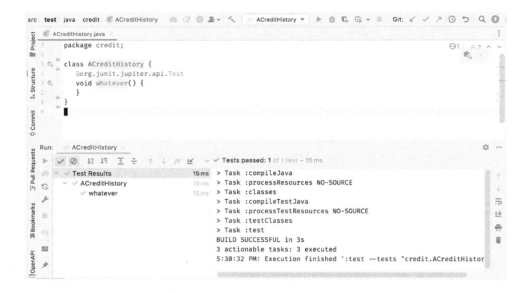

The built-in JUnit test runner appears at the bottom of the IDE. Its left-hand panel shows a summary of all the tests executed. Your summary shows that you ran the whatever test within ACreditHistory, that it succeeded (because it has a green check mark), and that it took 12 milliseconds to execute.

The test runner's right-hand panel shows different information depending on what's selected in the left-hand panel. By default, it tells you how many tests passed out of the number that were executed (yours: "1 of 1"). It also provides you with information captured as part of the JUnit process execution. (In this screenshot, the IDE is configured to use Gradle to execute the test via the build task, which also executes the tests.)

You now know something fundamental about how JUnit behaves: an empty test passes. More specifically and more usefully, a test whose method execution completes—without having encountered any failure points or throwing any exceptions—is a passing test.

Writing a First Real Test

An empty test isn't of much use. Let's devise a good first test.

You could start with a meaty test that adds a few credit scores, asks for the average, and then ascertains whether or not you got the right answer. This *happy path* test case—in contrast with negative or error-based tests—is not the only test you'd want to write, though. You have some other cases to consider for verifying arithmeticMean:

- What happens if you add only one credit rating?
- What happens if you don't add any credit ratings?
- Are there any *exceptional cases*—conditions under which a problem could occur? How does the code behave under these conditions?

Starting with a happy path test is one choice; you have other options. One is to start with the simplest test possible, move on to incrementally more complex tests, and finally to exceptional cases. Another option is to start with the exceptional cases first, then cover happy path cases in complexity order. Other ordering schemes are, of course, possible.

When writing unit tests for code you've already written, ultimately, the order really doesn't matter. But if you follow a consistent approach, you'll be less likely to miss something. Throughout this book, the progression you'll prefer will be to start with the simplest case, then move on to incrementally more complex happy path cases, and then to exception-based tests.

The Simplest Possible Case

The simplest case often involves *zero* or some concept of *nothing*. Calculating the arithmetic mean involves creating a credit history with nothing added to it. You think that an empty credit history should return an average of zero.

Update ACreditHistory with the following code, which replaces the whatever test with a new one:

utj3-credit-history/02/src/test/java/credit/ACreditHistory.java
```
Line 1  import org.junit.jupiter.api.Test;
   -    import static org.junit.jupiter.api.Assertions.assertEquals;

   -    class ACreditHistory {
   5        @Test
   -        void withNoCreditRatingsHas0Mean() {
   -            var creditHistory = new CreditHistory();
   -            var result = creditHistory.arithmeticMean();
   -            assertEquals(0, result);
  10        }
   -    }
```

Let's step through the updated lines in ACreditHistory.java.

Each of your tests will call one or more *assertion* methods to verify your assumptions about the system. That'll add up to piles of lines of assertions. Since these assertions are static methods, add a static import at 2 so that you don't have to constantly qualify your assertion calls.

Line 2: You simplify your test declaration by introducing an import statement for the @Test annotation.

The test name whatever wasn't much of a winner, so supply a new one at line 6. As with all tests you write, strive for a test name that summarizes what the test verifies. Here's a wacky idea: have the test name complete a sentence about the behavior it describes.

A Credit History...with no credit ratings...has a 0 mean

Your test describes a credit history object in a certain context—it has no credit ratings. You expect something to hold true about that credit history in that context: it has a zero mean. Your test name is a concise representation of that context and expected outcome:

```
ACreditHistory ... withNoCreditRatingsHas0Mean() { }
```

Was that a snort? No, you don't have to follow this test class naming convention, but it's as valid as any other. You'll read about alternative naming schemes at Documenting Your Tests with Consistent Names, on page 190.

On to the body of the code—where the work gets done. Your test first creates a CreditHistory instance (line 7). This new object allows your test to run from a clean slate, keeping it isolated from the effects of other tests. JUnit helps reinforce such isolation by creating a new instance of the test class—ACreditHistory—for each test it executes.

Your test next (at line 8) interacts with the CreditHistory test instance to exercise the behavior that you want to verify. Here, you call its arithmeticMean method and capture the return value in result.

Your test finally (at line 9) asserts that the expected (desired) result of 0 matches the actual result captured.

Your call to assertEquals uses JUnit's bread-and-butter assertion method, which compares a result with what you expect. The majority of your tests will use assertEquals. The rest will use one of many other assert forms that you'll learn in Chapter 5, Examining Outcomes with Assertions, on page 99.

An assertEquals method call *passes* if its two arguments match each other. It *fails* if the two arguments do not match. The test method as a whole fails if it encounters any assertion failures.

The hard part about learning assertEquals is remembering the correct order of its arguments. The value your test *expects* comes first; the *actual* value returned by the system you're testing second. The signature for assertEquals makes the order clear. If you ever forget, use your IDE to show it to you:

```
public static void assertEquals(int expected, int actual)
```

When you run your test, you'll see why the order for *expected* and *actual* arguments matters. You'll do that in the forthcoming section, Making It Fail, on page 14. Stick around!

Dealing with Failure

You previously learned to click on the little JUnit run icon next to the class declaration to execute all its tests. But you're going to be running tests quite often—potentially hundreds of times per day, and mousing about is a much slower, labor-intensive process. It behooves you to be more efficient. Repetitive stress injuries are real and unpleasant.

Any good IDE will show you the appropriate keyboard shortcut when you hover over a button. Hovering over the JUnit "run" button reveals Ctrl-Shift-R as the appropriate shortcut in my IDE. Hover over yours. Write down the shortcut it provides. Press it and run your tests. Press it again. And again. And remember it. And from here on out, for the thousands of times you will ultimately need to run your tests, use the keyboard. You'll go faster, and your tendons will thank you.

Your test is failing. Your JUnit execution should look similar to the following figure.

This information-rich view contains several pieces of information about your test's failing execution:

1. The JUnit panel to the left, which gives you a hierarchical listing of the tests executed, marks both the test class name ACreditHistory and the test method name withNoCreditRatingsHas0Mean with a yellow x. You can click on that test method name to focus on its execution details.

2. The JUnit panel to the right gets to the point with a statistical summary: Tests failed: 1 of 1 test That is, JUnit executed one test, and that sole test failed.

3. Below that redundantly phrased summary, JUnit shows the gory execution details for the test. The failure left behind an exception stack trace that tells you the test barfed before even reaching its assertion statement.

4. The stack trace screams at you in red text—the favored color of items designed to alert, like errors, stop signs, and poisoned lipstick. You have a divide-by-zero problem. The stack trace is linked to appropriate lines in the source, which allows you to quickly navigate to the offending code:

```
public int arithmeticMean() {
    var total = ratings.stream().mapToInt(CreditRating::rating).sum();
    return total / ratings.size(); // oops!
}
```

Your test added no credit ratings to the CreditHistory. As a result, ratings.size() returns a 0, and Java throws an ArithmeticException as its way of telling you it wants nothing to do with that sort of division. Oops!

Your exception-throwing test reveals another useful JUnit nugget: if code executed in a test run throws an exception that's not caught, that counts as a failing test.

Fixing the Problem

The unit test did its job: it notified you of a problem. Earlier, you decided that it's possible someone could call arithmeticMean before any credit ratings are added. You also decided that you don't want the code to throw an exception in that case; you instead want it to return a 0. The unit test captures and documents your choice.

Your unit test will continue to protect you from future *regressions*, letting you know anytime the behavior of arithmeticMean changes.

To get the failing test to pass—to fix your problem—add a *guard clause* to the arithmeticMean method in CreditHistory:

utj3-credit-history/03/src/main/java/credit/CreditHistory.java

```java
public int arithmeticMean() {
    if (ratings.isEmpty()) return 0;

    var total = ratings.stream().mapToInt(CreditRating::rating).sum();
    return total / ratings.size();
}
```

Run the tests again to see if your change did the trick. This time, kick them off by using the Project view (usually the upper-left-most tool window in IDEA and other IDEs). Drill down from the project at its top level until you can select the test/java directory, as shown in this figure:

A right-click brings up a near-freakishly large context menu:

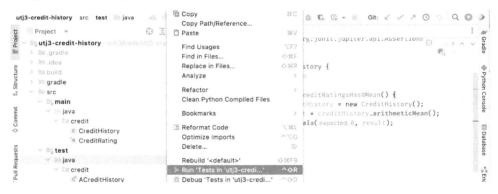

Select the option Run 'All Tests'. JUnit will execute all the tests within src/test/java. Success! Here's the passing test (as shown in the figure on page 14), where everything is a glorious green and devoid of stack trace statements.

Looks good, right? Feels good, right? Go ahead and hit that Ctrl-Shift-R keystroke (or its equivalent on your machine) to run the test again. Bask in the glory.

```
Run:    Tests in 'utj3-credit-history.test'                                          ⚙ —
  ▶ ✓ ⊘ ↓₂ ↓₂ ⊼ ÷ ↑ ↓ ⟲ ⟲  » ✓ Tests passed: 1 of 1 test – 16 ms
      ✓ Test Results                    16 ms  > Task :compileJava UP-TO-DATE            ↑
        ✓ ACreditHistory                16 ms  > Task :processResources NO-SOURCE        ↓
          ✓ withNoCreditRatingsHas0Mean 16 ms  > Task :classes UP-TO-DATE               ⇄
                                               > Task :compileTestJava UP-TO-DATE       ⇄
                                               > Task :processTestResources NO-SOURCE
                                               > Task :testClasses UP-TO-DATE           🖶
                                               > Task :test                            🗑
                                               BUILD SUCCESSFUL in 775ms
                                               3 actionable tasks: 1 executed, 2 up-to-date
                                               6:03:42 PM: Execution finished ':test'.
```

Moving On to a One-Based Test: Something's Happening!

Your zero-based test saved your bacon. Maybe a one-based test can do the same? Write a test that adds one and only one credit score:

utj3-credit-history/04/src/test/java/credit/ACreditHistory.java
```java
@Test
void withOneRatingHasEquivalentMean() {
    var creditHistory = new CreditHistory();
    creditHistory.add(new CreditRating(780));
    var result = creditHistory.arithmeticMean();
    assertEquals(780, result);
}
```

You might have quickly put that test in place by duplicating the zero-based test, adding a line to call creditHistory.add(), and changing the assertion.

Your new test passes. Are you done with it? No. Two critical steps remain:

1. Ensure you've seen it fail.
2. Clean it up.

Making It Fail

If you've never seen a test fail for the right reason, don't trust it.

The test you just wrote contains an assertion that expects arithmeticMean to return a specific value. "Failing for right reason" for this example would mean that arithmeticMean returns some value other than 780 (the expected value). Perhaps the calculation is incorrect, or perhaps the code never makes the calculation and returns some initial value.

You want to break your code so that the test fails. When it fails, ensure that the failure message JUnit provides makes sense. Let's try that.

utj3-credit-history/05/src/main/java/credit/CreditHistory.java

```java
    public void add(CreditRating rating) {
//        ratings.add(rating);
    }

    public int arithmeticMean() {
        if (ratings.isEmpty()) return 0;

        var total = ratings.stream().mapToInt(CreditRating::rating).sum();
        return total / ratings.size();
    }
```

The best way to break things is to comment out the line of code that adds to the credit history's ratings collection. Then, rerun the tests (using your new keyboard shortcut!). JUnit should now look like the following figure.

The JUnit process output on the right shows an exception stack trace. Behind the scenes, the code in JUnit's assertEquals method compares the expected value with the actual value. If they are the same, JUnit returns control to the test, allowing it to proceed. If the expected value differs from the actual value, JUnit throws an AssertionFailedError with some useful information attached to it.

Here's your test again, with the pertinent assertEquals method call highlighted.

utj3-credit-history/05/src/test/java/credit/ACreditHistory.java

```java
@Test
void withOneRatingHasEquivalentMean() {
    var creditHistory = new CreditHistory();
    creditHistory.add(new CreditRating(780));
    var result = creditHistory.arithmeticMean();
    assertEquals(780, result);
}
```

In other words, the assertion compares 780 against the value of result from the prior step. The message associated with the stack trace describes the comparison failure:

Expected :780 Actual :0

If you'd mistakenly swapped the order of the arguments to assertEquals, like this:

```
assertEquals(result, 780);
```

...then JUnit's error message would be inaccurate and confusing:

Expected :0 Actual :780

Your single-rating test doesn't expect 0; it expects 780. The 0 is the actual result emanating from the call to arithmeticMean, not 780.

You did see the test fail due to the assertEquals mismatch, so that's a good thing. Had you seen something different, it would be a reason to stop and investigate—something is probably wrong with the test in this case. If the test run shows an exception emanating from the production code, perhaps something isn't set up correctly in the test case. If the test run passes, perhaps your test isn't really doing what you think it is. You'd want to carefully re-read the test to see what you're missing or misrepresenting.

 Deliberately fail your tests to prove they're really doing something.

Corollary: Don't trust a test you've never seen fail.

It might seem easier to get a new test to fail by changing its assertion. For example, you might change your assertion to assertEquals(result, 9999), which you know would always result in a failing test.

But think of your tests as "documents of record" for each logical requirement. Prefer failing the test by changing the production code so that it no longer meets the requirement, not by altering the conditions of the test. It can require just a little more thought, but breaking production code will keep you out of trouble.

Programmers following the practice of test-driven development (TDD) *always* demonstrate test failure first to demonstrate that the code they write is responsible for making the test pass. See Chapter 11, Advancing with Test-Driven Development (TDD), on page 211 for more on how TDD practitioners build a cycle around this discipline.

JUnit's Exceptions

You can click the link of the first line in the stack trace to navigate precisely to the point where the exception emanated from the code—the assertEquals call.

(If you want to see the relevant execution path through JUnit's code itself, you can also click where JUnit says <6 internal lines>.)

All failed asserts throw an AssertionFailedError exception. JUnit catches this or any other exception thrown during test execution and adds one to its count of failing tests.

JUnit's choice to throw an exception means no more code in the test method gets executed. Any assertions following the first failing one also do not execute, a deliberate (and good) choice by its designers: Once your first assertion fails, all bets are off about the state of things. Executing subsequent assertions may be pointless.

You generally want your tests focused on a single (*unit*) behavior, which means, usually, you need only one assertion anyway. You'll dig deeper into this idea later in Test Smell: Multiple Assertions, on page 200.

Your probe to watch the test fail involved commenting out a line of code. You can now uncomment it and watch your test pass again, which should give you high confidence that your test properly demonstrates the right piece of behavior.

No More Screenshots

At this point, you've graduated…from screenshots! Now that you've seen what to expect in an IDE, you can move forward with learning about unit tests through raw Java code, presented *au naturel* rather than cloaked in screenshots. Much sleeker, much sexier.

You'll want to continue to increase your understanding of your IDE's implementation of JUnit. Try clicking on its various buttons and menus to learn more about its shortcuts and power.

Going forward in this book, you'll mostly see only the code pertinent to the current discussion (rather than large listings). Minimizing your need to flip about through the book to find code listings should help you keep your focus on the relevant code and discussion at hand.

Increasing Your ROI: Cleaning Up Tests

Always review your tests for opportunities to improve their readability. A few minutes of cleanup now can save countless developers from far more head-scratching time down the road.

Review your CreditHistory test. See if you can spot ways to improve things.

Scannability: Arrange—Act—Assert

With but four lines, your test is already a mass of code demanding close attention:

```
utj3-credit-history/06/src/test/java/credit/ACreditHistory.java
@Test
void withOneRatingHasEquivalentMean() {
    var creditHistory = new CreditHistory();
    creditHistory.add(new CreditRating(780));
    var result = creditHistory.arithmeticMean();
    assertEquals(780, result);
}
```

The test has little *scannability* (as Mike Hill calls it)—the ability to quickly locate and comprehend code without having to explicitly read it.[3] Someone wanting a quick understanding must scrutinize each of its four lines from top to bottom. This is the opposite of scannable, something I call *stepwise*.

Lines of stepwise code are the opposite of declarative. They're strongly linked to earlier steps, and reading one step alone often provides you with no useful information. Its intertwining of implementation details further compels you to slow down, lest you miss something.

The four stepwise lines here don't seem that terrible, but the problem definitely adds up—imagine thousands of similarly tedious tests.

Every test you write can be broken down into up to three steps. In order:

- *Arrange* the system so that it's in a useful state. This set-up step usually involves creating objects and calling methods or setting data on them. Your test arranges state by creating a CreditHistory object and adding a credit rating to it. The first part of your test name, withOneRating, echoes this state arrangement. Some tests won't have any *arrange* needs (for example, when you're making a static method call with literal or no arguments).

- *Act* upon the system so as to create the behavior you're trying to test. Your test acts on the credit history object by calling its arithmeticMean method.

- *Assert* (verify) that the system behaves the way you expect. Your test asserts that the arithmeticMean is calculated correctly.

---

3. https://www.geepawhill.org/2020/03/03/readability-and-scannability/.

Some of your tests will be functionally oriented, in which you invoke a method that returns a value. For these tests, you can often distill the three Arrange-Act-Assert (AAA) steps to a single line of test code:

```
assertEquals(42, new Everything().ultimateAnswer());
```

To make your tests align with at least one aspect of *scannable*, use blank lines to break them into AAA chunks:

```
utj3-credit-history/07/src/test/java/credit/ACreditHistory.java
@Test
void withOneRatingHasEquivalentMean() {
    var creditHistory = new CreditHistory();
    creditHistory.add(new CreditRating(780));

    var result = creditHistory.arithmeticMean();

    assertEquals(780, result);
}
```

Your test code now has some breathing room. AAA has the same effect as using paragraphs to break up a page of continuous text.

If all of your tests are similarly consistent, both organizationally and visually, a developer's eyes can immediately settle on the test part they're most interested in. That consistency alone can significantly reduce the time anyone must otherwise spend reading through any given test.

Test comprehension starts with reading its name. A well-named test summarizes the behavior that the example (the test code itself) demonstrates. You'll learn more about improving your test names in Tests as Documentation, on page 189.

Once you learn the test's intent through its name, you might next look at the *act* step. It will tell you how the test interacts with the system to trigger the behavior described by the test name.

Then, read the *arrange* step to see how the system gets into the proper state to be tested. Or, if you already know (or don't care) how things are arranged, focus instead on the *assert* step to see how the test verifies that the desired behavior occurred.

Ultimately, only you will know what parts of a test you need to focus on, and that interest will change from time to time. For example, if you must add a new behavior related to an existing one, you'll probably focus heavily on the *arrange* of the related test to understand how it sets up state. If you're instead trying to understand a specific behavior, you'll want to focus on how its test's *arrange* steps correlate with the expected result expressed in the *assert* step.

Quickly finding what you need is a key component of increasing your development speed, and a large part of succeeding is related to scannability.

 Follow Bill Wake's AAA mnemonic[4] and consistently (visually) chunk your tests as a valuable means of improving scannability.

Abstraction: Eliminating Boring Details

After chunking both tests using the Arrange—Act—Assert (*AAA*) pattern, your tests are more scannable:

```
utj3-credit-history/07/src/test/java/credit/ACreditHistory.java
@Test
void withOneRatingHasEquivalentMean() {
    var creditHistory = new CreditHistory();
    creditHistory.add(new CreditRating(780));

    var result = creditHistory.arithmeticMean();

    assertEquals(780, result);
}
```

But note that both tests repeat the same uninteresting line of code that creates a CreditHistory instance:

```
utj3-credit-history/07/src/test/java/credit/ACreditHistory.java
var creditHistory = new CreditHistory();
```

That line of code is, of course, necessary for each test to successfully execute, but you really don't have to *see* it in order to understand the tests.

JUnit provides a hook you can use to move common test initialization into a single place, which at the same time moves it away from the more relevant test code. The @BeforeEach annotation can mark one or more methods to be executed before each and every test.

```
utj3-credit-history/08/src/test/java/credit/ACreditHistory.java
import org.junit.jupiter.api.BeforeEach;
import org.junit.jupiter.api.Test;
import static org.junit.jupiter.api.Assertions.assertEquals;

class ACreditHistory {
    CreditHistory creditHistory;
```

---

4. https://xp123.com/3a-arrange-act-assert/

```
➤   @BeforeEach
➤   void createInstance() {
➤       creditHistory = new CreditHistory();
➤   }

    @Test
    void withNoCreditRatingsHas0Mean() {
       var result = creditHistory.arithmeticMean();

       assertEquals(0, result);
    }

    @Test
    void withOneRatingHasEquivalentMean() {
       creditHistory.add(new CreditRating(780));

       var result = creditHistory.arithmeticMean();

       assertEquals(780, result);
    }
}
```

The highlighted lines show a typical use for the @BeforeEach hook. The test declares a field named creditHistory and then initializes it in the annotated createInstance method. That allows you to remove the local initializations of creditHistory from both tests.

Here's how things happen when JUnit runs these two tests in ACreditHistory:

1. JUnit creates a new instance of ACreditHistory.

2. JUnit executes the createInstance method on this instance, which initializes the creditHistory field.

3. JUnit executes one of either withNoCreditRatingsHas0Mean or withOneRatingHas-EquivalentMean, depending on how Java returns the methods declared on a class. In other words, they don't run in an order you can depend on. That's okay. You want each test to stand completely on its own and not care about the order in which it's executed.

4. JUnit creates a new instance of ACreditHistory.

5. JUnit executes the createInstance method on this instance.

6. JUnit executes the other test, the one not already run.

Still fuzzy? Understandable. Put a System.out.println() call in the @BeforeEach hook, as well as in each of the two tests. Also, create a no-arg constructor and put a System.out.println() statement in that. Then run your tests; the output should jibe with the preceding list—you should see six println lines.

I just heard you say, "Big deal." Yep, you have removed a measly line from a couple of tests, but you have actually introduced more total lines in the source file.

The remaining tests are now as immediate and scannable as possible. Each AAA chunk is one line. You can visually scan past boring initialization code and instead focus on exactly what arrangement is needed to achieve the desired outcome. You can more quickly correlate the arrange and act steps and answer the question, "Why does this assertion pass?"

Your tests are highly *abstract*: They emphasize and document what's relevant in each test and de-emphasize necessary but boring details.

Most of your tests can be this concise, with a typical range from one to five statements. They'll be easier to write in the first place, easier to understand (and don't forget, "write once, read many"), and easier to change when requirements change. You'll find additional tips for keeping tests short and meaningful in Chapter 5, Examining Outcomes with Assertions, on page 99.

Eliminating Clutter and JUnit 5

Your test code may appear to violate longstanding Java conventions. Neither the class nor the test method signatures declare explicit modifiers. Older versions of JUnit did require the public modifier. In JUnit 5, classes and methods should have package-level access.

Omitting the extra keyword goes one more step toward emphasizing the abstraction of tests by eliminating one more bit of clutter. Your tests move in the direction of *documentation* and away from implementation details. They describe behaviors.

In a similar vein, you can omit the typical access modifier of private for fields.

If you're worried, don't be. None of your code will ever call test methods, and no one will violate their "exposed" fields.

ZOM: Zero and One Done, Now Testing Many

You've written a zero-based test (a test for the "zero" case) and a one-based test so far. It's time to slam out a many-based test:

```
utj3-credit-history/09/src/test/java/credit/ACreditHistory.java
@Test
void withMultipleRatingsDividesTotalByCount() {
    creditHistory.add(new CreditRating(780));
    creditHistory.add(new CreditRating(800));
    creditHistory.add(new CreditRating(820));
```

```
  var result = creditHistory.arithmeticMean();
  assertEquals(800, result);
}
```

You can create this test by copying the one-based test, duplicating a couple of lines in order to add a total of three credit ratings, and changing the expected value for the assertion. It should pass. Break it; it should fail. Fix it again and demonstrate that it passes. It's possible to do all of that within a total of about two minutes.

You might wonder if you need all three tests. The one-based test really doesn't differ much from the many-based test, and they don't execute anything differently with respect to code paths. It's a debatable point, and ultimately, it's up to you.

Prefer deleting tests that don't add any value in terms of "documenting variant behaviors." It was still useful for you to build tests using a zero-one-many (ZOM) progression, and it really didn't take any significant additional time to write all three tests. If you buy that, you should have no qualms about deleting the one-based test.

Delete it! Doing so allows you to simplify the test name: withMultipleRatingsDividesTotalByCount. Here's your final test class:

utj3-credit-history/10/src/test/java/credit/ACreditHistory.java
```java
import org.junit.jupiter.api.BeforeEach;
import org.junit.jupiter.api.Test;
import java.time.LocalDate;
import static org.junit.jupiter.api.Assertions.assertEquals;

class ACreditHistory {
   CreditHistory creditHistory;

   @BeforeEach
   void createInstance() {
      creditHistory = new CreditHistory();
   }

   @Test
   void withNoCreditRatingsHas0Mean() {
      var result = creditHistory.arithmeticMean();

      assertEquals(0, result);
   }

   @Test
   void withRatingsDividesTotalByCount() {
      creditHistory.add(new CreditRating(780));
      creditHistory.add(new CreditRating(800));
      creditHistory.add(new CreditRating(820));
```

```
    var result = creditHistory.arithmeticMean();

    assertEquals(800, result);
  }
}
```

 Always consider writing a test for each of Zero, One, and Many (ZOM) cases.

Covering Other Cases: Creating a Test List

Beyond the ZOM cases you've covered, you could brainstorm edge cases and exception-based tests. You'll explore doing that in later chapters.

As you write tests and continue to re-visit/re-read the code you're testing, you'll think of additional tests you should write. In fact, as you write the code yourself in the first place—before trying to write tests for it—think about and note the cases you'll need for that code.

Add the cases you think of to a *test list* to remember to write them. Cross them off as you implement or obviate them. You can do this on paper, in a notepad file, or even in the test class itself as a series of comments. (Perhaps in the form of TODO comments, which IDEs like IntelliJ IDEA and Eclipse will collect in a view as a set of reminders.) Things change, so don't expend the effort to code these tests just yet. You can read more on this highly useful tool in *Kent Beck's seminal book on TDD [Bec02].*

Congratulations!...But Don't Stop Yet

In this chapter, you got past one of the more significant challenges: getting a first test to pass using JUnit in your IDE. Congrats! Along with that achievement, you also learned:

- What it takes to write a test that JUnit can accept and run
- How to tell JUnit to run your tests
- How to interpret the test results provided by JUnit
- How to use the ZOM mnemonic to figure out what the next test might be
- How to structure a test using AAA

You've been reading about "units" throughout this chapter. Next up, you'll learn what a unit is, and you'll learn a number of tactics for testing some of the common units that you'll encounter.

CHAPTER 2

Testing the Building Blocks

In the previous chapter, you took a small piece of code and wrote a few JUnit tests around it. In the process, you learned how to structure your tests, execute them, how to interpret results, and what test to write next.

You've only scratched the surface of what it means to write tests for code. In this chapter, you'll examine several common code constructs and learn how to test them. These are the topics you'll cover:

- Testing pure functions
- Testing code with side effects
- How different designs can impact unit tests
- Writing tests for code involving lists
- Writing tests for code that throws exceptions
- Covering boundary conditions with tests

First, however, let's talk about the word *unit* in unit test.

Units

A software system is an organized collection of many *units*. A unit is the smallest piece of code that accomplishes a specific behavioral goal—a *concept*. Here are some examples of concepts:

- Capitalize the first letter of a word
- Move a passenger from the standby list to the boarding list
- Mark a passenger as upgraded
- Calculate the mean credit rating for an individual
- Throw an exception when a user is under 18 years old

Concepts can also represent generic or very common ideas in software:

- Add an item to a list
- Remove all items matching a predicate from a list
- Throw an exception when a string is non-numeric

Each of the above concepts requires perhaps one to three or four "atomic code concepts." Think of an atomic code concept (let's call it an *ACC*) as closer to an expression—the biggest chunk of code that you can read and understand at a glance. Each additional statement represents an additional ACC, as does each new lambda or function call in a pipeline.

An if statement with a single-line body would count as two ACCs: the conditional plus the statement that executes if it evaluates to true. The key notion is that both parts of the if must be read and understood separately.

 A *concise* implementation of a concept uses no more ACCs than needed.

Of course, you'll inevitably need to implement concepts requiring a handful or more ACCs. But for now, let's establish a fairly sensitive and arbitrary threshold. If your method requires five or more ACCs, consider the possibility that it's larger than a unit—that you could decompose it into smaller behavioral units (perhaps other methods or classes, which might be non-public).

Concise is great, but the code must also clearly impart all contextually pertinent intents. Succeeding requires that you are skilled in crafting clear, concise code. You'll see many examples of how to do that in this book.

You can implement any unit as a single *method*—a named block of code that can return a value and/or alter the state of an object. (Let's hope it's only one or the other—read about command-query separation in Command-Query Separation, on page 180.)

You can also choose to string a series of concepts together in a larger method rather than isolate each concept in a separate method. This is one of countless choices you make as a system designer. Each design choice has tradeoffs and implications, particularly when it comes to writing unit tests.

 A system's design is the complete set of choices made by its developers.

Let's discuss some of those design tradeoffs, starting with the question about representing units as a single method or not.

A Wee Bit Bigger Than a Unit?

Given the preceding definition of *unit*, does the following concept conform?

• Return a list of error messages for each field that fails validation checks

One practical scenario involving that concept is *validating data in a (simplistic) flight booking*. Booking data includes passenger name, departure date, age, and a list of airports representing an itinerary. The passenger name is required, the date must be later than right now, the age must be at least 18 (the airline disallows unaccompanied minors for a single-person booking), the itinerary must contain at least two airport codes (for example, DEN and PRG), and each of those airport codes must be valid.

To gather errors for these five requirements, the code must process five validation expressions. For each failing validation, the code must add a corresponding error message to a list.

Each validation would seemingly require two atomic code concepts—an if conditional and an addError expression—for a total of at least ten ACCs. Based on the dubious idea of an ACC count threshold, the validation concept is more than a unit. Here's a possible implementation:

```java
utj3-bookings/01/src/main/java/units/Booking.java
import java.time.LocalDateTime;
import java.util.ArrayList;
import java.util.List;
import java.util.Set;

public record Booking(
        String name,
        int age,
        LocalDateTime departureDate,
        List<String> itinerary) {
    private static final Set<String> AIRPORT_CODES = Set.of(
        "COS", "DEN", "DUB", "PRG");

    public List<String> validate() {
        var errorMessages = new ArrayList<String>();
        if (name == null || name.trim().isEmpty())
            errorMessages.add("Name is empty");
        if (age < 18)
            errorMessages.add("Minor cannot fly unaccompanied");
        if (!departureDate.isAfter(LocalDateTime.now()))
            errorMessages.add("Too late!");
```

```
    if (itinerary.size() < 2)
        errorMessages.add("Itinerary needs 2+ airport codes");
    if (!itinerary.stream().allMatch(
            airportCode -> AIRPORT_CODES.contains(airportCode)))
        errorMessages.add("Itinerary contains invalid airport code");
    return errorMessages;
    }
}
```

Simplification of the rules aside, validate looks like validation code you'd see in many real systems. The code itself isn't necessarily awful, but the high number of ACCs does beg for a cleaner approach. More validations are likely to come, and validate will only get worse.

You can write validation code in an infinite number of other ways. Some of those ways will represent much better choices—at least for certain contexts. If five requirements represent all the validation you'll ever do in your project, the code here is fine. Chances are good, though, that you have dozens more fields that need validating and dozens of new validations forthcoming. If that's your context, you have many better implementations. Some of them might involve the Javax validation framework.

An ACC limit is arbitrary but provides a good threshold that should remind you to stop and think. With practice, you'll quickly recognize when you can break methods into smaller chunks (a better solution most of the time). You can indeed write a sufficiently short unit that collects a list of error messages for each field that fails validation:

utj3-bookings/02/src/main/java/units/Booking.java
```
public List<String> validate() {
    return asList(
        new NameRequired(),
        new AgeMinimum(),
        new FutureDate(),
        new ItinerarySize(),
        new ItineraryAirports()).stream()
            .filter(Validation::isInvalid)
            .map(Validation::errorMessage)
            .toList();
}
```

The body of validate contains three smaller concepts:

- Create a stream referencing a list of validation objects
- Filter the stream down to a list of invalid validation objects
- Gather the error messages from each (invalid) validation object

Unfortunately, it reads as about eight ACCs since its concepts aren't cleanly separated. Understanding it requires stepwise reading.

The validation objects are instantiated from a set of five validation classes, each one of which isolates the conditional and error message. Here's one:

utj3-bookings/02/src/main/java/units/Booking.java
```
class AgeMinimum implements Validation {
   @Override
   public boolean isInvalid() {
      return age < 18;
   }

   @Override
   public String errorMessage() {
      return "Minor cannot fly unaccompanied";
   }
}
```

Each of the validation classes conforms to the Validation interface.

utj3-bookings/02/src/main/java/units/Validation.java
```
interface Validation {
    boolean isInvalid();

    String errorMessage();
}
```

The updated validate method won't be easier to test than it was before...yet. But you can further decompose it into two separate concepts:

- Pass a list of validation objects off to a validator
- Validate a list of validation objects (using the filter and gather steps described earlier)

You can move the validation concept to a new class, where it can be re-used by other validation interests:

utj3-bookings/03/src/main/java/units/Validator.java
```
import java.util.List;

public class Validator {
    public List<String> validate(List<Validation> validations) {
        return validations.stream()
                .filter(Validation::isInvalid)
                .map(Validation::errorMessage)
                .toList();
    }
}
```

Some tests for the Validator class:

```
utj3-bookings/03/src/test/java/units/AValidator.java
import org.junit.jupiter.api.Test;
import java.util.Collections;
import java.util.List;

import static org.junit.jupiter.api.Assertions.assertEquals;

public class AValidator {
    Validation passingValidation = new Validation() {
        @Override public boolean isInvalid() { return false; }
        @Override public String errorMessage() { return ""; }
    };

    Validation failingValidation = new Validation() {
        @Override public boolean isInvalid() { return true; }
        @Override public String errorMessage() { return "fail"; }
    };

    @Test
    void returnsEmptyListWhenAllValidationsPass() {
        assertEquals(Collections.emptyList(),
            new Validator().validate(List.of(passingValidation)));
    }

    @Test
    void returnsListOfFailingValidationMessages() {
        assertEquals(List.of(failingValidation.errorMessage()),
            new Validator().validate(List.of(
                failingValidation,
                passingValidation)));
    }
}
```

The logic for the Booking class method validate simplifies greatly:

```
utj3-bookings/03/src/main/java/units/Booking.java
public List<String> validate(Validator validator) {
    return validator.validate(validations());
}

List<Validation> validations() {
    return asList(
            new NameRequired(this),
            new AgeMinimum(this),
            new FutureDate(this),
            new ItinerarySize(this),
            new ItineraryAirports(this));
}
```

Each piece of the solution for validate now involves, at most, a handful of ACCs. The Validator class involves filtering a list on the predicate isInvalid, mapping each validation to an error message, then returning the result as a list. Each validation class contains two methods, each of which involves at most a couple of ACCs. In Booking, validate contains a single ACC, and validations declares a list of validator objects, which reads as a single ACC.

All of the units in the solution can now be understood at a glance. Most of them can be tested directly, resulting in simpler tests. (There are many ways to approach testing validate. Once you've worked through the first section of this book, read my adjunct article "Unit Testing Approaches"[1] for an in-depth discussion.)

 Small, single-purpose methods are the cornerstone of good design, which fosters easier unit testing.

Concepts as Building Blocks

One concept might be the basis for another. If you've provided an implementation of "capitalize a word" as a standalone method, you can incorporate it into the slightly larger concept of capitalizing all words within a sentence:

```java
public String capitalizeAllWords(String sentence) {
  return Arrays.stream(sentence.split(" "))
    .map(this::capitalize)
    .collect(joining(" "));
}
```

Implementing smaller concepts as methods provides numerous benefits:

- It's easy to derive a name that concisely summarizes the concept.
- You can re-use them in larger contexts without diminishing clarity.
- You can often digest their implementation at a glance.
- You can move them elsewhere more easily.
- You can write simpler, focused tests. Read on!

Testing the Simpler Things

A method that consistently returns the same value given the same arguments and that has no *side effects* is a *pure function*. A method has side effects when it results in any fields or arguments being changed or results in any external effects (such as a database or API call). These characteristics make pure functions easier to test than their opposite ilk—*impure functions*.

---

1. https://langrsoft.com/2024/07/03/unit-testing-approaches/

Code designed around (predominantly) pure functions is...wait for it...*functional* code. You'll look next at testing simple pure functions.

Test Pure Functions: Revisiting ZOM

In your first stab at unit testing in Chapter 1, Building Your First JUnit Test, on page 3, you started with a *Z*ero-based test, moved onto a *O*ne-based test, then a *M*any-based test before moving on to other tests. Tim Ottinger created the mnemonic ZOM[2] to capture this useful progression.

Following ZOM is sometimes all you need to do. It's not a panacea, though. Once you've worked through the progression, you'll want to explore *B*oundary and *E*xceptional behaviors. (If you add "*I*terate the interface definition" and "focus on creating *S*imple solutions" to the mix and move around some letters, you have James Grenning's spookier ZOMBIES acronym.)[3]

The capitalize method should uppercase the first letter of the word passed to it. You've also decided it must lowercase all other letters in the word.

utj3-units/01/src/main/java/units/StringUtils.java
```java
public class StringUtils {
    static String capitalize(String word) {
        var head = word.substring(0, 1);
        var tail = word.substring(1);
        return head.toUpperCase() + tail.toLowerCase();
    }
}
```

To verify capitalize, start with a zero-based test. That doesn't mean your test has to explicitly involve the number 0. A zero-based test can involve some other form of nothingness: an empty array or a null value, for example. A zero-based test for capitalize involves passing it an empty string:

utj3-units/01/src/test/java/units/SomeStringUtils.java
```java
import org.junit.jupiter.api.Test;
import static org.junit.jupiter.api.Assertions.assertEquals;
import static units.StringUtils.capitalize;

public class SomeStringUtils {
    @Test
    void returnsEmptyStringWhenEmpty() {
        assertEquals("", capitalize(""));
    }
}
```

---

2.   https://agileinaflash.blogspot.com/2012/06/simplify-design-with-zero-one-many.html

3.   http://blog.wingman-sw.com/tdd-guided-by-zombies

Empty string in, empty string out—simple stuff. It fails due to a StringIndex-OutOfBoundsException, a hiccup you can fix with a guard clause.

```
utj3-units/02/src/main/java/units/StringUtils.java
static String capitalize(String word) {
    if (word.isEmpty()) return "";

    var head = word.substring(0, 1);
    var tail = word.substring(1);
    return head.toUpperCase() + tail.toLowerCase();
}
```

Writing a test for the null value can sometimes be thought of as a zero-based test. Here, the code ignores null inputs completely—the assumption is that other code or mechanisms have ensured the string argument is not null. The behavior is undefined if capitalize gets called with null.

The choice to avoid a null check in capitalize might fly for some systems but not others. It's usually a valid choice for systems with good control over input. You end up with a lot fewer paranoid checks for null.

If you instead wanted capitalize to explicitly handle null inputs, you'd write a test for that case. And that test would document your choice.

 Tests capture intent. Absence of a test implies undefined (accidental) behavior. Write tests for all intents.

Moving to a test for one—one *letter*, that is. When passed a lowercase letter, capitalize should return an uppercase one:

```
utj3-units/02/src/test/java/units/SomeStringUtils.java
@Test
void uppercasesSingleLetter() {
    assertEquals("A", capitalize("a"));
}
```

Then a many-based test, in which you pass a bunch of letters to capitalize:

```
utj3-units/02/src/test/java/units/SomeStringUtils.java
@Test
void uppercasesFirstLetterOfLowercaseWord() {
    assertEquals("Alpha", capitalize("alpha"));
}
```

To test the last wrinkle—that the remainder of the letters are lowercased—you write a test for that variant of the input data:

utj3-units/02/src/test/java/units/SomeStringUtils.java

```
@Test
void lowercasesRemainderOfLetters() {
    assertEquals("Omega", capitalize("OMEGA"));
}
```

Testing pure functions is conceptually easy: call a method with some values, then assert against the result it returns.

Verifying Side Effects

An *impure function* creates side effects. The prototypical side effect: you call a void method that changes the value of one or more fields in the containing object. The Location class does just that in its move method (highlighted):

utj3-units/02/src/main/java/units/Location.java

```
import java.util.Objects;

public class Location {
    enum Heading {North, East, South, West}
    private int x, y;
    private Heading heading;

    public Location(int x, int y, Heading heading) {
        this.x = x;
        this.y = y;
        this.heading = heading;
    }
    public void move(int distance) {
        switch (heading) {
            case North -> y = y + distance;
            case East -> x = x + distance;
            case South -> y = y - distance;
            case West -> x = x - distance;
        }
    }

    public int getX() { return x; }
    public int getY() { return y; }
    public Heading getHeading() { return heading; }

    @Override
    public boolean equals(Object o) {
        if (this == o) return true;
        if (o == null || getClass() != o.getClass()) return false;
        Location location = (Location) o;
        return x == location.x && y == location.y && heading == location.heading;
    }
```

```
  @Override
  public int hashCode() { return Objects.hash(x, y, heading); }

  @Override
  public String toString() {
    return "(" + x + ", " + y + ", => " + heading + ')';
  }
}
```

Oh dear, that's a pile of code. While Location appears to have a lot going on, most of its code is boilerplate.

The Location class would be the sort of thing Java records are made for, but for one unfortunate circumstance: it creates *mutable* objects. A Location object's x and y fields are *mutated* (changed) when client code executes the move method.

Location looks like it demands a significant amount of testing. It's a lot longer than the CreditHistory class, for one (though probably nowhere near the size of a typical class in so many production systems). But let's see just what the testing effort will involve.

Testing gives you the guts to ship. You increase this confidence by ensuring that your code's unit behaviors work as expected.

 You gain the confidence to ship through testing.

You *don't* need to test code you didn't write as long as you think you can trust it. The equals and hashCode methods here were generated by an IDE, which should provide very high confidence that they work. If you later must manually change or directly invoke these methods, cover them with tests.

Developers wrote Location's toString method to help developers decipher problems and clarify failing tests. Don't feel compelled to test it, either. Do test toString if other production code depends on it, either explicitly or implicitly.

The only real behaviors in Location that remain for consideration are its ability to capture a location and to move to another location.

A first test for Location might create a location with an (x, y) coordinate and a heading, then ensure that it returns those initial values correctly. But that's terribly uninteresting and barely "behavior." The getters will get *exercised* (executed) as part of tests for other Location behavior. These tests will expose problems with the getters, however inconceivable.

Focus, then, on testing the one thing that could really break: move.

utj3-units/02/src/test/java/units/ALocation.java
```java
import org.junit.jupiter.api.Test;

import static org.junit.jupiter.api.Assertions.assertEquals;
import static units.Location.Heading.North;

public class ALocation {
    @Test
    void increasesYCoordinateWhenMovingNorth() {
        var location = new Location(0, 0, North);

        location.move(42);

        assertEquals(0, location.getX());
        assertEquals(42, location.getY());
        assertEquals(North, location.getHeading());
    }
}
```

The test first creates a location and then tells the location to move. It finally asserts that the y coordinate has changed appropriately (since you're moving north), but neither x nor the heading have changed.

Earlier, you learned to verify only one behavior per test method. This test does just that—it verifies that a move operation updates the x coordinate of a location and nothing else.

It would be nice and concise if you could consolidate the three assertions into a single line. You can, by comparing the altered location object to a newly-created instance:

utj3-units/03/src/test/java/units/ALocation.java
```java
@Test
void increasesYCoordinateWhenMovingNorth() {
    var location = new Location(0, 0, North);

    location.move(42);

    assertEquals(new Location(0, 42, North), location);
}
```

One fewer test statement means less extraneous cognitive load.

The move method is a void method; in other words, it returns no value. It's also a *command* (or *action* method)—its purpose is to allow you to *tell* an object to do something.

A command method can't return anything, so it must otherwise create some side effect to have a *raison d'etre*. It can alter any objects passed to it as arguments, it can alter the object's fields, or it can interact with something external that affects behavior. Or it can interact with another method that does one of those three things.

The code in move assigns new values to x and y depending on which case in the switch statement gets executed. These switch cases represent the potential side effects. It's the job of your tests to verify each one of these possible cases by tracking the state of both x and y.

Four cases, four tests. Here are the remaining three:

utj3-units/03/src/test/java/units/ALocation.java
```
@Test
void increasesXCoordinateWhenMovingEast() {
    var location = new Location(-2, 0, East);

    location.move(5);

    assertEquals(new Location(3, 0, East), location);
}

@Test
void decreasesYCoordinateWhenMovingSouth() {
    var location = new Location(-2, 5, South);

    location.move(9);

    assertEquals(new Location(-2, -4, South), location);
}

@Test
void decreasesXCoordinateWhenMovingWest() {
    var location = new Location(-2, 5, West);

    location.move(12);

    assertEquals(new Location(-14, 5, West), location);
}
```

You can create each test from scratch. Or you can copy a working test, paste it, and change the test data—as long as you go back and seek to eliminate redundancies across the tests.

All four tests contain the same three statements: create a location, call move on it, and then compare it to a new, expected location.

When only the data varies from test to test, you can use a *parameterized test* (see Executing Multiple Data Cases with Parameterized Tests, on page 131) to instead run one test many times, each with a different set of inputs and expected outcomes.

Let's consider, then discard, a couple more possibilities for testing the Location class:

1. The switch statement suggests a possibility that heading contains a value not represented in the case statements. But in this case, heading is an enum with four values, and you already have tests for all four values. (The compiler would also give you a warning otherwise.)

2. The heading parameter could be null. You could write a test that shows nothing happens if move gets called with a null heading. However, the notion of having no heading is probably nonsensical in the bigger application. Better solutions:

   - Default the heading to, say, North.
   - Throw an exception in the constructor if it's null.
   - Assume a *responsible* client calls move and never passes a null heading.

For now, make that last assumption, and don't worry about a null test.

Reflecting on Design

The more side effects your code creates, the more challenging it becomes to verify. If one method changes a field, its new value can unexpectedly break the behavior in other methods that interact with the field. These intertwinings of object state are one of the reasons you write tests.

How you design your code has a direct impact on how easy it is to change. A simpler design—more direct, more concise, and less intertwined—is better because it makes change cheaper.

A simpler design usually makes tests far easier to write, too. Fewer intertwinings of object state mean fewer pathways through the code that you must concern yourself with.

A simpler design makes for simpler testing.

The corollary to that important tip:

Tests that are hard to write usually imply less-than-ideal design. Fix the design.

Your tests for Location weren't so hard to write, and that's because there's not much entanglement within its code. Still, you'll want to look at a functional version. In Java, *records* provide the best place to get started—they create *immutable* objects by definition—objects whose state does not change after instantiation. It's a lot easier to reason about, and therefore test, when you don't have reason about complex ways in which the state can change.

utj3-units/03/src/main/java/units/FixedLocation.java
```java
public record FixedLocation(int x, int y, Heading heading) {
   public FixedLocation move(int distance) {
      return switch (heading) {
         case North -> new FixedLocation(x, y + distance, heading);
         case East -> new FixedLocation(x + distance, y, heading);
         case South -> new FixedLocation(x, y - distance, heading);
         case West -> new FixedLocation(x - distance, y, heading);
      };
   }
}
```

Holy hand grenade! Using Java records, all that other near-boilerplate gets blown away. You automagically get equals, hashCode, a useful toString, a constructor, and accessors. The code shrinks to a fraction of its stateful version. Take a look at what comparable tests look like.

utj3-units/03/src/test/java/units/AFixedLocation.java
```java
public class AFixedLocation {
   @Test
   void increasesYCoordinateWhenMovingNorth() {
      var location = new FixedLocation(0, 0, North);

      var newLocation = location.move(42);

      assertEquals(new FixedLocation(0, 42, North), newLocation);
   }

   @Test
   void increasesXCoordinateWhenMovingEast() {
      var location = new FixedLocation(-2, 0, East);

      var newLocation = location.move(5);

      assertEquals(new FixedLocation(3, 0, East), newLocation);
   }

   @Test
   void decreasesYCoordinateWhenMovingSouth() {
      var location = new FixedLocation(-2, 5, South);

      var newLocation = location.move(9);

      assertEquals(new FixedLocation(-2, -4, South), newLocation);
   }
```

```
@Test
void decreasesXCoordinateWhenMovingWest() {
    var location = new FixedLocation(-2, 5, West);

    var newLocation = location.move(12);

    assertEquals(new FixedLocation(-14, 5, West),newLocation);
}
}
```

Hmm. Not any better, really. But due to the functional nature of FixedLocation, you can inline all local variables to create single-statement assertions:

utj3-units/04/src/test/java/units/AFixedLocation.java
```
public class AFixedLocation {
    @Test
    void increasesYCoordinateWhenMovingNorth() {
        assertEquals(new FixedLocation(0, 42, North),
            new FixedLocation(0, 0, North).move(42));
    }

    @Test
    void increasesXCoordinateWhenMovingEast() {
        assertEquals(new FixedLocation(3, 0, East),
            new FixedLocation(-2, 0, East).move(5));
    }

    @Test
    void decreasesYCoordinateWhenMovingSouth() {
        assertEquals(new FixedLocation(-2, -4, South),
            new FixedLocation(-2, 5, South).move(9));
    }

    @Test
    void decreasesXCoordinateWhenMovingWest() {
        assertEquals(new FixedLocation(-14, 5, West),
            new FixedLocation(-2, 5, West).move(12));
    }
}
```

Each assertion now contains all the information needed to understand how the test example demonstrates what the test's name states. The tests are direct, and digestible almost at a glance.

You don't want to make Java into something it's not—a functional language. But moving in the direction of less state makes many things easier.

While each of the four tests involves a different set of data, their code is exactly the same. Each test creates a location, calls move, and asserts against a new location. You can cover the four data cases with a single test method that you inject data variants into—see Executing Multiple Data Cases with Parameterized Tests, on page 131).

Testing Common Code Circumstances

As you write more tests, you'll realize that you're often facing a number of common circumstances. Here's a handful of them:

- Add an item to a list
- Do something if a conditional is met
- Update all items in a list that match a predicate
- Remove all items matching a predicate from a list
- Throw an exception when a conditional is met

Lists and other collection types are a heavy part of most software development. You should be able to bang out tests involving lists without much thought.

In this section, you'll work through how you might write tests for each of those common needs. Hopefully, these examples will help you extrapolate and learn to write tests for other data structures (Maps, Sets, arrays, etc.) and operations (loops, streams, math, etc.).

Add an Item to a List

Here's some trivial code for a container class—DestinationList—that allows clients to add FixedLocation objects to it, one by one.

```
utj3-units/06/src/main/java/units/DestinationList.java
import java.util.ArrayList;
import java.util.List;

public class DestinationList {
    private List<FixedLocation> locations = new ArrayList<>();

    public void add(FixedLocation location) {
        locations.add(location);
    }

    public List<FixedLocation> getLocations() {
        return locations;
    }
}
```

At a glance, you pretty much know the code in DestinationList works. Doesn't matter, though—it's always possible for such a small amount of code to hide a mistake. The singular concept implemented in DestinationList—adding a location—involves three separate code points: a method to add the location to a list, a field that creates and initializes the list, and a method that returns the list. That lack of concision only increases the possibility of a defect.

DestinationList will change and grow as requirements for "add location" change or as other behaviors are added. Defects will be increasingly harder to spot.

Start testing now, before that "obvious" code sinks into a sea of "I'm not sure exactly what's going on!"

The Z in ZOM provides a good starting point and results in a guardrail test that will forever protect you:

utj3-units/06/src/test/java/units/ADestinationList.java
```java
import org.junit.jupiter.api.BeforeEach;
import org.junit.jupiter.api.Test;

import java.util.List;

import static org.junit.jupiter.api.Assertions.assertEquals;
import static org.junit.jupiter.api.Assertions.assertTrue;
import static units.FixedLocation.Heading.East;
import static units.FixedLocation.Heading.North;

class ADestinationList {
    private DestinationList list;

    @BeforeEach
    void create() {
        list = new DestinationList();
    }

    @Test
    void isEmptyWhenCreated() {
        assertTrue(list.getLocations().isEmpty());
    }
}
```

Do you really need both *one* and *many* tests? The only interesting behavior you've coded is your call to the add method defined on ArrayList:

utj3-units/06/src/main/java/units/DestinationList.java
```java
locations.add(location);
```

You trust ArrayList and its ability to support one location or scads of them. None of your code (for now) does anything differently when only one location is involved. Move directly to adding a *many* test:

utj3-units/06/src/test/java/units/ADestinationList.java
```java
@Test
void allowsAddingLocations() {
    list.add(new FixedLocation(1, 2, North));
    list.add(new FixedLocation(1, 3, East));

    assertEquals(
        List.of(
            new FixedLocation(1, 2, North),
            new FixedLocation(1, 3, East)),
        list.getLocations());
}
```

While it looks cut-and-dry, allowsAddingLocations involves some choices worth discussing. The test contains only two visual chunks. The second chunk represents the assert step, of course. Its assertion compares the result of calling getLocations to a List of two FixedLocation objects. The two objects in this comparison list are instantiated inline with the exact same values as when you constructed them in the arrange step.

In the assert, you are calling getLocations. By doing so, you are implying that getLocations isn't really what you're trying to verify (it's just an accessor), but you're instead using it to support your need to inspect the locations list.

Is the first chunk the arrange step or the act step? The test name says what behavior your test is trying to verify—the act of *adding* locations. That the two statements in the first chunk trigger the add behavior on the list means that they represent your act step. It's a subtle distinction. Some developers might consider the first chunk to be the test's arrange step, and maybe that's okay, but then there's no act step. It ain't much of a test without an act step.

The redundant FixedLocation instantiations may compel you to introduce a couple of local variables to help clarify the test. Creating such *test objects* can make it easier to *correlate* your test's inputs to the expected outcomes:

utj3-units/07/src/test/java/units/ADestinationList.java
```java
@Test
void allowsAddingLocations() {
   var locationOne = new FixedLocation(1, 2, North);
   var locationTwo = new FixedLocation(1, 3, East);

   list.add(locationOne);
   list.add(locationTwo);

   assertEquals(List.of(locationOne, locationTwo), list.getLocations());
}
```

Test objects are particularly useful when most, if not all, tests involve them. You can declare them as test-class-level constants with more memorable, domain-appropriate names:

utj3-units/08/src/test/java/units/ADestinationList.java
```java
static final FixedLocation ORIGIN = new FixedLocation(0, 0, East);
static final FixedLocation NORTHEAST = new FixedLocation(3, 3, North);

@Test
void allowsAddingLocations() {
   list.add(ORIGIN);
   list.add(NORTHEAST);

   assertEquals(List.of(ORIGIN, NORTHEAST), list.getLocations());
}
```

Such test objects also help de-emphasize details where they don't matter. That the northeast location is at (3, 3) and facing north is irrelevant in your allowsAddingLocations test. It only matters that NORTHEAST references an object distinct from ORIGIN.

Useful here, yet creating sample objects can be overkill. It's often easier to eyeball-compare the data by looking back and forth between the arrange and assert statements. As long as test intent remains clear, such trimmer tests can speed up efforts in both writing and understanding.

```
utj3-units/09/src/test/java/units/ADestinationList.java
@Test
void doesNotAddLocationAlreadyContained() {
   list.add(new FixedLocation(0, 0, East));
   list.add(new FixedLocation(3, 3, North));

   list.add(new FixedLocation(0, 0, East));

   assertEquals(
      List.of(new FixedLocation(0, 0, East),
              new FixedLocation(3, 3, North)),
      list.getLocations());
}
```

Any of the three forms (raw inline declarations, locally declared test objects, and globally accessible test objects) is acceptable. Here, the inline declarations clutter the tests a little too much. For now, use the constants.

Do Something if a Conditional Is Met

If the code you're testing involves a conditional (an if statement), you need *at least* two sets of tests: one set involving all the ways that the conditional can pass (in other words, return true), and one set involving all the ways that it can fail (return false). That way, your tests will cover both what happens if the if block executes and what happens if it does not.

A common behavioral need is to ensure that a collection doesn't take on duplicate elements. Here's a change to DestinationList that introduces such a conditional to the add method:

```
utj3-units/09/src/main/java/units/DestinationList.java
public void add(FixedLocation location) {
   if (locations.contains(location)) return;

   locations.add(location);
}
```

You already have one test that allows adding objects. Here it is again:

```
utj3-units/09/src/test/java/units/ADestinationList.java
@Test
void allowsAddingLocations() {
    list.add(ORIGIN);
    list.add(NORTHEAST);

    assertEquals(List.of(ORIGIN, NORTHEAST), list.getLocations());
}
```

The distinct names ORIGIN and DESTINATION imply that the two sample objects are distinct from each other. Write an additional test that involves attempting to add one of them, ORIGIN, a second time:

```
utj3-units/09/src/test/java/units/ADestinationList.java
@Test
void doesNotAddLocationWhenAlreadyContained() {
    list.add(ORIGIN);
    list.add(NORTHEAST);

    list.add(ORIGIN);

    assertEquals(List.of(ORIGIN, NORTHEAST), list.getLocations());
}
```

A final note on the Arrange—Act—Assert (AAA) organization here: you are still trying to verify the behavior of adding (or not adding) locations. The first two lines in the test arrange things by adding a couple of locations. You then see the act step that isolates the addition of a duplicate location. This breakout helps readers focus on how to trigger the happy path of the if statement—you attempt to add an object whose details match those of one already added.

Update All Items in a List That Match a Predicate

The job of the method moveLocationsWithHeading is to iterate all locations and update those whose heading matches a target (passed-in) heading. The update involves changing to new x and y coordinates.

A map operation suits your needs. Each location is mapped either to the same location, if its heading does not match, or to a new FixedLocation with updated coordinates (since FixedLocations are immutable). The collected stream is then assigned back to the DestinationList's locations field.

```
utj3-units/09/src/main/java/units/DestinationList.java
public void moveLocationsWithHeading(Heading heading, int x, int y) {
    this.locations = locations.stream()
        .map(location -> location.heading().equals(heading)
            ? new FixedLocation(x, y, heading)
            : location)
        .toList();
}
```

Here's an approach for testing the moveLocationsWithHeading:

- Create a list with two FixedLocation objects, one with the heading you want to target (for example, East). The other object should have a different heading.

- Call the method moveLocationsWithHeading and pass it the targeted heading (East); also pass new values for x and y.

- Ensure that the updated list in DestinationList contains a list of two elements. The location with the targeted location should reflect the new x and y values; the other location should remain unchanged.

Here's what the new test looks like:

utj3-units/09/src/test/java/units/ADestinationList.java
```
@Test
void updatesMatchingLocationsWithNewCoordinates() {
   list.add(new FixedLocation(0, 0, East));
   list.add(new FixedLocation(1, 1, North));

   list.moveLocationsWithHeading(East, 2, 3);

   assertEquals(List.of(
        new FixedLocation(2, 3, East),
        new FixedLocation(1, 1, North)),
      list.getLocations());
}
```

You'll note you're not using test objects here. Test objects de-emphasize most details, but for this test, you need to show whether specific values (x and y) change, or don't, based on another value (the heading). By directly instantiating FixedLocation objects, you can visually correlate the details between arrange inputs and assert expected outputs.

Remove All Items Matching a Predicate from a List

Another method on DestinationList allows clients to remove all locations that exceed a specified distance from a point:

utj3-units/09/src/main/java/units/DestinationList.java
```
public void removeLocationsFurtherThan(int x, int y, int distance) {
   this.locations = locations.stream()
      .filter(location -> distanceBetween(location, x, y) < distance)
      .toList();
}

private double distanceBetween(FixedLocation point, int x, int y) {
   return Math.sqrt(
      Math.pow(x - point.x(), 2) + Math.pow(y - point.y(), 2));
}
```

Your test looks similar to the test for moveLocationsWithHeading. It creates three locations, two of which have a distance from (0, 0) that is greater than the value of 9 passed in the act step. The assertion verifies that only the location with a shorter distance remains.

utj3-units/09/src/test/java/units/ADestinationList.java

```java
@Test
void retainsLocationsLessThanDistance() {
    list.add(new FixedLocation(0, 5, North));
    list.add(new FixedLocation(0, 10, North));
    list.add(new FixedLocation(0, 15, North));

    list.removeLocationsFurtherThan(0, 0, 9);

    assertEquals(List.of(
        new FixedLocation(0, 5, North)),
      list.getLocations());
}
```

This test purposefully uses simplistic test data. Each of the three highlighted locations added as part of arranging the test is on the vertical (y) axis. As a result, the distance between each location and (0, 0) (the passed-in point) is the same as its y coordinate.

The simple-data approach to removeLocationsFurtherThan keeps the test easy to understand, but it means you're ignoring the complexity in distanceBetween. That means you'll need to demonstrate that the logic in distanceBetween is correct for non-zero values of x.

You have a few options for verifying the distance calculations:

- You can write more tests that interact with removeLocationsFurtherThan. These tests represent a slightly indirect way to verify the distance calculation and demand a few more lines of code.

- You can expose distanceBetween as a package-level method, which would allow ADestinationList to directly test it. But distanceBetween as a concept is out of place in DestinationList. The job of DestinationList is to manage a list of destinations, not to calculate distances between a FixedLocation and a point.

- You can make distanceBetween a concept better associated with FixedLocation, and move the method to that class. After moving the method, you can test it directly in FixedLocation.

Here's the relevant code after the move:

```
utj3-units/10/src/main/java/units/DestinationList.java
public void removeLocationsFurtherThan(int x, int y, int distance) {
    this.locations = locations.stream()
        .filter(location -> location.distanceFrom(x, y) < distance)
        .toList();
}
```

```
utj3-units/10/src/main/java/units/FixedLocation.java
double distanceFrom(int x, int y) {
    return Math.sqrt(Math.pow(x - x(), 2) + Math.pow(y - y(), 2));
}
```

In the context of FixedLocation, the method name distanceBetween could use a little improvement. It's been renamed to distanceFrom here. (A trick for deriving names: utter the phrase that describes how the method is used in context, for example, "we ask for the *distance from* a fixed location for a point.")

Now, you can quickly write a number of very focused tests that exhaust your ideas about how to test the distance calculation:

```
utj3-units/10/src/test/java/units/AFixedLocation.java
import org.junit.jupiter.api.Test;
import static org.junit.jupiter.api.Assertions.assertEquals;
import static units.FixedLocation.Heading.*;

public class AFixedLocation {
    final static FixedLocation.Heading h = North;

    @Test
    void is0WhenCoordinatesAreTheSame() {
        assertEquals(0, new FixedLocation(1, 2, h).distanceFrom(1, 2));
    }

    @Test
    void is5InClassicHypotenuseCase() {
        assertEquals(5.0, new FixedLocation(0, 0, h).distanceFrom(3, 4));
    }

    @Test
    void isNearSomeDoubleValue() {
        assertEquals(5.6568, new FixedLocation(10, 13, h).distanceFrom(14, 9),
            0.0001);
    }

    @Test
    void worksWithNegativeNumbers() {
        assertEquals(23.7697,
            new FixedLocation(-7, 13, h).distanceFrom(2, -9),
            0.0001);
    }
}
```

The first two tests verify the zero case and a simple example. The last two involve distance calculations that return interesting floating point quantities. (Stylistic note: since the heading is irrelevant to these tests, naming it h helps de-emphasize it.)

Assertions against code involving complex calculations too often provide insufficient insight into what the code is doing. The expected value is mathematically correct, but there's no easy way to correlate it to the input values from just reading the act and assert.

To derive the expected value for such a calculation, you can hand-calculate it. You can also cross-check by using an independent source for verification, such as an online app.

Due to limitations on how floating point values are captured, comparing two floating point values can result in unexpected discrepancies. For this reason, JUnit provides a form of assertEquals that takes a delta value as the third argument. This delta represents a tolerance. How much can the two numbers be off before JUnit fails the assertion?

In the test, define a heading constant arbitrarily set to North. While the heading is required each time you construct a FixedLocation, it's completely irrelevant to the tests. Name this constant h, to de-emphasize the constructor argument and thus minimize the clutter it otherwise adds to the tests.

Throw an Exception When a Conditional Is Met

In Chapter 1, Building Your First JUnit Test, on page 3, you wrote tests for arithmeticMean in CreditHistory. The first test you wrote was a zero case:

utj3-credit-history/10/src/test/java/credit/ACreditHistory.java
```
@Test
void withNoCreditRatingsHas0Mean() {
    var result = creditHistory.arithmeticMean();

    assertEquals(0, result);
}
```

That test described and verified the highlighted behavior in arithmeticMean:

utj3-credit-history/10/src/main/java/credit/CreditHistory.java
```
public int arithmeticMean() {
    if (ratings.isEmpty()) return 0;

    var total = ratings.stream().mapToInt(CreditRating::rating).sum();
    return total / ratings.size();
}
```

You've been asked to change the code—oh no! The product owner has been schooled by a mathematician and wants arithmeticMean to throw an exception when there are no credit ratings.

Pretend to panic for a moment ("But I'll have to retest everything!"), then make the trivial change:

```
utj3-credit-history/11/src/main/java/credit/CreditHistory.java
public int arithmeticMean() {
    if (ratings.isEmpty()) throw new IllegalStateException();

    var total = ratings.stream().mapToInt(CreditRating::rating).sum();
    return total / ratings.size();
}
```

Because you changed your code, run your tests. Hope at least one test will fail due to your change of the behavior that the tests cover. Dream that *only* the test ACreditHistory::withNoCreditRatingsHas0Mean fails since it's the only test directly related to the changed behavior. Rejoice when your hopes and dreams (paltry as they are) come true: withNoCreditRatingsHas0Mean fails and for the right reason—an IllegalStateException was thrown. Hooray!

The desired behavior is in place. A test is failing. Time to fix the incorrect test.

JUnit 5 gives you a way to verify that a piece of test code throws an exception:

```
utj3-credit-history/12/src/test/java/credit/ACreditHistory.java
@Test
void withNoCreditRatingsThrows() {
    assertThrows(IllegalStateException.class,
        () -> creditHistory.arithmeticMean());
}
```

In its simplest form, JUnit's assertThrows method takes on two arguments. The first represents the type of exception you expect to be thrown (IllegalStateException.class in this case). The second argument is a lambda whose body contains the code that you expect will throw the appropriate exception. In your case, you're expecting the call to arithmeticMean to throw the exception.

When handling an assertThrows statement within a test, JUnit executes the lambda in the context of a try/catch block. If the lambda barfs an exception, the catch block catches the barfage and JUnit marks the test as passing as long as the exception type matches. Otherwise, JUnit marks the test as a failure since no exception was thrown.

Because your requirements changed, you updated the code and then verified that your change broke a specific test. That seems so...reactionary. Maybe you should take control of things.

If you view the unit tests as a way of characterizing all your code units, collectively they become the requirements in an odd but useful little "requirements by example" manner. Your test names describe the behavioral needs. Each test provides an example of one of those behaviors.

Such well-named requirements-by-example (tests) can quickly answer questions others (or even you) might ask: "hey, what does the system do when we try to calculate the arithmetic mean and there are no credit ratings?" Everyone is happy, you have an immediate answer, and you're highly confident it's correct because all of your tests are passing.

One way to take control: invert your approach to unit testing—drive a requirements change by *first* updating the tests that relate to the change. After observing that the updated tests fail (because you've not yet updated the system with the new requirement), you can make the necessary changes and then run all tests to ensure you're still happy.

Once you feel increased control by test-driving changes, your next thought might be, "what if I drove in all new functionality this way?" You can, and doing so is known as *Test-Driven Development (TDD)*. See Chapter 11, Advancing with Test-Driven Development (TDD), on page 211 for a rundown of what TDD looks like and why it might help even more. Get a little excited about it—because TDD is also a lot of fun—but for now, you should continue your unit testing journey.

Testing that an exception is thrown when expected is as important as testing any other code. You'll also want to verify that *other* code responds properly to the situation when an exception *is* thrown. Doing so is a slightly trickier technique; visit Testing Exception Handling, on page 65 for details.

Exploring Boundaries with CORRECT

The zero, one, many, and exception-based tests will cover most of your typical needs when testing code. But you'll also want to consider adding tests for cases that a happy path through the code might not hit. These *boundary* conditions represent scenarios that involve the edges of the input domain.

You can employ the CORRECT acronym, devised by Andy Hunt and Dave Thomas for the *first edition of this book [HT03]*, to help you think about potential boundary conditions. For each of these items, consider whether or not similar conditions can exist in the method that you want to test and what might happen if these conditions are violated:

- Conformance—Does the value conform to an expected format, such as an email address or filename? What does the method do when passed an invalid format? Does a string parameter support upper or mixed case?

- Ordering—Is the set of values ordered or unordered as appropriate? What happens if things happen out of chronological order, such as an HTTP server that returns an OPTIONS response after a POST instead of before?

- Range—Is the value within reasonable minimum and maximum values? Can any computations result in numeric overflow? range

- Reference—Does the object need to be in a certain state? What happens if it's in an unexpected state? What if the code references something external that's not under its direct control?

- Existence—Does the value exist (is it non-null, nonzero, present in a set)? What if you pass a method empty values (0, 0.0, "", null)?

- Cardinality—Are there exactly enough values? Have you covered all your bases with ZOM? Can it handle large volumes? Is there a notion of too many? What if there are duplicates in a list that shouldn't allow them (for example, a roster of classroom students)?

- Time (absolute and relative)—Is everything happening in order? At the right time? In time?

Many of the defects you'll code in your career will involve similar corner cases, so you'll positively want to cover them with tests.

Summary

You have worked through writing tests for a number of common unit scenarios. Your own "real" code test will, of course, be different and often more involved. Still, how you approach writing tests for your code will be similar to the approaches you've learned here.

Much of the code you try to test will be dependent on other classes that are volatile, slow, or even incomplete. In the next chapter, you'll learn how to use test doubles (colloquially referred to as mock objects or mocks) to break those dependencies so that you can test.

CHAPTER 3

Using Test Doubles

You can test a lot of your system using the information you've learned over the prior two chapters. But not all units are going to be similarly easy to test.

It's a safe bet you find your own system hard to test. Perhaps you think the first two chapters made it look too easy. "It must be nice to have a system that supports writing unit tests out of the box, but it doesn't match my reality," says Joe.

In this chapter, you'll learn how to employ *test doubles* to break dependencies on pain-inducing collaborators. A test double is a stand-in (think "stunt double") for the dependencies that make your code hard to test. You're probably already familiar with the name of one kind of test double—a *mock object*.

With test doubles, you gain a tool that will help you get past the ever-present unit testing hurdle of troublesome dependencies.

A Testing Challenge

You're testing an AddressRetriever. Given a latitude and longitude, its retrieve method returns an appropriately populated Address object.

utj3-mock-objects/01/src/main/java/com/langrsoft/domain/AddressRetriever.java
```
import com.fasterxml.jackson.core.JsonProcessingException;
import com.fasterxml.jackson.databind.DeserializationFeature;
import com.fasterxml.jackson.databind.ObjectMapper;
import com.langrsoft.util.HttpImpl;

public class AddressRetriever {
    private static final String SERVER =
        "https://nominatim.openstreetmap.org";

    public Address retrieve(double latitude, double longitude) {
        var locationParams =
            "lon=%.6f&lat=%.6f".formatted(latitude, longitude);
        var url =
            "%s/reverse?%s&format=json".formatted(SERVER, locationParams);
```

```
➤          var jsonResponse = new HttpImpl().get(url);

           var response = parseResponse(jsonResponse);

           var address = response.address();
           var country = address.country_code();
           if (!country.equals("us"))
               throw new UnsupportedOperationException(
                   "intl addresses unsupported");

           return address;
       }

    private Response parseResponse(String jsonResponse) {
        var mapper = new ObjectMapper().configure(
           DeserializationFeature.FAIL_ON_UNKNOWN_PROPERTIES, false);
        try {
           return mapper.readValue(jsonResponse, Response.class);
        } catch (JsonProcessingException e) {
           throw new RuntimeException(e);
        }
    }
}
```

At first glance, testing retrieve appears straightforward—it's only about ten lines long with one conditional and a short helper method. Then you notice code that appears to make a live HTTP get request (highlighted in AddressRetriever). Hmm.

Sure enough, the HttpImpl class interacts with Apache's HttpComponents client to execute a REST call:

utj3-mock-objects/01/src/main/java/com/langrsoft/util/HttpImpl.java
```java
import java.io.IOException;
import java.net.URI;
import java.net.http.HttpClient;
import java.net.http.HttpRequest;
import java.net.http.HttpResponse.BodyHandlers;

public class HttpImpl implements Http {
  @Override
  public String get(String url) {
    try (var client = HttpClient.newHttpClient()) {
      var request = HttpRequest.newBuilder().uri(URI.create(url)).build();
      try {
        var httpResponse = client.send(request, BodyHandlers.ofString());
        return httpResponse.body();
      } catch (IOException | InterruptedException e) {
        throw new RuntimeException(e);
      }
    }
  }
}
```

The HttpImpl class implements the HTTP interface:

utj3-mock-objects/01/src/main/java/com/langrsoft/util/Http.java
```java
public interface Http {
    String get(String url);
}
```

You trust HttpImpl because you find an integration test for it in ./src/test/java/com/langrsoft/util. But you also know that HttpImpl's code interacts with an external service over HTTP—a recipe for unit testing trouble. Any tests you write for retrieve in AddressRetriever will ultimately trigger a live HTTP call. That carries at least two big implications:

- The tests against the live call will be slow compared to the bulk of your other fast tests.

- You can't guarantee that the Nominatim HTTP API will be available or return consistent results. It's out of your control.

A test version of the API would give you control over availability. Your builds and local dev environments would need to start/restart the service as appropriate. It would also be slow in comparison (see Fast Tests, on page 66).

You want a way to focus on unit testing the rest of the logic in retrieve—the code that preps the HTTP call and the code that handles the response—isolated from the HTTP dependency.

Replacing Troublesome Behavior with Stubs

The challenge for testing is the code in HttpImpl that calls a real endpoint. To fix the problem, your test can supplant HttpImpl's live call with logic that instead returns mocked-up data. You'll create an implementation of HttpImpl known as a *stub*: It will *stub* out the real code with a simplified version.

 A stub is a test double that supplants real behavior with a method that returns a hardcoded value.

HTTP is a *functional interface*: It contains exactly one abstract method declaration (for get). As a result, you can dynamically and concisely declare an implementation of HTTP using a lambda:

utj3-mock-objects/02/src/test/java/com/langrsoft/domain/AnAddressRetriever.java
```java
Http http = url ->
    """
        {"address":{
          "house_number":"324",
```

```
            "road":"Main St",
            "city":"Anywhere",
            "state":"Colorado",
            "postcode":"81234",
            "country_code":"us"}}
        """;
```

The stub returns a hardcoded JSON string, backward engineered from the parsing code in retrieve. Consider it an alternate implementation of the HTTP interface, suitable for use only by a test.

Injecting Dependencies into Production Code

The HTTP stub gets you halfway toward being able to write your test. You must also tell AddressRetriever to use your stub instead of a "real" HttpImpl object. You do so using *dependency injection,* a fancy term for passing the stub to an AddressRetriever instance. You can *inject* a stub in a few ways; here, you'll inject it via the constructor:

utj3-mock-objects/02/src/main/java/com/langrsoft/domain/AddressRetriever.java
```
public class AddressRetriever {
    private static final String SERVER =
        "https://nominatim.openstreetmap.org";
➤   private final Http http;

➤   public AddressRetriever(Http http) {
➤       this.http = http;
➤   }

    public Address retrieve(double latitude, double longitude) {
        var locationParams =
            "lon=%.6f&lat=%.6f".formatted(latitude, longitude);
        var url =
            "%s/reverse?%s&format=json".formatted(SERVER, locationParams);

➤       var jsonResponse = http.get(url);

        var response = parseResponse(jsonResponse);
        // ...
    }
    // ...
```

The call to http.get(url) in retrieve (highlighted) no longer creates a private instance of HTTP. It now dereferences the http field, which points to the stub when executed in the context of the test you can now write.

utj3-mock-objects/02/src/test/java/com/langrsoft/domain/AnAddressRetriever.java
```
import com.langrsoft.util.*;
import org.junit.jupiter.api.Test;
import static org.junit.jupiter.api.Assertions.assertEquals;
import static org.junit.jupiter.api.Assertions.assertThrows;
```

```java
class AnAddressRetriever {
    @Test
    void answersAppropriateAddressForValidCoordinates() {
        Http http = url ->
            """
                {"address":{
                  "house_number":"324",
                  "road":"Main St",
                  "city":"Anywhere",
                  "state":"Colorado",
                  "postcode":"81234",
                  "country_code":"us"}}
                """;
        var retriever = new AddressRetriever(http);

        var address = retriever.retrieve(38, -104);

        assertEquals("324", address.house_number());
        assertEquals("Main St", address.road());
        assertEquals("Anywhere", address.city());
        assertEquals("Colorado", address.state());
        assertEquals("81234", address.postcode());
    }
}
```

When the test runs:

- It creates an AddressRetriever, passing it the HTTP stub instance.

- When executed, the retrieve method formats a URL using parameters passed to the method. It then calls the get method on http.

- The stub returns the JSON string you hardcoded in the test.

- The rest of the retrieve method parses the hardcoded JSON string and populates an Address object accordingly.

- The test verifies elements of the returned Address object.

The retrieve method is oblivious to whether http references a stub or the real implementation. In this example, the stub represents a "single use test case" for purposes of one test. Add another test that creates a completely different stub:

utj3-mock-objects/02/src/test/java/com/langrsoft/domain/AnAddressRetriever.java
```java
@Test
void throwsWhenNotUSCountryCode() {
    Http http = url -> """
        {"address":{ "country_code":"not us"}}""";
    var retriever = new AddressRetriever(http);
```

```
assertThrows(UnsupportedOperationException.class,
    () -> retriever.retrieve(1.0, -1.0));
}
```

This second test takes advantage of the fact that AddressRetriever code looks only at country_code, throwing an exception when it is anything but the lowercase string "us".

Changing Your Design to Support Testing

You changed the design of AddressRetriever. Before, it created an HttpImpl instance in retrieve as a private detail. Now, a client using AddressRetriever must pass an HTTP-derived object to its constructor (or use a dependency injection tool):

```
var retriever = new AddressRetriever(new HttpImpl());
```

Changing design to simplify testing might seem odd, but doing so lets you write the tests that increase your confidence to ship.

You're not limited to constructor injection; you can inject stubs in many other ways. Some ways require no changes to the interface of your class. You can use setters instead of constructors, you can override factory methods, you can introduce abstract factories, and you can even use tools such as Google Guice or Spring that do the injection somewhat magically.

Adding Smarts to Your Stub: Verifying Parameters

Your HTTP stub always returns the same hardcoded JSON string, regardless of the latitude/longitude passed to get. That's a small hole in testing. If the AddressRetriever doesn't pass the parameters properly, you have a defect.

You are not exercising the real behavior of HttpImpl (which already has tests). You're exercising the rest of retrieve's code based on a return value that HttpImpl might cough up. The only thing left to cover is verifying that retrieve correctly interacts with HttpImpl.

As a quick stab at a solution, add a guard clause to the stub that verifies the URL passed to the HTTP method get. If it doesn't contain the expected parameter string, explicitly fail the test at that point:

utj3-mock-objects/03/src/test/java/com/langrsoft/domain/AnAddressRetriever.java
```
@Test
void answersAppropriateAddressForValidCoordinates() {
    Http http = url -> {
        if (!url.contains("lat=38") ||
            !url.contains("lon=-104"))
            fail("url " + url + " does not contain correct params");
```

```
        return """
          {"address":{
            "house_number":"324",
            "road":"Main St",
            "city":"Anywhere",
            "state":"Colorado",
            "postcode":"81234",
            "country_code":"us"}}
          """;
};
var retriever = new AddressRetriever(http);

var address = retriever.retrieve(38, -104);
// ...
```

The stub has a little bit of smarts now...meaning it's no longer a stub. It's closer to being a *mock*. A mock, like a stub, lets you provide test-specific behavior. It can also self-verify, as in this example, by ensuring that expected interactions with collaborators (an HTTP implementation here) occur.

The "smart stub" pays off—your test now fails. Did you spot the defect earlier?

utj3-mock-objects/03/src/main/java/com/langrsoft/domain/AddressRetriever.java
```
public Address retrieve(double latitude, double longitude) {
    var locationParams = "lon=%.6f&lat=%.6f".formatted(latitude, longitude);
    var url = "%s/reverse?%s&format=json".formatted(SERVER, locationParams);

    var jsonResponse = http.get(url);
    // ...
}
```

Fixing the problem involves swapping the two query parameter names:

utj3-mock-objects/04/src/main/java/com/langrsoft/domain/AddressRetriever.java
```
var locationParams = "lat=%.6f&lon=%.6f".formatted(latitude, longitude);
```

 Using a mock, your test can verify that a method was called *and* with the right arguments.

Simplifying Testing Using a Mock Tool

Hand-grown smart stubs are kind of a bad idea. A stub is a simple test construct that returns a hard-coded value. Adding logic in the middle of it is a recipe for wasted time when you get the logic wrong (you eventually will)—which turns it into a smart-ahh...never mind.

You'll instead represent your stub using Mockito,[1] the *de facto* standard "mock" library for Java. Using the tool will keep your tests safer and simpler when you need test doubles. It handles the smarts, so you don't have to.

Here's the test updated to use Mockito:

utj3-mock-objects/05/src/test/java/com/langrsoft/domain/AnAddressRetriever.java

```java
// ...
import static org.mockito.ArgumentMatchers.contains;
import static org.mockito.Mockito.mock;
import static org.mockito.Mockito.when;

class AnAddressRetriever {
    Http http = mock(Http.class);

    @Test
    void answersAppropriateAddressForValidCoordinates() {
        when(http.get(contains("lat=38.000000&lon=-104.000000"))).thenReturn(
            """
            {"address":{
              "house_number":"324",
              "road":"Main St",
              "city":"Anywhere",
              "state":"Colorado",
              "postcode":"81234",
              "country_code":"us"}}
            """);
        var retriever = new AddressRetriever(http);

        var address = retriever.retrieve(38, -104);
        // ...
    }
    // ...
}
```

The field http is initialized with a call to Mockito's static mock method, which synthesizes an object that implements the HTTP interface. This mock object tracks when methods are called and with what arguments.

The first statement in the test (in its arrange step) sets up an *expectation* on the mock. It tells the mock object to *expect* that the get method *might* be called. If the method is indeed called (at any point later during test execution), and with an argument containing the substring "lat=38.000000&lon=-104.000000", the mock object will return the specified hard-coded JSON string.

If the get method is not called, or if it's called but doesn't contain the expected lat-long string, the mock object returns null. The contains method is what

---

1.   https://site.mockito.org

Mockito refers to as *matcher*. More typically, you wouldn't use a matcher like contains, but would instead specify the exact argument expected.

The second statement in the test, as before, injects the Mockito mock into the AddressRetriever via its constructor. Replacing your stub with Mockito doesn't require changing any production code.

When the retrieve method is called during the "act" step of the test, its code interacts with the Mockito mock. If the Mockito mock's expectations are met—if the production code calls http.get(url) as expected, the mock returns the hardcoded JSON string, and the test passes. If not, the test fails.

It would be better if your mock didn't have to know the exact encoding order of the latitude and longitude query params. Mockito lets you supply two distinct matchers using the and matcher:

utj3-mock-objects/06/src/test/java/com/langrsoft/domain/AnAddressRetriever.java
```java
import static org.mockito.AdditionalMatchers.and;
// ...
    @Test
    void answersAppropriateAddressForValidCoordinates() {
        when(http.get(
            and(contains("lat=38.000000"), contains("lon=-104.000000"))))
            .thenReturn(
                // ...
    }
```

Both contains matchers have to hold true for the test to pass.

With the happy path test for retrieve out of the way, you can update the not-as-happy-path test, throwsWhenNotUSCountryCode, to use Mockito:

utj3-mock-objects/05/src/test/java/com/langrsoft/domain/AnAddressRetriever.java
```java
@Test
void throwsWhenNotUSCountryCode() {
    when(http.get(anyString())).thenReturn("""
        {"address":{ "country_code":"not us"}}""");
    var retriever = new AddressRetriever(http);

    assertThrows(UnsupportedOperationException.class,
        () -> retriever.retrieve(1.0, -1.0));
}
```

Your happy path test, answersAppropriateAddressForValidCoordinates, demonstrated that retrieve correctly formats its arguments into a query parameter string. Accordingly, you don't need to similarly worry about doing so in this second test. You can use the Mockito matcher method anyString() to indicate that the test should pass as long as a string object is passed to the get method.

The when(...).thenReturn(...) pattern is one of a number of ways to set up mocks using Mockito, but it's probably the simplest to understand and code. It distills the effort of setting up a mock into what's essentially a one-liner that immediately makes sense to someone reading the code.

Injecting Mocks with Mockito

Using constructor injection may require you to change your class's interface. A dependency injection (DI) tool like Spring DI, Google Guice, or PicoContainer can eliminate the need for that change. You can also use Mockito, which provides nominal built-in DI capabilities. It's not as sophisticated as the other two tools, but it might be all you need. To use Mockito's DI:

- Annotate the test class with @ExtendWith(MockitoExtension.class).
- Annotate the http field with @Mock. Mockito initializes it as a mock object.
- Annotate the retriever field with @InjectMocks. Mockito creates an instance of retriever and injects any @Mock fields into it.

utj3-mock-objects/07/src/test/java/com/langrsoft/domain/AnAddressRetriever.java
```
// ...
import org.junit.jupiter.api.extension.ExtendWith;
import org.mockito.Mock;
import org.mockito.InjectMocks;
import org.mockito.junit.jupiter.MockitoExtension;

@ExtendWith(MockitoExtension.class)
class AnAddressRetriever {
    @InjectMocks
    AddressRetriever retriever;

    @Mock
    Http http;

    @Test
    void answersAppropriateAddressForValidCoordinates() {
        when(http.get(and(contains("lat=38.000000"),
                          contains("lon=-104.000000"))))
            // ...
    }
    // ...
}
```

When injecting mock objects, Mockito first seeks an appropriate constructor—in this case, one that takes on an HTTP instance. If it finds none, it seeks an appropriate setter method, and then finally, a field with the matching type.

To try this feature, eliminate AddressRetriever's constructor and initialize an http field:

utj3-mock-objects/07/src/main/java/com/langrsoft/domain/AddressRetriever.java
```java
public class AddressRetriever {
    private static final String SERVER =
        "https://nominatim.openstreetmap.org";
    private Http http = new HttpImpl(); // this cannot be final

    // look ma, no constructor!

    public Address retrieve(double latitude, double longitude) {
        // ...
    }
    // ...
}
```

From the test, Mockito magically finds your http field and injects the mock instance into it (overwriting what was already there)!

Production clients no longer need to pass a value for http into the AddressRetriever since it's initialized to the appropriate production object.

Downsides: mucking with privates violates many folks' design sensibilities. Also, Mockito injection is slow, adding almost a full second to the test run on my machine. Ensure its inclusion doesn't pig out the overall execution time of your test suite.

Verifying a Method Was Called…or Not

As an alternative to when(…).thenReturn(…), you might want to verify that a certain method was called with the proper arguments as part of processing. The typical case for this need is when you're invoking a *consumer*—a method that has side effects but returns nothing. Mockito helps you verify that such a method was called with its verify functionality.

Update the AddressRetriever to tell an Auditor instance to add audit information when the country code returned is a non-U.S. country code:

utj3-mock-objects/08/src/main/java/com/langrsoft/domain/AddressRetriever.java
```java
public class AddressRetriever {
    private Auditor auditor = new ApplicationAuditor();
    // ...
    public Address retrieve(double latitude, double longitude) {
    // ...
        var country = address.country_code();
        if (!country.equals("us")) {
            auditor.audit("request for country code: %s".formatted(country));
            throw new UnsupportedOperationException(
                "intl addresses unsupported");
        }
```

```
        return address;
    }
    // ...
}
```

For now, the audit method in ApplicationAuditor does nothing; some other team member is coding it. You need only the interface declaration in order to write your test:

utj3-mock-objects/08/src/main/java/com/langrsoft/domain/Auditor.java
```
public interface Auditor {
    void audit(String message);
}
```

Add a test that proves audit is called for a non-U.S. country code. Use Mockito's verify method, which acts as an assertion. If the audit method is called with exactly the same String argument, the test passes.

utj3-mock-objects/08/src/test/java/com/langrsoft/domain/AnAddressRetriever.java
```
➤   import static org.mockito.Mockito.verify;
    // ...
    @Test
    void auditsWhenNonUSAddressRetrieved() {
        when(http.get(anyString())).thenReturn("""
            {"address":{ "country_code":"not us"}}""");

        assertThrows(UnsupportedOperationException.class,
            () -> retriever.retrieve(1.0, -1.0));

➤       verify(auditor).audit("request for country code: not us");
    }
    // ...
}
```

Note the difference regarding parentheses placement between verify and when:

```
verify(someObject).method();
when(someObject.method()).thenReturn(...);
```

Add a second test to verify that audit is *not* called when the country code is "us". You can add a second argument to verify that represents the number of times you expect verify to be invoked. In this case, you can specify that you expect it never to be called. Provide an any() matcher as the argument to the audit method, indicating that the method will never be called with anything.

utj3-mock-objects/08/src/test/java/com/langrsoft/domain/AnAddressRetriever.java
```
➤   import static org.mockito.Mockito.never;
➤   import static org.mockito.ArgumentMatchers.any;
    // ...
    @Test
    void doesNotOccurWhenUSAddressRetrieved() {
```

```
    when(http.get(anyString())).thenReturn("""
        {"address":{ "country_code":"us"}}""");

    retriever.retrieve(1.0, -1.0);

➤   verify(auditor, never()).audit(any());
}
```

Both verify and when contain numerous nuances and options. Make sure you peruse the Mockito docs[2] for more on these and other features.

Testing Exception Handling

Exception handling is often an afterthought. The happy path is the first thing in the mind of most developers; that's human nature. After they get a solution working, a developer revisits the code and thinks about what might go wrong. They add exception-handling logic to all the places (hopefully) it looks like it needs it.

Currently, AddressRetriever doesn't handle errors thrown by the HTTP get method, which could occur for a number of reasons. You've decided that retrieve shouldn't propagate the exception but should instead return null.

Mockito will help you set up a test to emulate get throwing an exception. Rather than returning a value when an expectation is met, as you've been doing throughout this chapter, you tell Mockito to throw an exception:

utj3-mock-objects/09/src/test/java/com/langrsoft/domain/AnAddressRetriever.java
```java
@Test
void returnsNullWhenHttpGetThrows() {
➤   when(http.get(anyString())).thenThrow(RuntimeException.class);

    var address = retriever.retrieve(38, -104);

    assertNull(address);
}
```

Your implementation requires a try/catch block to trap the potential exception emanating from get. The unsightliness of the construct—six, count 'em, *six* vertical lines of code—is worth isolating by extracting to a separate method:

utj3-mock-objects/09/src/main/java/com/langrsoft/domain/AddressRetriever.java
```java
public class AddressRetriever {
    private Auditor auditor = new ApplicationAuditor();
    private static final String SERVER =
        "https://nominatim.openstreetmap.org";
    private Http http = new HttpImpl(); // this cannot be final
```

---

2. https://site.mockito.org/javadoc/current/org/mockito/Mockito.html

```
    public Address retrieve(double latitude, double longitude) {
    // ...
        var jsonResponse = get(url);
        if (jsonResponse == null) return null;
        // ...
    }

    private String get(String url) {
        try {
            return http.get(url);
        }
        catch (Exception e) {
            return null;
        }
    }
    // ...
}
```

Mockito's thenThrow stub helps your tests describe how the system deals with errors. Also important: writing tests to describe how and when code propagates errors. You'll learn about that in Expecting Exceptions, on page 112.

Fast Tests

Mock objects are essential for creating unit tests that aren't beholden to volatile external dependencies, such as the Nominatim API. An added bonus of employing mock objects: you gain tremendously faster tests.

Tremendously? There's no unit testing standard for what *fast* and *slow* mean. Perhaps it's personal: if you're unwilling to wait for tests to complete and instead, forego or defer running them, they're too slow.

Here's another way to characterize a test's speed: if it runs code that ultimately interacts with external dependencies—databases, files, and network calls—it's slow. If the test otherwise executes Java code that interacts only with more Java code and no external dependencies, it's usually fast.

Slow tests take many dozens, hundreds, or thousands of milliseconds to execute. Fast tests each take, at most, a few milliseconds to execute.

Milliseconds add up. Consider a suite of 2500 unit tests. If the average execution time of each test is 200ms, running them all takes over eight minutes. If, instead, each test takes 5ms, running them all takes less than 15 seconds.

You might run an eight-plus-minute test suite two or three times a day. You can run a 15-second suite many times per hour.

With an eight-minute suite, you might also concede and run a small subset after making changes. But you'll start unwittingly breaking code elsewhere, not finding out until much later.

Keep your tests fast! Minimize dependencies on code that executes slowly. If all your tests interact with code that makes one or more database calls, directly or indirectly, all your tests will be slow.

Fast tests support the most effective way to build software: incrementally. Testing as you go verifies that each new behavior works and doesn't break other code, letting you frequently and confidently integrate code changes.

 Fast tests empower continual, confident software development.

A Mélange of Important Test Double Tips

- A good mock-based test is three lines: a one-line arrange step with a highly readable smart stub declaration, followed by one-line act and assert steps. That's a test anyone can quickly read, understand, and trust.

- In answersAppropriateAddressForValidCoordinates, the expected parameter string of "lat=38.000000&lon=-104.000000" correlates clearly with the act arguments of 38.0 and -104.0. Creating correlation between arrange and assert isn't easy sometimes, but it saves developers from digging about for understanding. Without such correlation, tests using mocks can be hard to follow.

- Mocks supplant real behavior. Ask yourself if you're using them safely. Does your mock really emulate the way the production code works? Does the production code return other formats you're not thinking of? Does it throw exceptions? Does it return null? You'll want a different test for each of these conditions.

- Does your test really trigger use of a mock, or does it run real production code? Try turning off the mock and letting your code interact with the production class to see what happens (it might be as subtle as a slightly slower test run). Step-debug if needed.

- Try temporarily throwing a runtime exception from the production code. If your test bombs as a result, you know you're hitting the production code. (Don't forget and accidentally push that throw into production!)

- Use test data that you know is *not* what a production call would return. Your test passed neat, whole numbers for latitude and longitude. You also know Anywhere is not a real city in Colorado. If you were using the real HttpImpl class, your test expectations would fail.

- The code you're mocking is getting replaced with a test double and is not getting tested. A mock represents gaps in test coverage. Make sure you have an appropriate higher-level test (perhaps an integration test) that demonstrates end-to-end use of the real class.

- Using DI frameworks can slow down your test runs considerably. Consider injecting your dependencies by hand—it turns out to be fairly easy to do.

- When using DI frameworks, prefer injecting via a real, exposed interface point—typically the constructor. Cleverness creates complexity and cultivates contempt.

 A mock creates a hole in unit testing coverage. Write integration tests to cover these gaps.

Possibly the most important when it comes to test doubles: avoid using them, or at least minimize their pervasiveness. If a large number of tests require test doubles, you're allowing your troublesome dependencies to proliferate too much. Reconsider the design.

A couple of avoidance policies:

- Rather than have a class depend on the persistence layer, push the responsibility out. Have a client retrieve the relevant data, then inject that.

- If collaborator classes don't have troublesome dependencies, let your tests interact with their real code rather than mock them.

Mocks are great tools, but they can also create great headaches. Take care.

Summary

In this chapter, you learned the important technique of introducing stubs and mocks to emulate the behavior of dependent objects. Your tests don't have to interact with live services, files, databases, and other troublesome dependencies! You also learned how to use Mockito to simplify your effort in creating and injecting mocks.

You also learned Mockito's core features, but it can do much more:

- Verify that methods were called in order
- Capture and assert against an argument passed to a mock method
- Spy on a method, which results in the *real* method getting called

Now that you're empowered with enough unit testing fundamentals to survive, it's time to explore some bigger-picture unit testing topics: code coverage, integration testing, and tests for multithreaded code.

CHAPTER 4

Expanding Your Testing Horizons

At this point, you've worked through the core topics in unit testing, including JUnit and unit testing fundamentals, how to test various scenarios, and how to use test doubles to deal with dependencies.

In this chapter, you'll review a few topics that begin to move outside the sphere of "doing unit testing":

- Code coverage and how it can help (or hurt)
- Challenges with writing tests for multithreaded code
- Writing integration tests

Improving Unit Testing Skills Using Code Coverage

Code coverage metrics measure the percentage of code that your unit tests execute (exercise) when run. Ostensibly, code that is covered is working, and code that is not covered represents the risk of breakage.

From a high level, tests that exhaust all relevant pieces of code provide 100 percent coverage. Code with no tests whatsoever has 0 percent coverage. Most code lies somewhere in between.

Many tools exist that will calculate coverage metrics for Java code, including JaCoCo, OpenClover, SonarQube, and Cobertura. IntelliJ IDEA ships with a coverage tool built into the IDE.

Numerous coverage metrics exist to measure various code aspects. Function coverage, for example, measures the percentage of functions (methods) exercised by tests. Some of the other metrics include line, statement, branch, condition, and path coverage.

Line and statement coverage metrics are similar. Line coverage measures source lines exercised. Since a line can consist of multiple statements, some tools measure statement coverage.

Branch, condition, and path coverage metrics are similarly related. Branch coverage measures whether all branches of a conditional statement (for example, both true and false branches of an if statement) are executed. Condition coverage measures whether all conditionals (including each in a complex conditional) have evaluated to both true and false. Path coverage measures whether every possible route through the code has been executed.

Most of the popular Java coverage tools support calculating line and branch coverage. You'll learn about these in this section.

Understanding Statement Coverage

Consider a Batter class that tracks a baseball batter's strike count. A batter is out after three strikes. A swing-and-a-miss with the bat—a strike—increments the strike count. A foul ball (a ball hit out of play) also increments the strike count unless the batter already has two strikes.

```
utj3-coverage/01/src/main/java/util/Batter.java
public class Batter {
   private int strikeCount = 0;

   public void foul() {
      if (strikeCount < 2)
         strikeCount++;
   }

   public void strike() {
      strikeCount++;
   }

   public int strikeCount() {
      return strikeCount;
   }
}
```

Note the strike method. If none of your tests trigger its execution, its coverage is 0 percent. If your tests *do* result in a call to strike, its whopping one line of code gets exercised, and thus the recorded coverage is 100 percent.

The foul method contains a conditional. It increments strikeCount only if there are fewer than two strikes. A conditional, implemented in Java with an if statement, demands at least two tests—one that forces the conditional block to execute (because the conditional expression resolved to true) and one that bypasses the if block code.

The following test covers the special case—when two strikes already exist.

```
utj3-coverage/01/src/test/java/util/ABatter.java
@Test
void doesNotIncrementStrikesWhenAtTwo() {
    batter.strike();
    batter.strike();

    batter.foul();

    assertEquals(2, batter.strikeCount());
}
```

If you run this test "with coverage" (that's the actual text on an IDEA menu item), the if statement conditional evaluates to false because strikeCount is not less than two. As a result, the if-statement body doesn't execute, and strikeCount is not incremented.

Here's a tool window showing the summary coverage metrics:

Method coverage shows that three of three possible methods defined on the Batter class were exercised. That's not terribly interesting or useful.

Line coverage shows that three of four lines were exercised across those three methods—one of the lines didn't get covered when the test ran. In this case, it's because you only ran one test in ABatter. Run them all to attain 100 percent line coverage.

The real value of a coverage tool is that it shows exactly what lines are exercised and what lines are not. IDEA's coverage tool window shows colored markers in the gutter (the gray strip left of the source code) to the immediate right of the line numbers. It marks executed lines as green, lines not executed as red, and lines *partially* covered (read on) as yellow as shown in the figure on page 74.

The increment operation (strikeCount++) is marked red because it is never executed.

Uncovered code is one of two things: dead or risky.

It can be near-impossible to determine whether code is ever needed or used. "All dead" code (as opposed to mostly dead code, which might have some

```
 C  Batter.java  ×

 2      package util;

 1
 3      public class Batter {
 1          private int strikeCount = 0;
 2
 3          public void foul() {
 4              if (strikeCount < 2)
 5                  strikeCount
 6          }
 7
 8          public void strike() {
 9              strikeCount++;
10          }
11
12          public int strikeCount() {
13              return strikeCount;
14          }
15      }
16
```

future resurrected purpose) can waste time in many ways. Like a vampire, dead code sucks time: when you read it, when it shows up in search results, and when you mistakenly start making changes (true stories here) to it.

When you encounter uncovered, mostly dead code, bring it into the sunlight of your whole team. If it doesn't shrivel away under their scrutiny, cover the code with tests. Otherwise, delete it.

 Unit tests declare intent. If you test *every* intent, you can safely delete untested code.

Add a second test involving only a single strike to get 100 percent coverage in foul:

utj3-coverage/01/src/test/java/util/ABatter.java
```
@Test
void incrementsStrikesWhenLessThan2() {
    batter.strike();

    batter.foul();

    assertEquals(2, batter.strikeCount());
}
```

Conditionals and Code Coverage

Line coverage is an unsophisticated metric that tells you only whether a line of code was executed or not. It doesn't tell you if you've explored different data cases. For example, if a method accepts an int, did you test it with 0? With negative numbers and very large numbers? A coverage tool doesn't even tell you if the tests contain any assertions. (Yes, some clever developers do that to make their coverage numbers look better.)

Complex conditionals often represent insufficiently covered paths through your code. You create complex conditionals when you produce Boolean expressions involving the logical operators OR (||) and AND (&&).

Suppose you write one test that exercises a complex conditional using only the OR operator. The line coverage metric will credit your tests for the entire line containing the complex conditional as long as any one of its Boolean expressions resolves to true. But you won't have ensured that all the other Boolean expressions behave as expected.

Conditional coverage tools can help you pinpoint deficiencies in your coverage of conditionals.

Take a look at the next intended increment of the Batter code, which supports tracking balls and walks. It introduces the notion of whether or not a batter's turn at home plate is "done," meaning that they either struck out or walked (hits and fielding outs would come later). The method isDone implements that complex conditional.

utj3-coverage/02/src/main/java/util/Batter.java
```java
public class Batter {
   private int strikeCount = 0;
   private int ballCount = 0;

   public void foul() {
      if (strikeCount < 2)
         strikeCount++;
   }

   public void ball() {
      ballCount++;
   }

   public void strike() {
      strikeCount++;
   }

   public int strikeCount() {
      return strikeCount;
   }

   public boolean isDone() {
      return struckOut() || walked();
   }
```

```java
    private boolean walked() {
        return ballCount == 4;
    }

    private boolean struckOut() {
        return strikeCount == 3;
    }
}
```

A new test is added to the test class to cover a strikeout case:

```java
utj3-coverage/02/src/test/java/util/ABatter.java
@Test
void whenStruckOut() {
    batter.strike();
    batter.strike();
    batter.strike();

    assertTrue(batter.isDone());
}
```

IDEA supports the branch coverage metric, but it is turned off by default. Turn it on and run all the tests in ABatter. Your code coverage summary now includes a column for Branch Coverage %:

```java
public class Batter {
    public void foul() {
        if (strikeCount < 2)
            strikeCount++;
    }

    public void ball() {
        ballCount
    }

    public void strike() {
        strikeCount++;
    }

    public int strikeCount() {
        return strikeCount;
    }

    public boolean isDone() {
        return struckOut() || walked();
    }

    private boolean walked() {
        ballCount
    }

    private boolean struckOut() {
        return strikeCount == 3;
    }
}
```

Element ▲	Class, %	Method, %	Line, %	Branch, %
util	100% (1/1)	71% (5/7)	75% (6/8)	50% (4/8)
Batter	100% (1/1)	71% (5/7)	75% (6/8)	50% (4/8)

The summary pane shows that you have a branch coverage deficiency; currently, it measures only 50 percent. Again, the more revealing aspect is how the coverage tool marks code within the editor for Batter. The isDone method is marked with yellow to indicate that not all branches of the complex conditional are covered. A call to struckOut occurs, but not to walked.

The struckOut method is also marked as partially covered. If you click on the yellow marker, IDEA reveals the coverage data:

```
Hits: 1
Covered 1/2 branches
```

In other words, the method was invoked ("hit") one time. Full branch coverage of a simple Boolean conditional would require getting hit twice—once where it evaluates to true and once where it gets evaluated to false.

To garner full coverage for ABatter, you'll need to add a couple of tests to not only exercise the walked method but to also ensure that you have a test in which the entire expression in isDone returns false.

utj3-coverage/03/src/test/java/util/ABatter.java
```java
@Test
void isDoneWithWalk() {
    for (var i = 0; i < 4; i++)
        batter.ball();

    assertTrue(batter.isDone());
}

@Test
void isNotDoneWhenNeitherWalkNorStrikeout() {
    assertFalse(batter.isDone());
}
```

How Much Coverage Is Enough?

Any one of your unit tests will exercise only a very small percentage of code—a unit's worth. If you want 100 percent coverage, write unit tests for every unit you add to your system. Emphasize testing the *behaviors*, not the methods. Use tools like ZOM to help you think through the different *cases* and their outcomes.

On the surface, it would seem that higher code coverage is good and lower coverage is not so good. But your manager craves a single number that says, "Yup, we're doing well on our unit testing practice," or "No, we're not writing enough unit tests."

To satisfy your manager, you'd unfortunately need to first determine what *enough* means. Obviously, 0 percent is not enough. And 100 percent would be great, but is it realistic? The use of certain frameworks can make it nearly impossible to hit 100 percent without some trickery.

Most folks out there (the purveyors of Emma included) suggest that coverage under 70 percent is *in*sufficient. I agree.

Many developers also claim that attempts to increase coverage represent diminishing returns on value. I disagree. Teams that habitually write unit tests *after* they write code achieve coverage levels of 70 percent with relative ease. Unfortunately, that means the remaining 30 percent of their code remains untested, often because it's difficult, hard-to-test code. Difficult code hides more defects, so at least a third of your defects will probably lie in this untested code.

 Jeff's Theory of Code Coverage: the amount of costly code increases in the areas of least coverage.

The better your design, the easier it is to write tests. Revisit Chapter 8, Refactoring to Cleaner Code, on page 147 and Chapter 9, Refactoring Your Code's Structure, on page 169 to understand how to better structure your code. A good design coupled with the will to increase coverage will move you *in the direction of* 100 percent, which should lead to fewer defects. You might not reach 100 percent, and that's okay.

Developers practicing TDD (see Chapter 11, Advancing with Test-Driven Development (TDD), on page 211) achieve percentages well over 90 percent, largely by definition. They write a test for each new behavior they're about to code. Those who do TDD, myself included, rarely look at the coverage numbers. TDD makes coverage a self-fulfilling prophecy.

Coverage percentages can mislead. You can easily write a few tests that blast through a large percentage of code yet assert little of use. Most tools don't even care if your tests have no assertions (which means they're not really tests). The tools certainly don't care if your tests are cryptic or prolix or if they assert nothing useful. Too many teams spend a fortune writing unit tests with decent coverage numbers but little value.

Unfortunately, managers always want a single number they can use to measure success. The code-coverage number is but a surface-level metric that means little if the tests stink. And if someone tells the team that the metric goal matters most, the tests will stink.

A downward code coverage *trend* is probably useful information, however. Your coverage percentage should either increase or become stable over time as you add behavior.

The Value in Code Coverage

If you write your tests after you write the corresponding code, you'll miss numerous test cases until you improve your skills and habits. Even if you try TDD and write tests first for all unit behaviors, you'll still find yourself sneaking in untested logic over time.

As you're learning, lean on the visual red-yellow-and-green annotations that the tools produce.

 Use code-coverage tools to help you understand where your code lacks coverage or where your team is trending downward.

Do your best to avoid the code coverage metric debate and convince your leadership that the metric is not for them. It will ultimately create problems when used for anything but educational purposes.

Testing Multithreaded Code

It's hard enough to write code that works as expected. That's one reason to write unit tests. It's dramatically harder to write *concurrent* code that works and even harder to verify that it's safe enough to ship.

In one sense, testing application code that requires concurrent processing is technically out of the realm of *unit* testing. It's better classified as integration testing. You're verifying that you can integrate the notion of your application-specific logic with the ability to execute portions of it concurrently.

Tests for threaded code tend to be slower because you must expand the scope of execution time to ensure that you have no concurrency issues. Threading defects sometimes sneakily lie in wait, surfacing long after you thought you'd stomped them all out.

There are piles of ways to approach multithreading in Java and, similarly, piles of ways for your implementation to go wrong: deadlock, race conditions, livelock, starvation, and thread interference, to name a few. One could fill a book (or at least several chapters) covering how to test for and correct all of these policies. I'm not allowed to fill that much paper, so you'll see only a short example that highlights a couple of key thoughts.

Tips for Testing Multithreaded Code

Here's a short list of techniques for designing and analyzing multithreaded code that minimizes concurrency issues:

- Minimize the overlap between threading controls and application code. Rework your design so that you can unit test the bulk of application code in the absence of threads. Write thread-focused tests for the small remainder of the code.

- Trust the work of others. Java incorporates Doug Lea's set of concurrency utility classes in java.util.concurrent. Don't code producer/consumer yourself by hand, for example; it's too easy to get wrong. Do take advantage of Lea's BlockingQueue implementations, and capitalize on his painstaking efforts to get them right.

- Avoid and isolate concurrent updates, which cause most problems.

- Profile the codebase using static concurrency analysis tools, which can identify potential problems (including deadlocks) based on coded interactions between threads.

- Profile the runtime behavior of your system using dynamic analysis tooling such as VisualVM or YourKit. These tools can monitor thread state, analyze thread dumps, detect deadlocks, and more.

- Write a test that demonstrates a potential concurrency problem, then exacerbate it to the point where the test always fails. You might reduce the number of threads, increase the number of requests being tested, or temporarily introduce sleep to expose timing issues. Tools like Thread Weaver can also help you force and test different thread interleavings.

  - Add only the concurrency control that makes the test pass. Synchronization blocks and locks may be necessary, but using them inappropriately can degrade performance (while still not solving the real concurrency problems).

  - When your fix consistently passes, remove any artificialities like sleep.

- Don't introduce concurrency controls like locks, synchronized blocks, or atomic variables until you've actually demonstrated a concurrency problem (hopefully with a failing test).

Let's take a quick look at one example of fixing a concurrency issue.

Exacerbating a Threading Issue

You'll work on a bit of code from iloveyouboss, a job-search website designed to compete with sites like Indeed and Monster. It takes a different approach to the typical job posting site: It attempts to match prospective employees with potential employers and vice versa, much as a dating site would. Employers and employees both create profiles by answering a series of multiple-choice or yes-no questions. The site scores profiles based on criteria from the other party and shows the best potential matches from the perspective of both the employee and employer. (The author reserves the right to monetize the site, make a fortune, retire, and do nothing but support the kind readers of this book.)

The ProfileMatcher class, a core piece of iloveyouboss, collects all of the relevant profiles. Provided with a set of criteria (essentially the preferred answers to relevant questions), the ProfileMatcher method scoreProfiles iterates all profiles added. For each profile matching the criteria, ProfileMatcher collects both the profile and its score—zero if the profile is not a match for the criteria and a positive value otherwise.

utj3-iloveyouboss2/01/src/main/java/iloveyouboss/domain/ProfileMatcher.java
```java
import java.util.*;
import java.util.concurrent.*;

public class ProfileMatcher {
    private List<Profile> profiles = new ArrayList<>();

    public void addProfile(Profile profile) {
        profiles.add(profile);
    }

    ExecutorService executorService =
        Executors.newFixedThreadPool(8);

    public Map<Profile, Integer> scoreProfiles(Criteria criteria)
        throws ExecutionException, InterruptedException {
        var profiles = new HashMap<Profile, Integer>();

        var futures = new ArrayList<Future<Void>>();
        for (var profile: this.profiles) {
            futures.add(executorService.submit(() -> {
                profiles.put(profile,
                    profile.matches(criteria) ? profile.score(criteria) : 0);
                return null;
            }));
        }

        for (var future: futures)
            future.get();

        executorService.shutdown();
        return profiles;
    }
}
```

To be responsive, scoreProfiles calculates matches in the context of separate threads, implemented using futures. Each profile iterated gets managed by a single future. That future is responsible for adding the profile and score to the profiles variable, initialized to an empty HashMap. That concurrent update is the source of the problem your test will uncover.

utj3-iloveyouboss2/01/src/test/java/iloveyouboss/domain/AProfileMatcher.java

```java
import org.junit.jupiter.api.Test;
import org.junit.jupiter.api.extension.ExtendWith;
import org.mockito.junit.jupiter.MockitoExtension;

import java.util.List;
import java.util.function.Function;

import static iloveyouboss.domain.Weight.REQUIRED;
import static iloveyouboss.domain.Weight.WOULD_PREFER;
import static java.util.stream.IntStream.range;
import static org.junit.jupiter.api.Assertions.assertEquals;

@ExtendWith(MockitoExtension.class)
class AProfileMatcher {
    ProfileMatcher matcher = new ProfileMatcher();

    @Test
    void returnsScoreForAllProfiles() throws Exception {
        var questions = createQuestions(50);
        int profileCount = 500;
        var half = profileCount / 2;
        range(0, half).forEach(id ->
            matcher.addProfile(createProfile(
                questions, id, i -> nonMatchingAnswer(questions.get(i)))));
        range(half, profileCount).forEach(id ->
            matcher.addProfile(createProfile(
                questions, id, i -> matchingAnswer(questions.get(i)))));
        var criteria = createCriteria(questions);

        var results = matcher.scoreProfiles(criteria);

        assertEquals(half,
            results.values().stream().filter(score -> score == 0).count());
        assertEquals(half,
            results.values().stream().filter(score -> score > 0).count());
    }

    private Profile createProfile(
            List<BooleanQuestion> questions,
            int id,
            Function<Integer, Answer> answerFunction) {
        var profile = new Profile(String.valueOf(id));
        range(0, questions.size()).forEach(i ->
            profile.add(answerFunction.apply(i)));
        return profile;
    }

    private Criteria createCriteria(List<BooleanQuestion> questions) {
        var questionCount = questions.size();
        var criteria = new Criteria();
        range(0, 5).forEach(i ->
            criteria.add(new Criterion(
                matchingAnswer(questions.get(i)), REQUIRED)));
```

```
    range(5, questionCount).forEach(i ->
        criteria.add(new Criterion(
            matchingAnswer(questions.get(i)), WOULD_PREFER)));
    return criteria;
    }

    private List<BooleanQuestion> createQuestions(int questionCount) {
        return range(0, questionCount)
            .mapToObj(i -> new BooleanQuestion("question " + i))
            .toList();
    }

    Answer matchingAnswer(Question question) {
        return new Answer(question, Bool.TRUE);
    }

    Answer nonMatchingAnswer(Question question) {
        return new Answer(question, Bool.FALSE);
    }
}
```

The test returnsScoreForAllProfiles should fail most of the time and occasionally pass. If you have difficulty getting it to fail, alter the size of the thread pool, the number of questions (currently 50), and/or the number of profiles (500). Try to get it to fail at least 9 out of 10 times. I got it to consistently fail with 200 questions and 2000 profiles.

A simple solution is to wrap the shared HashMap in a *synchronized map*, which makes it a thread-safe Java construct:

utj3-iloveyouboss2/02/src/main/java/iloveyouboss/domain/ProfileMatcher.java
```
public class ProfileMatcher {
    private List<Profile> profiles = new ArrayList<>();

    public void addProfile(Profile profile) {
        profiles.add(profile);
    }

    ExecutorService executorService =
        Executors.newFixedThreadPool(8);

    public Map<Profile, Integer> scoreProfiles(Criteria criteria)
        throws ExecutionException, InterruptedException {
        var profiles =
            Collections.synchronizedMap(new HashMap<Profile, Integer>());

        var futures = new ArrayList<Future<Void>>();
        for (var profile: this.profiles) {
            futures.add(executorService.submit(() -> {
                profiles.put(profile,
                    profile.matches(criteria) ? profile.score(criteria) : 0);
```

```
          return null;
      }));
    }

    for (var future: futures)
      future.get();

    executorService.shutdown();
    return profiles;
  }
}
```

Ensure that your test passes consistently—with the same numbers as it was consistently failing with—after making this small change.

Perhaps the better approach, however, is to have each future return a map with a single key-value pair of profile and score. This avoids the modification to a shared data store. The individual-key maps can all be aggregated into a single HashMap as part of a loop that blocks on future.get for all futures:

utj3-iloveyouboss2/03/src/main/java/iloveyouboss/domain/ProfileMatcher.java

```
public Map<Profile, Integer> scoreProfiles(Criteria criteria)
    throws ExecutionException, InterruptedException {
➤   var futures = new ArrayList<Future<Map<Profile, Integer>>>();
    for (var profile : profiles)
      futures.add(executorService.submit(() ->
➤        Map.of(profile,
➤                profile.matches(criteria) ? profile.score(criteria) : 0)));

➤   var finalScores = new HashMap<Profile, Integer>();
➤   for (var future: futures)
➤     finalScores.putAll(future.get());

    executorService.shutdown();
    return finalScores;
  }
}
```

Any exacerbation aside, the performance test will be slow due to the numerous iterations and larger data volumes typically wanted for such a test. It takes several hundred milliseconds on my machine, far too much for a single test. Mark it as "slow," and run it separately from your suite of fast unit tests. See Creating Arbitrary Test Groups Using Tags, on page 137.

Writing Integration Tests

The QuestionRepository class talks to an H2 database using the Java Persistence API (JPA). You might correctly guess that this data class is used in many places throughout the application and that testing each of those places will require the use of a test double.

Here's the code for the class:

utj3-iloveyouboss2/01/src/main/java/iloveyouboss/persistence/QuestionRepository.java

```java
import iloveyouboss.domain.BooleanQuestion;
import iloveyouboss.domain.PercentileQuestion;
import iloveyouboss.domain.Persistable;
import iloveyouboss.domain.Question;
import jakarta.persistence.EntityManager;
import jakarta.persistence.EntityManagerFactory;
import jakarta.persistence.Persistence;

import java.time.Clock;
import java.util.List;
import java.util.function.Consumer;

public class QuestionRepository {
    private Clock clock = Clock.systemUTC();

    private static EntityManagerFactory getEntityManagerFactory() {
        return Persistence.createEntityManagerFactory("h2-ds");
    }

    public Question find(Long id) {
        try (var em = em()) {
            return em.find(Question.class, id);
        }
    }

    public List<Question> getAll() {
        try (var em = em()) {
            return em.createQuery("select q from Question q",
                Question.class).getResultList();
        }
    }

    public List<Question> findWithMatchingText(String text) {
        try (var em = em()) {
            var queryString =
                "select q from Question q where q.text like :searchText";
            var query = em.createQuery(queryString, Question.class);
            query.setParameter("searchText", "%" + text + "%");
            return query.getResultList();
        }
    }

    public long addPercentileQuestion(String text, String... answerChoices) {
        return persist(new PercentileQuestion(text, answerChoices));
    }

    public long addBooleanQuestion(String text) {
        return persist(new BooleanQuestion(text));
    }
```

```java
    void setClock(Clock clock) {
        this.clock = clock;
    }

    void deleteAll() {
        executeInTransaction(em ->
            em.createNativeQuery("delete from Question").executeUpdate());
    }

    private EntityManager em() {
        return getEntityManagerFactory().createEntityManager();
    }

    private void executeInTransaction(Consumer<EntityManager> func) {
        try (var em = em()) {
            var transaction = em.getTransaction();
            try {
                transaction.begin();
                func.accept(em);
                transaction.commit();
            } catch (Exception t) {
                if (transaction.isActive()) transaction.rollback();
            }
        }
    }

    private long persist(Persistable object) {
        object.setCreateTimestamp(clock.instant());
        executeInTransaction(em -> em.persist(object));
        return object.getId();
    }
}
```

Most of the code in QuestionRepository is simple delegation to the JPA. The class contains little in the way of interesting logic. That's good design. QuestionRepository isolates the dependency on JPA from the rest of the system.

From a testing stance, does it make sense to write a unit test against Question-Repository? You could write unit tests in which you stub all of the relevant interfaces, but it would take a good amount of effort, the tests would be difficult, and in the end, you wouldn't have proven much. Particularly, unit testing QuestionRepository won't prove that you're using JPA correctly. Defects are fairly common in dealings with JPA because three different pieces of detail must all work correctly in concert: the Java code, the mapping configuration (located in src/META-INF/persistence.xml in your codebase), and the database itself.

The only real way to know if QuestionRepository works is to have it interact with a real database. You can write tests to do so, but they'll be *integration tests*, not unit tests. They'll also be one to two orders of magnitude slower than unit tests.

The world of integration testing is huge, and this section is tiny, but hopefully, it provides a few ideas on when you'll want integration tests and how you might approach crafting them.

The Data Problem

You want the vast majority of your JUnit tests to be fast. No worries—if you isolate all of your persistence interaction to one place in the system, you'll have a reasonably small amount of code that must be integration tested.

When you write integration tests for code that interacts with the real database, the data in the database and how it gets there are important considerations. To verify that database query operations return expected results, for example, you must either insert appropriate data or assume it already exists.

Assuming that data is already in the database will create problems. Over time, the data will change without your knowledge, breaking tests. Also, divorcing the data from the test code makes it a lot harder to understand why a particular test passes or not. The meaning of the data with respect to the tests is lost by dumping it all into the database.

 As much as possible, integration tests should create and manage their own data.

If your tests will be running against your database on your own machine, the simplest route might be for each test to start with a clean database (or one pre-populated with necessary reference data). Each test then becomes responsible for adding and working with its own data. This minimizes intertest dependency issues, where one test breaks because of data that another test left lying around. (Those can be a headache to debug!)

If you can only interact with a shared database for your testing, then you'll need a less intrusive solution. One option: if your database supports it, you can initiate a transaction in the context of each test and then roll it back. (The transaction handling is usually relegated to @BeforeEach and @AfterEach methods.)

You'll also want your integration tests to execute as part of your build process. Whatever solution you derive for the tests must work both on your machine as well as in the build server's environment.

Ultimately, integration tests are harder to write, execute, and maintain. They tend to break more often, and when they do break, debugging the problem can take considerably longer. But a dependable testing strategy demands you include some.

If you find yourself adding interesting logic either before or after interaction with the live interactions (to the database in this example), find a way to extract that logic to another class. Write unit tests against it there.

 Integration tests are essential but challenging to design and maintain. Minimize their number and complexity by maximizing the logic you verify in unit tests.

Clean-Room Database Tests

Your tests for the repository empty the database both before and after each test method's execution:

utj3-iloveyouboss2/01/src/test/java/iloveyouboss/persistence/AQuestionRepository.java
```java
import iloveyouboss.domain.Question;
import org.junit.jupiter.api.AfterEach;
import org.junit.jupiter.api.BeforeEach;
import org.junit.jupiter.api.Test;

import java.time.ZoneId;
import java.util.Date;
import java.util.List;

import static java.time.Clock.fixed;
import static java.util.Arrays.asList;
import static org.junit.jupiter.api.Assertions.assertEquals;

class AQuestionRepository {
    QuestionRepository repository = new QuestionRepository();

    @BeforeEach
    void setUp() {
        repository.deleteAll();
    }

    @AfterEach
    void tearDown() {
        repository.deleteAll();
    }

    @Test
    void findsPersistedQuestionById() {
        var id = repository.addBooleanQuestion("question text");

        var question = repository.find(id);

        assertEquals("question text", question.getText());
    }
```

```java
@Test
void storesDateAddedForPersistedQuestion() {
    var now = new Date().toInstant();
    repository.setClock(fixed(now, ZoneId.systemDefault()));
    var id = repository.addBooleanQuestion("text");

    var question = repository.find(id);

    assertEquals(now, question.getCreateTimestamp());
}

@Test
void answersMultiplePersistedQuestions() {
    repository.addBooleanQuestion("q1");
    repository.addBooleanQuestion("q2");
    repository.addPercentileQuestion("q3", "a1", "a2");

    var questions = repository.getAll();

    assertEquals(asList("q1", "q2", "q3"), extractText(questions));
}

@Test
void findsMatchingEntries() {
    repository.addBooleanQuestion("alpha 1");
    repository.addBooleanQuestion("alpha 2");
    repository.addBooleanQuestion("beta 1");

    var questions = repository.findWithMatchingText("alpha");

    assertEquals(asList("alpha 1", "alpha 2"), extractText(questions));
}

private List<String> extractText(List<Question> questions) {
    return questions.stream().map(Question::getText).toList();
}
}
```

Clearing the data *before* gives your tests the advantage of working with a clean slate.

Clearing the data *after* each test runs is just being nice, not leaving data around cluttering shared databases.

When trying to figure out a problem, you might want to take a look at the data after a test completes. To do so, comment out the call to clearData call in the @AfterEach method.

Your tests aren't focused on individual methods; instead, they're verifying behaviors that are inextricably linked. To verify that you can retrieve or find elements, you must first insert them. To verify that you've inserted elements, you retrieve them.

Ensure you run coverage tools to verify that all the code is getting tested. The tests for QuestionRepository show that it's completely covered with tests. Also, if you use integration tests to cover some small portions of code rather than unit tests, your system-wide unit test code coverage numbers will suffer a little. If that concerns you, you might be able to merge the numbers properly (the tool jacoco:merge[1] works for JaCoCo).

Exploratory Unit Testing

The unit tests you've learned to build capture your best understanding of the intents in the code. They cover known edge cases and typical use cases.

Some code may demand further exploration. For example, complex code, code that seems to keep breaking as you uncover more nuances about the input data, or code that incurs a high cost if it were to fail. Systems requiring high reliability or security might incur significant costs from unit-level failures.

Numerous kinds of developer-focused tests exist to help you with such exploratory testing. Many of them verify at the integration level—load tests, failover tests, performance tests, and contract tests, to name a few. You can learn about some of these in Alexander Tarlinder's book *Developer Testing*.[2]

Following is an overview of two *unit*-level testing tactics: fuzz testing and property testing, which can be considered forms of what's known as *generative testing*. These sorts of tests require additional tooling above and beyond JUnit, and thus, you're only getting an introduction to them in this book. (That's one excuse among a few, and I'm sticking with it.)

Not covered at all: *mutation testing*, which involves tools that make small changes to your production code to see if such changes break your tests. If your tests don't break, the mutation tests suggest you might have insufficient test coverage.

Fuzz Testing

With fuzz testing, you use a tool to provide a wide range of random, unexpected, or invalid inputs to your code. It can help you identify edge cases in your code that you're otherwise unlikely to think of when doing traditional unit testing.

---

1. https://www.jacoco.org/jacoco/trunk/doc/merge-mojo.html
2. https://www.informit.com/store/developer-testing-building-quality-into-software-9780134431802

This URL creator code combines server and document strings into a valid URL string:

```
utj3-iloveyouboss2/03/src/main/java/util/URLCreator.java
import java.net.MalformedURLException;
import java.net.URL;
import static java.lang.String.format;

public class URLCreator {
    public String create(String server, String document)
            throws MalformedURLException {
        if (isEmpty(document))
            return new URL(format("https://%s", server)).toString();
        return new URL(
            format("https://%s/%s", server, clean(document))).toString();
    }

    private boolean isEmpty(String document) {
        return document == null || document.trim().equals("");
    }

    private String clean(String document) {
        return document.charAt(0) == '/'
            ? document.substring(1)
            : document;
    }
}
```

Here are the tests:

```
utj3-iloveyouboss2/03/src/test/java/util/AURLCreator.java
import org.junit.jupiter.api.Test;
import org.junit.jupiter.params.ParameterizedTest;
import org.junit.jupiter.params.provider.NullSource;
import org.junit.jupiter.params.provider.ValueSource;
import java.net.MalformedURLException;
import static org.junit.jupiter.api.Assertions.assertEquals;

class AURLCreator {
    URLCreator urlCreator = new URLCreator();

    @Test
    void returnsCombinedURLStringGivenServerAndDocument()
            throws MalformedURLException {
        assertEquals(
            "https://example.com/customer?id=123",
            urlCreator.create("example.com", "customer?id=123"));
    }

    @ParameterizedTest
    @NullSource
```

```java
@ValueSource(strings = { "", " \n\t\r " })
void buildsURLGivenServerOnly(String document)
        throws MalformedURLException {
    assertEquals(
        "https://example.com",
        urlCreator.create("example.com", document));
}

@Test
void eliminatesRedundantLeadingSlash() throws MalformedURLException {
    assertEquals(
        "https://example.com/customer?id=123",
        urlCreator.create("example.com", "/customer?id=123"));
}
}
```

Code like this tends to grow over time as you think of additional protections to add. The third test deals with the case where the caller of the create method prepends the document with a forward slash—"/employee?id=42", for example. Someone likely wasn't sure if the slash needed to be provided or not. The developer, as a result, updated the code to allow either circumstance.

With fuzz testing, you'll likely add more protections and corresponding tests as the fuzzing effort uncovers additional problems.

You can write fuzz tests using the tool Jazzer:[3]

utj3-iloveyouboss2/03/src/test/java/util/AURLCreatorFuzzer.java
```java
import com.code_intelligence.jazzer.api.FuzzedDataProvider;
import com.code_intelligence.jazzer.junit.FuzzTest;
import java.net.MalformedURLException;

public class AURLCreatorFuzzer {
    @FuzzTest
    public void fuzzTestIsValidURL(FuzzedDataProvider data)
            throws MalformedURLException {
        var server = data.consumeString(32);
        var document = data.consumeRemainingAsString();
        new URLCreator().create(server, document);
    }
}
```

Fuzz test methods are annotated with @FuzzTest, and passed a data provider. From this data provider (a wrapper around some random stream of data), you can extract the data you need. The test fuzzTestIsValidUrl first extracts a 32-character string to be passed as the server, then uses the remaining incoming data as the document.

---

3. https://github.com/CodeIntelligenceTesting/jazzer

To run fuzzing with Jazzer, first create a directory in your project's test resources. Derive its name from your fuzzer class's package plus the fuzzer class name plus the word Inputs:

```
utj3-iloveyouboss2/src/test/resources/util/AURLCreatorFuzzerInputs
```

Then run your tests with the environment variable setting JAZZER_FUZZ=1. The fuzzing tool will display failures and add the inputs causing the failures to files within the resource directory you created.

The fuzzer should report that an input containing an LF (line feed character; ASCII value 10) represents an invalid character for a URL. You, as the developer, get to decide how you want the code to deal with that, if at all.

You can also collect a number of inputs in the test resources directory. With the JAZZER_FUZZ environment variable turned off, Jazzer will use these inputs to run what effectively become regression test inputs.

Property Testing

Another form of unit testing is *property testing*, where your tests describe invariants and postconditions, or *properties*, about the expected behavior of code. Property testing tools, such as jqwik,[4] will test these invariants using a wide range of automatically generated inputs.

Your primary reason for using property tests is to uncover edge cases and unexpected behaviors by virtue of exploring a broader range of inputs.

Here's an implementation for the insertion sort algorithm, which performs terribly but is a reasonable choice if your input array is small (or if your inputs are generally almost sorted already):

utj3-iloveyouboss2/03/src/main/java/util/ArraySorter.java
```java
public class ArraySorter {
    public void inPlaceInsertionSort(int[] arr) {
        for (var i = 1; i < arr.length - 1; i++) {
            var key = arr[i];
            var j = i - 1;

            while (j >= 0 && arr[j] > key) {
                arr[j + 1] = arr[j];
                j = j - 1;
            }
            arr[j + 1] = key;
        }
    }
}
```

---

4.   https://jqwik.net

Using jqwik, you define @Property methods that get executed by the JUnit test runner. The following set of properties for ArraySorter describes three properties: an already-sorted array should remain sorted, an array with all the same elements should remain unchanged, and a random array should be sorted in ascending order:

```
utj3-iloveyouboss2/03/src/test/java/util/ArraySorterProperties.java
import static java.util.Arrays.fill;
import static java.util.Arrays.sort;
import net.jqwik.api.*;
import java.util.Arrays;

public class ArraySorterProperties {
   ArraySorter arraySorter = new ArraySorter();

   @Property
   boolean returnsSameArrayWhenAlreadySorted(@ForAll int[] array) {
      sort(array);
      var expected = array.clone();

      arraySorter.inPlaceInsertionSort(array);

      return Arrays.equals(expected, array);
   }

   @Property
   boolean returnsSameArrayWhenAllSameElements(@ForAll int element) {
      var array = new int[12];
      fill(array, element);
      var expected = array.clone();

      arraySorter.inPlaceInsertionSort(array);

      return Arrays.equals(expected, array);
   }

   @Property
   boolean sortsAscendingWhenRandomUnsortedArray(@ForAll int[] array) {
      var expected = array.clone();
      sort(expected);

      arraySorter.inPlaceInsertionSort(array);

      return Arrays.equals(expected, array);
   }
}
```

Taking the last method as an example: sortsAscendingForRandomUnsortedArray represents a postcondition that should hold true for all (@ForAll) input arrays (array). The property implementation clones the incoming array and sorts it using Java's built-in sort, capturing the result as expected. It sorts the incoming array, then returns the result of comparing that sort to expected.

Jqwik, a sophisticated and highly flexible tool, calls the property one thousand times by default. And, beauty! The last property fails, and consistently so, given those thousand inputs.

The array sort code represents a good fit for property testing. You might think to write a handful of test cases (ZOM, certainly). But there are some cases that can be hard to think of. Property testing can help uncover those cases.

Yes, there's a defect in the insertion sort. The jqwik tool should identify the problem. See if you can figure out and fix the defective code.

Summary

In this chapter, you rounded out your knowledge of core unit testing concepts with a few (mostly unrelated) topics that look at bigger concerns surrounding unit testing:

- Code coverage, a concept that can help you learn where your unit testing is deficient

- Testing multithreaded code, a tricky and sophisticated challenge

- Integration tests, which verify code and its interaction with external dependencies that might be out of your control

Now that you've worked through foundational concepts regarding unit testing, you'll take a deeper look into the preferred tool for Java unit testing, JUnit. The next three chapters will explore JUnit in-depth, providing useful insights and nuggets on how to best take advantage of its wealth of features.

Part II

Mastering JUnit with "E"s

You can accomplish most of your unit testing needs with a small fraction of JUnit's robust capabilities. In this part, you'll learn to streamline your day-to-day unit testing activities by delving into the three "E"s of JUnit: Examining outcomes with assertions, Establishing organization in your tests, and Executing your tests.

CHAPTER 5

Examining Outcomes with Assertions

You've learned the most important features of JUnit in the prior four chapters of this book, enough to survive but not thrive. Truly succeeding with your unit testing journey will involve gaining proficiency with your primary tool, JUnit. In this and the next couple of chapters, you'll explore JUnit in significant detail. First, you'll focus on JUnit's means of verification—its assertion library.

Assertions (or *asserts*) in JUnit are static method calls that you drop into your tests. Each assertion is an opportunity to verify that some condition holds true. If an asserted condition does not hold true, the test stops executing right there and JUnit reports a test *failure*.

To abort the test, JUnit throws an exception object of type AssertionFailedError. If JUnit catches AssertionFailedError, it marks the test as failed. In fact, JUnit marks any test as failed that throws an exception not caught in the test body.

In order to use the most appropriate assertion for your verification need, you'll want to learn about JUnit's numerous assertion variants.

In examples to this point, you've used the two most prevalent assertion forms, assertTrue and assertEquals. Since you'll use them for the bulk of your tests, you'll first examine these assertion workhorses more deeply. You'll then move on to exploring the numerous alternative assertion choices that JUnit provides.

In some cases, the easiest way to assert something won't be to compare to an actual result but to instead verify an operation by inverting it. You'll see a brief example of how.

You'll also get an overview of AssertJ, a third-party assertion library that allows you to write "fluent" assertions. Such assertions can make your tests considerably easier to read. They can also provide more precise explanations about why a test is failing.

Using the Core Assertion Forms

The bulk of your assertions will use either assertTrue or assertEquals. Let's review and refine your knowledge of these two assertion workhorses. Let's also see how to keep your tests streamlined by eliminating things that don't add value.

The Most Basic Assertion Form: assertTrue

The most basic assert form accepts a Boolean expression or reference as an argument and fails the test if that argument evaluates to false.

```
org.junit.jupiter.api.Assertions.assertTrue(someBooleanExpression);
```

Here's an example demonstrating the use of assertTrue:

```
utj3-junit/01/src/test/java/scratch/AnAccount.java
@Test
void hasPositiveBalanceAfterInitialDeposit() {
    var account = new Account("an account name");

    account.deposit(50);

    Assertions.assertTrue(account.hasPositiveBalance());
}
// ...
```

Technically, you could use assertTrue for every assertion you had to write. But an assertTrue failure tells you only that the assertion failed and nothing more. Look for more precise assertions such as assertEquals, which reports what was expected vs. what was actually received when it fails. You'll find test failures easier to understand and resolve as a result.

Eliminating Clutter

As documents that you'll spend time reading and re-reading, you'll want to streamline your tests. You learned in the first chapter (see Chapter 1, Building Your First JUnit Test, on page 3) that the public keyword is unnecessary when declaring both JUnit test classes and test methods. Such additional keywords and other unnecessary elements represent *clutter*.

 Streamline your tests by eliminating unnecessary clutter.

You'll be scanning lots of tests to gain a rapid understanding of what your system does and where your changes must go. Getting rid of clutter makes it easier to understand tests at a glance.

Asserts pervade JUnit tests. Rather than explicitly scope each assert call with the class name (Assertion), use a static import:

```java
import static org.junit.jupiter.api.Assertions.assertTrue;
```

The result is a de-cluttered, more concise assertion statement:

```java
utj3-junit/01/src/test/java/scratch/AnAccount.java
@Test
void hasPositiveBalanceAfterInitialDeposit() {
    var account = new Account("an account name");

    account.deposit(50);

➤    assertTrue(account.hasPositiveBalance());
}
```

Generalized Assertions

Here's another example of assertTrue which explains how a result relates to some expected outcome:

```java
utj3-junit/01/src/test/java/scratch/AnAccount.java
@Test
void depositIncreasesBalance() {
    var account = new Account("an account name");
    var initialBalance = account.getBalance();

    account.deposit(100);

    assertTrue(account.getBalance() > initialBalance);
}
```

A test name—depositIncreasesBalance—is a general statement about the behavior you want the test to demonstrate. Its assertion—assertTrue(balance > initialBalance)—corresponds to the test name, ensuring that the balance has increased as an outcome of the deposit operation. The test does not *explicitly* verify by how much the balance increased. As a result, you might describe its assert statement as a *generalized* assertion.

Eliminating More Clutter

The preceding examples depend on the existence of an initialized Account instance. You can create an Account in a @BeforeEach method (see Initializing with @BeforeEach and @BeforeAll, on page 124 for more information) and store a reference to it as a field on the test class:

```java
utj3-junit/02/src/test/java/scratch/AnAccount.java
class AnAccount {
    Account account;
```

```java
@BeforeEach
void createAccount() {
    account = new Account("an account name");
}

@Test
void hasPositiveBalanceAfterInitialDeposit() {
    account.deposit(50);

    assertTrue(account.hasPositiveBalance());
}
// ...
}
```

JUnit creates a new instance of the test class for each test (see Observing the JUnit Lifecycle, on page 127 for further explanation). That means you can also safely initialize fields at their point of declaration:

utj3-junit/03/src/test/java/scratch/AnAccount.java
```java
class AnAccount {
    Account account = new Account("an account name");

    @Test
    void hasPositiveBalanceAfterInitialDeposit() {
        // ...
    }
    // ...
}
```

Use assertEquals for Explicit Comparisons

Your test names should be generalizations of behavior, but each test should present a specific example with a specific result. If the test makes a deposit, you know what the new balance amount should be. In most cases, you should be explicit with your assertion and verify the actual new balance.

The assertion assertEquals compares an expected answer to the actual answer, allowing you to explicitly verify an outcome's value. It's overloaded so that you can appropriately compare all primitive types, wrapper types, and object references. (To compare two arrays, use assertArrayEquals instead.) Most of your assertions should probably be assertEquals.

Here's the deposit example again, asserting by how much the balance increased:

utj3-junit/01/src/test/java/scratch/AnAccount.java
```java
@Test
void depositIncreasesBalanceByAmountDeposited() {
    account.deposit(50);
```

```
account.deposit(100);

assertEquals(150, account.getBalance());
}
```

You design the example for each test, and you know the expected outcome. Encode it in the test with assertEquals.

Assertion Messages: Redundant Messages for Assertions

Most verifications are self-explanatory, at least in terms of the code bits they're trying to verify. Sometimes, it's helpful to have a bit of "why" or additional context to explain an assertion. "Just why does this test expect the total to be 42?"

Most JUnit assert forms support an optional final argument named message. The message argument allows you to supply a nice verbose explanation of the rationale behind the assertion:

utj3-junit/01/src/test/java/scratch/AnAccount.java
```
@Test
void balanceRepresentsTotalOfDeposits() {
    account.deposit(50);
    account.deposit(51);

    var balance = account.getBalance();

    assertEquals(101, balance, "account balance must be total of deposits");
}
```

The assertion message displays when the test fails:

```
account balance must be total of deposits ==> expected: <101> but was: <102>
```

If you prefer lots of explanatory comments, you might get some mileage out of assertion messages. However, this is the better route:

- Test only one behavior at a time
- Make your test names more descriptive

In fact, if you demonstrate only one behavior per test, you'll usually only need a single assertion. The name of the test will then naturally describe the reason for that one assertion. No assertion failure message is needed.

 Well-written tests document themselves.

Elements like explanatory constants, helper methods, and intention-revealing variable names go a long way toward making tests accessible and to the point. The existence of comments and assertion messages in unit tests is a smell that usually indicates stinky test design. In Chapter 10, Streamlining Your Tests, on page 189, you'll step through an example of test clean-up.

In well-written tests, the assertion message becomes redundant clutter, just one more thing to have to wade through and maintain.

Improved test failure messages can provide a small benefit since figuring out the meaning or implication of an assertion failure can be frustrating. Rather than use assertion failure messages, however, take a look at AssertJ, which provides *fluent assertions* that generate more detailed failure messages.[1]

Assertion messages can also provide value when you employ parameterized tests, which are a JUnit mechanism for running the same test with a bunch of different data. See Executing Multiple Data Cases with Parameterized Tests, on page 131.

Other Common JUnit Assertion Forms

While assertEquals and assertTrue would cover almost all the assertions you'll need to write, you'll want to learn about the other forms that JUnit supports. Choosing the best assertion for the job will keep your tests concise and clear.

In this section, you'll be introduced to the majority of JUnit's other assertion forms, including assertFalse, assertNotEquals, assertSame, assertNotSame, assertNull, and assertNotNull. You'll also get an experience-based opinion on the value and best uses for each variant.

assertFalse

Nobody doesn't dislike double negatives (or triple negatives, so says my editor). To help you say things "straight up" in your tests, JUnit provides some inverse assertions. Here's assertFalse—the opposite of assertTrue—in action:

```
utj3-junit/01/src/test/java/scratch/AnAccount.java
@Test
void doesNotHavePositiveBalanceWhenAccountCreated() {
    assertFalse(account.hasPositiveBalance());
}
```

You can code the equivalent by using assertTrue if you're in a contrary mood:

```
utj3-junit/01/src/test/java/scratch/AnAccount.java
@Test
void doesNotHavePositiveBalanceWhenAccountCreated() {
    assertTrue(!account.hasPositiveBalance());
}
```

---

1. https://assertj.github.io/doc/

Paraphrased, it reads awkwardly: "assert true...not account has positive balance" and represents the kind of logic that trips many of us up. Keep the double negatives out of your tests. Use assertFalse when it's easier to read than assertTrue.

assertNotEquals

Appropriate use of assertNotEquals is much rarer. If you know what the answer should be, use assertEquals to say that. Use of assertNotEquals otherwise may represent making what you might call a *weak assertion*—one that doesn't fully verify a result.

Some sensible cases for using assertNotEquals:

- You really don't have a way of knowing what the answer should be.

- You've explained (in another test, perhaps) what an actual answer might be, and with this test, you want to emphasize that it can't possibly be some other specified value.

- It would require too much data detail to explicitly assert against the actual result.

Let's try an example. For any card game (for example, poker), you must shuffle the deck of playing cards prior to dealing any cards from it. Here's a starter implementation of a Deck class, showing that shuffling occurs in its constructor:

utj3-junit/01/src/main/java/cards/Deck.java
```java
public class Deck {
    private LinkedList<Card> cards;

    public Deck() {
        cards = newDeck();
        Collections.shuffle(cards);
    }

    static LinkedList<Card> newDeck() {
        var cards = new LinkedList<Card>();
        for (var i = 1; i <= 13; i++) {
            cards.add(new Card(i, "C"));
            cards.add(new Card(i, "D"));
            cards.add(new Card(i, "H"));
            cards.add(new Card(i, "S"));
        }
        return cards;
    }

    public Card deal() {
        return cards.removeFirst();
    }
```

```
List<Card> remaining() {
    return cards;
}
}
```

You want to verify that the shuffling did actually occur:

utj3-junit/01/src/test/java/cards/ADeck.java
```
public class ADeck {
    Deck deck = new Deck();

    // ... other Deck tests here ...

    @Test
    void hasBeenShuffled() {
        var cards = deck.remaining();

        assertNotEquals(Deck.newDeck(), cards);
    }

}
```

You might be thinking, "Hey, that looks like a weak assertion!" It is, in a way—you do not know whether or not the deck has been *properly* shuffled. But that's not the job of the Deck class. The Deck class here *invokes* a shuffle rather than implementing it, using a method from the Java API. You can trust that Collections.shuffle() randomizes the order of a collection appropriately, though you might need a better random shuffler if you're a casino.

Since you can trust the Java API, you don't need to prove the quality of its shuffle. But your unit test does need to verify that the cards were actually shuffled. You can do this in a number of somewhat complex ways, such as by using test doubles (see Chapter 3, Using Test Doubles, on page 53) or injecting a seeded random number generator to use for shuffling.

Ensuring that the order of cards in an instantiated Deck is not equal to the cards returned by Deck.newDeck() is sufficient and simple. It demonstrates that some operation occurred to change the order. (Note that this weak assertion also has a slim possibility of failing in the one case where it shuffles to the deck's starting order. Highly unlikely in your lifetime. Run the test again if you chance upon that serendipitous moment.)

Yes, someone could replace the call to Collections.shuffle() with shoddy shuffle code—for example, something that moved one card from the front to the back of the deck. But don't worry—no one would do that.

Unit tests don't exist to protect you from willful destructiveness. A determined saboteur can break your system without breaking any tests.

Avoid weak assertions like assertNotEquals unless you have no choice
or they emphasize what you really want your test to say.

assertSame

Also infrequently used, assertSame verifies that two references point to the same
object in memory.

Your challenge: minimize the use of memory in a scheduling application where
there might need to be many millions of Time objects. (This example is based
on "Working with Design Patterns: Flyweight.")[2] Most of these Times will be on
the quarter hour (11:15, 14:30, 10:15) because that's how we usually like to
schedule things. Some small subset will be at odd times, like 3:10 or 4:20,
because some people do odd things at odd times, dude.

The idea of the flyweight pattern is to have a single object pool, which allows
for multiple interested parties to share objects that have the same values.
(This works great for immutable objects, not so great otherwise.) Your application can reduce its memory footprint significantly as a result.

Here are the two production classes involved:

utj3-junit/01/src/main/java/time/Time.java
```java
import static java.lang.String.format;

public record Time(byte hour, byte minute) {
   static String key(byte hour, byte minute) {
      return format("%d:%d", hour, minute);
   }

   @Override
   public String toString() {
      return key(hour, minute);
   }
}
```

utj3-junit/01/src/main/java/time/TimePool.java
```java
import java.util.HashMap;
import java.util.Map;

public class TimePool {
   private static Map<String, Time> times = new HashMap<>();

   static void reset() {
      times.clear();
   }
```

---

2.   https://www.developer.com/design/working-with-design-patterns-flyweight/

```java
    public static Time get(byte hour, byte minute) {
        return times.computeIfAbsent(Time.key(hour, minute),
            k -> new Time(hour, minute));
    }
}
```

Here are a couple of tests:

utj3-junit/01/src/test/java/time/ATimePool.java

```java
public class ATimePool {
    @BeforeEach
    void resetPool() {
        TimePool.reset();
    }

    @Test
    void getReturnsTimeInstance() {
        byte four = 4;
        byte twenty = 20;
        assertEquals(new Time(four, twenty), TimePool.get(four, twenty));
    }

    @Test
    void getWithSameValuesReturnsSharedInstance() {
        byte ten = 10;
        byte five = 5;
        var firstRetrieved = TimePool.get(ten, five);

        var secondRetrieved = TimePool.get(ten, five);

        assertSame(firstRetrieved, secondRetrieved);
    }
}
```

The highlighted line in the second test demonstrates the use of assertSame. The arrange step calls the get method on the TimePool to retrieve a first Time object, then makes the same call a second time in the act step. The assert step verifies that the two Time objects are one and the same.

assertNotSame

assertNotSame verifies that two references point to different objects in memory.

You might use assertNotSame to verify that an object "persisted" in memory—in a hash map, for example—is a different instance than the one stored. Otherwise, changes to the "live" object would also alter the persisted object. Here's some code to demonstrate:

utj3-junit/01/src/test/java/persistence/AnInMemoryDatabase.java

```java
package persistence;

import org.junit.jupiter.api.Test;
```

```java
import static org.junit.jupiter.api.Assertions.*;

class AnInMemoryDatabase {
    @Test
    void objectCopiedWhenAddedToDatabase() {
        var db = new InMemoryDatabase();
        var customer = new Customer("1", "Smelt, Inc.");

        db.add(customer);

        var retrieved = db.data.get("1");
        assertNotSame(retrieved, customer);
    }
}
```

The test creates an InMemoryDatabase and adds a customer via the database's add method.

utj3-junit/01/src/main/java/persistence/InMemoryDatabase.java
```java
import java.util.HashMap;
import java.util.Map;

public class InMemoryDatabase {
    Map<String, Customer> data = new HashMap<>();

    public void add(Customer customer) {
        data.put(customer.id(), new Customer(customer));
    }
}
```

In the add method in the production code, the highlighted line shows the use of a copy constructor on the Customer record to ensure that a new instance is added to the HashMap named data.

Without making that copy—with this line instead as the implementation for the add method:

utj3-junit/01/src/main/java/persistence/InMemoryDatabase.java
```java
data.put(customer.id(), customer);
```

...the test fails.

One way to think about unit tests is they add protections—and corresponding explanations—for the little things that are important but not necessarily obvious, like the need for creating a copy in this example.

> Unit tests not only safeguard but also describe the thousands of choices in your system.

assertNull

assertNull is equivalent to doing assertEquals(null, someValue).

The InMemoryDatabase class needs a public way for clients to retrieve customers by their id. Here's an implementation of a get method:

```
utj3-junit/01/src/main/java/persistence/InMemoryDatabase.java
public class InMemoryDatabase {
   Map<String, Customer> data = new HashMap<>();
   // ...
   public Customer get(String id) {
      return data.getOrDefault(id, null);
   }
}
```

How many tests do you need to cover that method? The word "Or" in getOrDefault is a solid hint that you'll want at least two. In this listing, the first test is the "happy path" case where a Customer is successfully retrieved:

```
utj3-junit/01/src/test/java/persistence/AnInMemoryDatabase.java
InMemoryDatabase db = new InMemoryDatabase();

@Test
void returnsCustomerCorrespondingToId() {
   var customer = new Customer("42", "Mr Creosote");
   db.add(customer);

   var retrieved = db.get("42");

   assertEquals(customer, retrieved);
}

@Test
void returnsNotNullForNonexistentKey() {
   assertNull(db.get("42"));
}
```

The second test demonstrates the use of assertNull: if you attempt to retrieve anything (42 in this case) from a newly created db (into which nothing has been inserted), it should return null.

assertNotNull

assertNotNull is the opposite of assertNull, naturally. It's used to assert that a reference points to something, not nothing.

Like assertNotEquals, many uses of assertNotNull are dubious.

Some folks new to JUnit introduce assertNotNull checks for references to newly instantiated objects:

utj3-junit/01/src/test/java/persistence/AnInMemoryDatabase.java

```
@Test
void returnsCustomerCorrespondingToId() {
    var customer = new Customer("42", "Mr Creosote");
    assertNotNull(customer); // bogus! this can't fail
    db.add(customer);

    var retrieved = db.get("42");

    assertEquals(customer, retrieved);
}
```

However, that assertNotNull can never fail. The only way that the customer variable, initialized in the first line of the test, can ever end up null is if the Customer constructor throws an exception. If an exception *is* thrown, the next line of code—the assertNotNull statement—is never executed. If no exception is thrown, the customer reference will point to a (non-null) object, so the assertNotNull will never fail if it does get executed. Don't do that.

assertNotNull is only useful when you need to demonstrate that a reference points to a value and you don't care at all what that value is. Otherwise—if you can determine the expected value—assertNotNull is a weak assertion. You'd be better off using assertEquals to compare the reference to its actual value.

You'll know when, on rare occasions, you should reach for assertNotNull. Otherwise...don't do that.

An Added Assortment of Asserts

But wait—there's more!

The org.junit.jupiter.api.Assertions class in JUnit provides a few more assertions that are not described here. Without perusing the users's guide or the voluminous Javadoc for the class, you wouldn't know these assertions existed. Here they are with brief descriptions of what they do.

assertLinesMatch	asserts that two lists or streams of strings match; can involve regular expressions and "fast forwarding"
assertAll	asserts that all supplied executables do not throw exception
assertInstanceOf	asserts that the actual value is an instance of the expected type
assertIterableEquals	asserts that the provided Iterable references are deeply equal
assertTimeout	asserts that an executable completes execution within a specified duration
assertTimeout Preemptively	like assertTimeout, but runs the executable in a separate thread

Expecting Exceptions

In addition to ensuring that the happy path through your code works, you also need to verify the unhappy cases. For example, you'll want to write tests that demonstrate when code can throw exceptions. These tests are necessary to provide a full understanding of the behaviors to developers who must work with the code.

The ever-evolving Java language has driven the continual development of JUnit as well—there are no fewer than four ways to write exception-based tests in JUnit. You'll take a look at a couple of these.

Let's examine a simple case: ensure the Account code throws an InsufficientFunds-Exception when a client attempts to withdraw more than the available balance.

Newer School: assertThrows

The assertThrows assertion, available in JUnit since version 4.13, should cover all your needs when writing exception-based tests. Prefer it over the other mechanisms.

The most useful assertThrows form takes two arguments: the type of the exception expected to be thrown and an executable object (usually a lambda, but potentially a method reference). The executable contains the code expected to throw the exception.

When the assertion gets executed by JUnit, the code in the lambda is run. If that code throws no exception, the assertion fails. If the code in the lambda does throw an exception, the test passes if the type of the exception object matches or is a subclass of the expected exception type.

Here's assertThrows in action. The lambda argument to assertThrows attempts to withdraw 100 from a newly created account (that is, one with no money):

```
utj3-junit/01/src/test/java/scratch/AnAccount.java
import static org.junit.jupiter.api.Assertions.assertThrows;
// ...

    @Test
    void throwsWhenWithdrawingTooMuch() {
        var thrown = assertThrows(InsufficientFundsException.class,
            () -> account.withdraw(100));
        assertEquals("balance only 0", thrown.getMessage());
    }
```

Calling assertThrows returns the exception object. This test assigns it to the thrown variable to allow asserting against its message string.

Don't add extraneous code to the lambda. You don't want a false positive where the test passes because the *wrong* line of code threw the expected exception.

Code in withdraw passes the assertThrows statement by throwing an InsufficientFundsException when the amount to withdraw exceeds the balance:

utj3-junit/01/src/main/java/scratch/Account.java

```
void withdraw(int dollars) {
    if (balance < dollars) {
        throw new InsufficientFundsException("balance only " + balance);
    }
    balance -= dollars;
}
```

Old School

Prior to the availability of assertThrows, you had at least three options in JUnit for expecting exceptions: Using try/catch, annotations, and rules. You may see some of these solutions if you maintain older systems. Annotations and rules aren't supported by JUnit 5, so I won't cover them here. I'll show you what they look like, though, so you can understand what you're seeing.

Here's an example of the annotations-based mechanism:

```
@Test(expected=InsufficientFundsException.class)
public void throwsWhenWithdrawingTooMuch() {
    account.withdraw(100);
}
```

If you see expected= as an argument to the @Test annotation, visit the JUnit 4 documentation on @Test for further explanation.[3]

Here's what the use of the rules-based mechanism (added in JUnit 4.7) might look like:

```
public class SimpleExpectedExceptionTest {
    @Rule
    public ExpectedException thrown= ExpectedException.none();

    @Test
    public void throwsException() {
        thrown.expect(NullPointerException.class);
        thrown.expectMessage("happened");

        // ... code that throws the exception
    }
// ...
```

---

3.   https://junit.org/junit4/javadoc/4.12/org/junit/Test.html

If you see an ExpectedException instantiated and annotated with @Rule, visit JUnit 4's documentation for ExpectedException for further explanation.[4]

If it's not obvious, "old school" is pejorative. (I'm allowed to say it, though, 'cause I'm old.) Don't use these old constructs if you can help it.

Use of try/catch

JUnit's first releases supported only "roll-your-own" mechanisms for exception handling, based on the use of Java's try/catch construct. Here's the comparable Account code for expecting an InsufficientFundsException:

```
@Test
void throwsWhenWithdrawingTooMuch() {
   try {
      account.withdraw(100);
      fail();
   } catch (InsufficientFundsException expected) {
      assertEquals("balance only 0", expected.getMessage());
   }
}
```

When JUnit executes code within a try block that *does* throw an exception, control is transferred to the appropriate catch block and executed. In the example, since the code indeed throws an InsufficientFundsException, control transfers to the assertEquals statement in the catch block, which verifies the exception object's message contents.

You can deliberately fail the test by commenting out the withdrawal operation in Account's withdraw method. Do that to see firsthand what JUnit tells you.

If the call to withdraw does *not* throw an exception, the next line executes. When using the try/catch mechanism, the last line in the try block should be a call to org.junit.Assert.fail(). As you might guess, JUnit's fail method throws an Assertion-FailedError so as to abort and fail the test.

The try/catch idiom represents the rare case where it might be okay to have an empty catch block—perhaps you don't care about the contents of the exception. Naming the exception variable expected helps reinforce to the reader that we expect an exception to be thrown and caught.

Think about other things that you might want a test to assert after an exception has been thrown. Examine any important post-conditions that must hold true. For example, it might be of value to assert that the account balance didn't change after the failed withdrawal attempt.

---

4.   https://junit.org/junit4/javadoc/4.12/org/junit/rules/ExpectedException.html

You might occasionally see the try/catch mechanism used in older code. If so, you can leave it alone (you now know how it works), or you can streamline your test by replacing it with assertThrows.

Assert That Nothing Happened: assertDoesNotThrow

As with a lot of other assertion forms, JUnit provides a converse to assertThrows—specifically, the 'assertDoesNotThrow' method. In its simplest form, it takes an executable object (a lambda or method reference). If the invocation of code in the executable doesn't throw anything, the assertion passes; otherwise, it fails.

Every once in a while, you'll think you might want to use assertDoesNotThrow...the only problem is, it really doesn't assert anything about what the executed code *does* do. Try finding a way to test that elusive "something."

You might find assertDoesNotThrow useful as the catch-all in a series of tests. Suppose you have a validator that throws an exception in a couple of cases and otherwise does nothing:

```
utj3-junit/01/src/test/java/scratch/ANameValidator.java
class NameValidationException extends RuntimeException {}

class NameValidator {
    long commaCount(String s) {
        return s.chars().filter(ch -> ch == ',').count();
    }

    void validate(String name) {
        if (name.isEmpty() ||
            commaCount(name) > 1)
            throw new NameValidationException();
    }
}
```

You need two tests to demonstrate that validate throws an exception for each of the two negative cases:

```
utj3-junit/01/src/test/java/scratch/ANameValidator.java
import org.junit.jupiter.api.Test;

import static org.junit.jupiter.api.Assertions.assertDoesNotThrow;
import static org.junit.jupiter.api.Assertions.assertThrows;

class ANameValidator {
    NameValidator validator = new NameValidator();

    @Test
    void throwsWhenNameIsEmpty() {
        assertThrows(NameValidationException.class, () ->
            validator.validate(""));
    }
```

```
@Test
void throwsWhenNameContainsMultipleCommas() {
    assertThrows(NameValidationException.class, () ->
        validator.validate("Langr, Jeffrey,J."));
}
}
```

...and one test with assertDoesNotThrow to show nothing happens otherwise:

utj3-junit/01/src/test/java/scratch/ANameValidator.java
```
@Test
void doesNotThrowWhenNoErrorsExist() {
    assertDoesNotThrow(() ->
        validator.validate("Langr, Jeffrey J."));
}
```

Use assertDoesNotThrow if you must, but maybe explore a different design first. For the example here, changing the validator to expose a Boolean method would do the trick.

Exceptions Schmexceptions, Who Needs 'em?

Most tests you write will be more carefree, happy path tests where exceptions are highly unlikely to be thrown. But Java acts as a bit of a buzzkill, insisting that you acknowledge any checked exception types.

Don't clutter your tests with try/catch blocks to deal with checked exceptions. Instead, let those exceptions loose! The test can just throw them:

utj3-junit/01/src/test/java/scratch/SomeAssertExamples.java
```
@Test
void readsFromTestFile() throws IOException {
    var writer = new BufferedWriter(new FileWriter("test.txt"));
    writer.write("test data");
    writer.close();
    // ...
}
```

You're designing these positive tests so you know they won't throw an exception except under truly *exceptional* conditions. Even if an exception does get thrown unexpectedly, JUnit will trap it for you and report the test as an *error* instead of a *failure*.

Alternate Assertion Approaches

Most of the assertions in your tests will be straight-up comparisons of expected outcomes to actual outcomes: is the average credit history 780? Sometimes, however, direct comparisons aren't the most effective way to describe the expected outcome.

For example, suppose you've coded the method fastHalf that uses bit shifting to perform integer division by two. The code is trivial, as are some core tests:

utj3-junit/01/src/main/java/util/MathUtils.java
```java
public class MathUtils {
    static long fastHalf(long number) {
        return number >> 1;
    }
}
```

utj3-junit/01/src/test/java/util/SomeMathUtils.java
```java
import org.junit.jupiter.api.Test;
import static org.junit.jupiter.api.Assertions.assertEquals;
import static util.MathUtils.fastHalf;

public class SomeMathUtils {
    @Nested
    class FastHalf {
        @Test
        void isZeroWhenZero() {
            assertEquals(0, fastHalf(0));
        }

        @Test
        void roundsDownToZeroWhenOne() {
            assertEquals(0, fastHalf(1));
        }

        @Test
        void dividesEvenlyWhenEven() {
            assertEquals(11, fastHalf(22));
        }

        @Test
        void roundsDownWhenOdd() {
            assertEquals(10, fastHalf(21));
        }

        @Test
        void handlesNegativeNumbers() {
            assertEquals(-2, fastHalf(-4));
        }
```

You might want another test to verify the utility works with very large numbers:

utj3-junit/01/src/test/java/util/SomeMathUtils.java
```java
@Test
void handlesLargeNumbers() {
    var number = 489_935_889_934_389_890L;
    assertEquals(244_967_944_967_194_945L, fastHalf(number));
}
```

But, oh, that's ugly, and it's hard for a test reader to quickly verify.

You've demonstrated that fast half works for 0, 1, many, and negative number cases. For very large numbers, rather than show many-digit barfages in the test, you can write an assertion that emphasizes the *inverse* mathematical relationship between input and output:

```
utj3-junit/01/src/test/java/util/SomeMathUtils.java
@Test
void handlesLargeNumbers() {
    var number = 489_935_889_934_389_890L;
    assertEquals(number, fastHalf(number) * 2);
}
```

Mathematical computations represent the canonical examples for verifying via inverse relationships: you can verify division by using multiplication, addition by using subtraction, square roots by squares, and so on. Other domains where you can verify using inverse operations include cryptography, accounting, physics, computer graphics, finance, and data compression.

Cross-checking via inversion ensures that everything adds up and balances, much like the general ledger in a double-entry bookkeeping system. It's not a technique you should reach for often, but it can occasionally help make your tests considerably more expressive. You might find particular value in inversion when your test demands voluminous amounts of data.

Be careful with the code you use for verification! If both the actual routine and the assertion share the same code (perhaps a common utility class you wrote), they could share a common defect.

Third-Party Assertion Libraries

JUnit provides all the assertions you'll need, but it's worth taking a look at the third-party assertion libraries available—AssertJ, Hamcrest, Truth, and more. These libraries primarily seek to improve upon the expressiveness of assertions, which can help streamline and simplify your tests.

Let's take a very quick look at AssertJ, a popular choice, to see a little bit of its power. AssertJ offers *fluent assertions*, which are designed to help tests flow better and read more naturally. A half-dozen simple examples should get the idea across quickly. Each of the examples assumes the following declaration:

```
String name = "my big fat acct";
```

The core AssertJ form reverses JUnit order. You specify the *actual* value first as an argument to an assertThat method that *all* assertions use. You then make a chained call to one of many methods that complete or continue the assertion.

Here's what an AssertJ assertion looks like when applied to the common need of comparing one object to another—isEqualTo is analogous to assertEquals in JUnit:

utj3-junit/01/src/test/java/scratch/SomeAssertJExamples.java
```
assertThat(name).isEqualTo("my big fat acct");
```

So far, so simple. To note:

- You can take advantage of autocomplete to flesh out the assertion.
- The assertion reads like an English sentence, left to right.

AssertJ provides numerous inversions of positively stated assertions. Thus, the converse of isEqualTo is isNotEqualTo:

utj3-junit/01/src/test/java/scratch/SomeAssertJExamples.java
```
assertThat(name).isNotEqualTo("plunderings");
```

A few more examples follow. Most of them speak for themselves, and that's part of the point.

You can use chaining to specify multiple expected outcomes in a single statement. The following assertion passes if the name references a string that both starts with "my" and ends with "acct":

utj3-junit/01/src/test/java/scratch/SomeAssertJExamples.java
```
assertThat(name)
    .startsWith("my")
    .endsWith("acct");
```

A type-checking example:

utj3-junit/01/src/test/java/scratch/SomeAssertJExamples.java
```
assertThat(name).isInstanceOf(String.class);
```

Using regular expressions:

utj3-junit/01/src/test/java/scratch/SomeAssertJExamples.java
```
assertThat(name).containsPattern(
    compile("\\s+(big fat|small)\\s+"));
```

AssertJ contains numerous tests around lists:

utj3-junit/01/src/test/java/scratch/SomeAssertJExamples.java
```
@Test
public void simpleListTests() {
    var names = List.of("Moe", "Larry", "Curly");

    assertThat(names).contains("Curly");
    assertThat(names).contains("Curly", "Moe");
    assertThat(names).anyMatch(name -> name.endsWith("y"));
    assertThat(names).allMatch(name -> name.length() < 6);

}
```

The third list assertion passes if *any* one or more of the elements in the list ends with the substring "y". (The strings "Larry" or "Curly" here make it pass.)

The fourth assertion passes if *all* of the elements in the list have a length less than 6. (They do.)

(Caveat: The preceding asserts that verify only part of a string might be considered weak assertions. You likely need to verify more.)

AssertJ's failing fluent assertions provide far more useful failure messages than what JUnit might give you. Here's a failing assertion for the list of names:

utj3-junit/01/src/test/java/scratch/SomeAssertJExamples.java
```
assertThat(names).allMatch(name -> name.length() < 5);
```

... and here's the failure message generated by AssertJ:

```
Expecting all elements of:
  ["Moe", "Larry", "Curly"]
to match given predicate but these elements did not:
  ["Larry", "Curly"]
```

Knowing exactly why the assert failed should speed up your fix.

AssertJ allows you to express your assertions in the most concise manner possible, particularly as things get more complex. Occasionally, your tests will need to extract specific data from results in order to effectively assert against it. With JUnit, doing so might require one or more lines of code before you can write the assertion. With AssertJ, you might be able to directly express your needs in a single statement.

The Power of Fluency

Let's look at a small example that still demonstrates some of AssertJ's power. The example uses two classes:

- a Flight class that declares a segment field of type Segment
- a Segment class containing the fields origin, destination, and distance

utj3-junit/01/src/test/java/scratch/SomeAssertJExamples.java
```
record Segment(String origin, String destination, int distance) {
    boolean includes(String airport) {
        return origin.equals(airport) || destination.equals(airport);
    }
}

record Flight(Segment segment, LocalDateTime dateTime) {
    Flight(String origin, String destination,
           int distance, LocalDateTime dateTime) {
```

```
      this(new Segment(origin, destination, distance), dateTime);
   }

   boolean includes(String airport) {
      return segment.includes(airport);
   }
}
```

The following AssertJ assertion compares against a list of Flight objects stored in the variable flights:

```
utj3-junit/01/src/test/java/scratch/SomeAssertJExamples.java
@Test
void filterAndExtract() {
   // ...
   assertThat(flights)
      .filteredOn(flight -> flight.includes("DEN"))
      .extracting("segment.distance", Integer.class)
      .allMatch(distance -> distance < 1700);
}
```

The call to filteredOn returns a subset of flights involving the flight code "DEN".

The call to extracting applies an AssertJ property reference ("segment.distance") to each "DEN" flight. The reference tells AssertJ to first retrieve the segment object from a flight, then retrieve the distance value from that segment as an Integer.

Yes, you could manually code an equivalent to the AssertJ solution, but the resulting code would lose the declarative nature that AssertJ can provide. Your test would require more effort to both write and read. In contrast, AssertJ's support for method chaining creates a fluent sentence that you can read as a single concept.

Regardless of whether you choose to adopt AssertJ or another third-party assertions library, streamline your tests so they read as concise documentation. A well-designed assertion step minimizes stepwise reading.

Eliminating Non-Tests

Assertions are what make a test an automated test. Omitting assertions from your tests would render them pointless. And yet, some developers do exactly that in order to meet code coverage mandates easily. Another common ruse is to write tests that exercise a large amount of code, then assert something simple—for example, that a method's return value is not null.

Such *non-tests* provide almost zero value at a significant cost in time and effort. Worse, they carry an increasingly negative return on investment: you must expend time on non-tests when they fail or error, when they appear in search results ("is that a real test we need to update or do we not need to worry about it?"), and when you must update them to keep them running (for example, when a method signature gets changed).

 Eliminate tests that verify nothing.

Summary

You've learned numerous assertion forms in this chapter. You also learned about AssertJ, an alternate assertions library.

Initially, you'll survive if you predominantly use assertEquals for most assertions, along with an occasional assertTrue or assertFalse. You'll want to move to the next level quickly, however, and learn to use the most concise and expressive assertion for the situation at hand.

Armed with a solid understanding of how to write assertions, you'll next dig into the organization of test classes so that you can most effectively run and maintain related groups of tests.

CHAPTER 6

Establishing Organization in JUnit Tests

Your JUnit learnings so far include:

- How to run JUnit and understand its results
- How to group related test methods within a test class
- How to group common test initialization into a @BeforeEach method
- A deep dive into JUnit assertions (the previous chapter)

Generally, you want at least one test class for each production class you develop. In this chapter, you'll dig into the topic of test organization within a test class. You'll learn about:

- The parts of a test
- Initializing and cleaning up using lifecycle methods
- Grouping related tests with nested classes
- The JUnit test execution lifecycle
- Avoiding dependency challenges by never ordering tests
- Executing multiple test cases for a single test using parameterized tests

The Parts of an Individual Test

A handful of chapters ago (see Scannability: Arrange—Act—Assert, on page 18), you learned how AAA provides a great visual mnemonic to help readers quickly understand the core parts of a test.

Some developers refer to a "four-phase test,"[1] where each test can be broken into (wait for it) four parts or phases:

- Set up state/data in what's sometimes called a *fixture*. Think of a fixture as the context in which a test runs—its world, so to speak. The fixture is

---

1. http://xunitpatterns.com/Four%20Phase%20Test.html

managed for you by JUnit; you'll learn more about that in this chapter as part of the JUnit test execution lifecycle.

- Interact with the system to execute what you want to verify.

- Do the verification (assert).

- Tear down the fixture—clean up any side effects, if necessary. This typically involves cleaning up resources that a test might have used and that could impact the execution of other tests. In this chapter, you'll read about doing such clean-up with @AfterEach and @AfterAll JUnit hooks.

For every intent and purpose, AAA is the first three parts of a four-part test. Arrange, act, assert ≈ setup, execute, verify.

Turns out that the fourth part, "tear down," is and should be rare in *unit* tests, in which you seek to avoid (mostly by design) interaction with the things that you must clean up. If you feel AAA cheats you out of that fourth phase, you can add a fourth "A"...for *ANNIHILATION!* (If the violence disturbs you, just mentally go with "After." Keep calm and carry on.)

Setting Up and Tearing Down Using Lifecycle Methods

You learned about @BeforeEach in your first JUnit example (see Chapter 1, Building Your First JUnit Test, on page 3). Let's take a closer look at this initialization hook, as well as some other useful hooks that JUnit provides.

Initializing with @BeforeEach and @BeforeAll

In Abstraction: Eliminating Boring Details, on page 20, you learned to use @BeforeEach to put common initialization in one place. Methods annotated with @BeforeEach are executed before each test in scope.

JUnit also provides another initialization hook known as @BeforeAll, which you must declare as a static method. Each method annotated with @BeforeAll gets executed once per test class and prior to the execution of anything else within that class. Its primary use is to ensure that slowly executing initializations (for example, anything involving a database) only have to execute once. Otherwise, prefer using @BeforeEach.

If you find yourself using @BeforeAll more than once in a blue moon, you may be testing behaviors bigger than units. That may be okay, but it might suggest you have opportunities for reducing the dependencies in your system. See Chapter 3, Using Test Doubles, on page 53 for ideas on how to do that.

If your test needs demand that you initialize a few things before each test is run, you can declare multiple @BeforeEach methods in the test class's scope, each with a different name. These don't run in any useful order, just as test methods do not.

Creating additional @BeforeEach methods allows you to use their methods name to describe what's going on in each initialization. Of course, you can also lump all your initialization into a single @BeforeEach method as long as it's easy for other developers to understand what's going on when reading through your lump.

You can have multiple (static) @BeforeAll methods in a test class.

Using @AfterEach and @AfterAll for Cleanup

JUnit bookends the initialization hooks @BeforeEach and @BeforeAll with corresponding "teardown" lifecycle methods @AfterEach and @AfterAll. These methods allow you to clean up resources on test completion. Both @AfterEach and @AfterAll are guaranteed to run (as long as the JUnit process itself doesn't crash), even if any tests throw exceptions.

Within @AfterEach, for example, you might close a database connection or delete a file. If you write integration (non-unit) tests in JUnit, these teardown hooks are essential.

Most *unit* tests, however, shouldn't interact with code that requires clean-up. The typical, hopefully rare case is when multiple tests alter the state of a static field.

If you do have a clean-up need, try to redesign your code to eliminate it. Use dependency injection (see Injecting Dependencies into Production Code, on page 56) and/or mock objects (see Chapter 3, Using Test Doubles, on page 53) as appropriate.

Even when you do have a legitimate clean-up need, adding code to @AfterEach or @AfterAll is mostly only being nice. Suppose the general assumption is that all tests clean up after themselves—seems like a fair testing standard, yes? The problem is that eventually, someone will forget to properly clean up in another test elsewhere. If your test fails as a result, it may take some real time to figure out which one of possibly thousands of tests is the culprit.

 Each of your tests is responsible for ensuring it executes in a clean, expected state.

You can usually design your code so almost no *unit* tests require clean-up, but you may still need @AfterEach in a tiny number of places.

Organizing Related Tests into Nested Classes

As your classes grow by taking on more behaviors, you'll need more and more tests to describe the new behaviors. Use your test class size as a hint: if you declare several dozen tests in one test source file, chances are good that the class under test is too large. Consider splitting the production class up into two or more classes, which also means you'll want to split the test methods across at least two or more test classes.

You may still end up with a couple dozen test methods in one test class. A larger test class can not only be daunting from a navigational sense, but it can also make it harder to find all tests that relate to each other.

To help group related tests, you might consider starting each related test's name with the same thing. Here are three tests describing how withdrawals work in the Account class:

```
@Test void withdrawalReducesAccountBalance() { /* ... */ }
@Test void withdrawalThrowsWhenAmountExceedsBalance() { /* ... */ }
@Test void withdrawalNotifiesIRSWhenAmountExceedsThreshold() { /* ... */ }
```

A better solution, however, is to group related tests within a JUnit @Nested class:

```
@Nested
class Withdrawal {
    @Test void reducesAccountBalance() { /* ... */ }
    @Test void throwsWhenAmountExceedsBalance() { /* ... */ }
    @Test void notifiesIRSWhenAmountExceedsThreshold() { /* ... */ }
}
```

You can create a number of @Nested classes within your test class, similarly grouping all methods within it. The name of the nested class, which describes the common behavior, can be removed from each test name.

You can also use @Nested classes to group tests by context—the state established by the arrange part of a test. For example:

```
class AnAccount
    @Nested
    class WithZeroBalance {
        @Test void doesNotAccrueInterest() { /* ... */ }
        @Test void throwsOnWithdrawal() { /* ... */ }
    }
```

```
  @Nested
  class WithPositiveBalance {
    @BeforeEach void fundAccount() { account.deposit(1000); }
    @Test void accruesInterest() { /* ... */ }
    @Test void reducesBalanceOnWithdrawal() { /* ... */ }
  }
}
```

Tests are split between those needing a zero-balance account (WithZeroBalance) and those needing a positive account balance (WithPositiveBalance).

Observing the JUnit Lifecycle

You've learned about using before and after hooks and how to group related tests into nested classes. Using a skeleton test class, let's take a look at how these JUnit elements are actually involved when you run your tests.

AFundedAccount contains six tests. Per its name, all tests can assume that an account exists and has a positive balance. An account object gets created at the field level and subsequently funded within a @BeforeEach method. Here's the entire AFundedAccount test class, minus all the intricate details of each test.

utj3-junit/01/src/test/java/scratch/AFundedAccount.java

```java
import org.junit.jupiter.api.*;

class AFundedAccount {
    Account account = new Account("Jeff");
    AFundedAccount() {
        // ...
    }

    @BeforeEach
    void fundAccount() {
        account.deposit(1000);
    }

    @BeforeAll
    static void clearAccountRegistry() {
        // ...
    }

    @Nested
    class AccruingInterest {

        @BeforeEach
        void setInterestRate() {
            account.setInterestRate(0.027d);
        }

        @Test
        void occursWhenMinimumMet() {
            // ...
        }
```

```
    @Test
    void doesNotOccurWhenMinimumNotMet() {
        // ...
    }

    @Test
    void isReconciledWithMasterAccount() {
        // ...
    }
    }
    @Nested
    class Withdrawal {
    @Test
    void reducesAccountBalance() {
        // ...
    }

    @Test
    void throwsWhenAmountExceedsBalance() {
        // ...
    }

    @Test
    void notifiesIRSWhenAmountExceedsThreshold() {
        // ...
    }
    }
}
```

While you could choose to instantiate the account field in a @BeforeEach method, there's nothing wrong with doing field-level initialization, particularly if there's not much going on. The field declaration in AFundedAccount initializes an account with some arbitrary name, so it's not interesting enough to warrant a @BeforeEach method. But if your common initialization is at all interesting or requires a series of statements, you'd definitely want it to occur within a @BeforeEach method.

The use of @Nested makes for well organized test results when you run your tests:

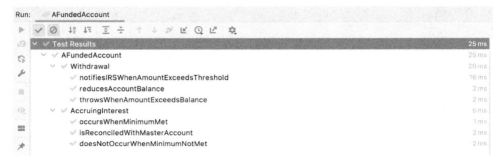

You can clearly see the grouping of related tests, which makes it easier to find what you're looking for. The visual grouping also makes it easier to spot the glaring absence of necessary tests as well as review their names for consistency—with other tests or with your team's standards for how tests are named.

I instrumented each of the @BeforeEach methods, the @Test methods, and the constructors (implicitly defined in the listing) with System.out statements. Here's the output when the tests are run:

```
@BeforeAll::clearAccountRegistry
AFundedAccount(); Jeff balance = 0
        Withdrawal
                @BeforeEach::fundAccount
                notifiesIRSWhenAmountExceedsThreshold
AFundedAccount(); Jeff balance = 0
        Withdrawal
                @BeforeEach::fundAccount
                reducesAccountBalance
AFundedAccount(); Jeff balance = 0
        Withdrawal
                @BeforeEach::fundAccount
                throwsWhenAmountExceedsBalance
AFundedAccount(); Jeff balance = 0
        Accruing Interest
                @BeforeEach::fundAccount
                @BeforeEach::setInterestRate
                occursWhenMinimumMet
AFundedAccount(); Jeff balance = 0
        Accruing Interest
                @BeforeEach::fundAccount
                @BeforeEach::setInterestRate
                accruesNoInterestWhenMinimumMet
AFundedAccount(); Jeff balance = 0
        Accruing Interest
                @BeforeEach::fundAccount
                @BeforeEach::setInterestRate
                doesNotOccurWhenMinimumNotMet
```

The static @BeforeAll method executes first.

The output shows that a new instance of AFundedAccount is constructed for each test executed. It also shows that the account is, as expected, properly initialized with a name and zero balance.

Creating a new instance for each test is part of JUnit's deliberate design. It helps ensure each test is isolated from side effects that other tests might create.

JUnit creates a new instance of the test class for each test method that runs.

The @BeforeEach method fundAccount, declared within the top-level scope of the AFundedAccount class, executes prior to each of all six tests.

The @BeforeEach method setInterestRate, declared within the scope of AccruingInterest, executes only prior to each of the three tests defined within that nested class.

Avoiding Dependency Despair: Don't Order Your Tests!

JUnit tests don't run in their declared (top to bottom) order. In fact, they don't run in any order that you'd easily be able to determine or depend on, such as alphabetically. (They're likely returned in the order that a call to java.lang.Class.getMethods() returns, which is "not sorted and not in any particular order," per its Javadoc.)

You might be tempted to *think* you want your tests to run in a specific order: "I'm writing a first test around newly created accounts, which have a zero balance. A second test can add $100 to the account, and I can verify that amount. I can then add a test that runs third, in which I'll deposit $50 and ensure that the new balance is $150."

While JUnit 5 provides a way to force the ordering of test execution, using it for *unit* tests is a bad idea. Depending on test order might help you avoid redundantly stepping through common setup in multiple test cases. But it will usually lead you down the path to wasted time. For example, say you're running tests, and the fourth test fails. Was it because of a real problem in the production code? Or was it because one of the preceding three tests (which one?) left the system in some newly unexpected state?

With ordered tests, you'll also have a harder time understanding any test that's dependent on other tests. Increasing dependencies is as costly in tests as it is in your production code.

 Unit tests should verify *isolated units* of code and not depend on any order of execution.

Rather than creating headaches by forcing the order of tests, use @BeforeEach to reduce the duplication of common initialization. You can also extract helper methods to reduce redundancy and amplify your tests' abstraction level.

Executing Multiple Data Cases with Parameterized Tests

Many of your system's behaviors will demand several distinct test cases. For example, you'll often end up with at least three tests as you work through the progression of zero-one-many.

Defining separate test methods allows you to explicitly summarize their distinct behaviors in the test names:

```
storesEmptyStringWhenEmpty
storesInputStringWhenContainingOneElement
storesCommaSeparatedStringWhenContainingManyElements
```

Often, the three test cases will be structured exactly the same—all the statements within it are the same, but the input and expected output data differ. You can streamline the redundancies across these tests with things like helper methods and @BeforeEach methods if it bothers you.

Sometimes, when you have such redundancy across tests, there's no interesting way to name them distinctly. For example, suppose you have tests for code that converts Arabic numbers into Roman equivalents:

utj3-junit/01/src/main/java/util/RomanNumberConverter.java
```java
public class RomanNumberConverter {
    record Digit(int arabic, String roman) {}

    Digit[] conversions = {
        new Digit(1000, "M"),
        new Digit(900, "CM"),
        new Digit(500, "D"),
        new Digit(400, "CD"),
        new Digit(100, "C"),
        new Digit(90, "XC"),
        new Digit(50, "L"),
        new Digit(40, "XL"),
        new Digit(10, "X"),
        new Digit(9, "IX"),
        new Digit(5, "V"),
        new Digit(4, "IV"),
        new Digit(1, "I")
    };

    public String toRoman(int arabic) {
        return Arrays.stream(conversions).reduce(
            new Digit(arabic, ""),
            (acc, conversion) -> {
                var digitsRequired = acc.arabic / conversion.arabic;
```

```
        return new Digit(
            acc.arabic - digitsRequired * conversion.arabic,
            acc.roman + conversion.roman.repeat(digitsRequired));
    }).roman();
  }
}
```

Neither the algorithm nor the behavior changes based on the inputs. Were you to code this as separate JUnit tests, there'd be little useful distinction between the test names:

utj3-junit/01/src/test/java/util/ARomanNumberConverter.java
```
import org.junit.jupiter.api.Test;
import static org.junit.jupiter.api.Assertions.assertEquals;

class ARomanNumberConverter {
   RomanNumberConverter converter = new RomanNumberConverter();

   @Test
   void convertsOne() {
      assertEquals("I", converter.toRoman(1));
   }

   @Test
   void convertsTwo() {
      assertEquals("II", converter.toRoman(2));
   }

   @Test
   void convertsThree() {
      assertEquals("III", converter.toRoman(3));
   }

   // ... so wordy!
}
```

It's tedious to create separate tests for each case, and their names add little real value. You could lump them all in a single test method but then the individual cases wouldn't be isolated from each other.

Fortunately, JUnit supports a special form of test known as a *parameterized test*. You create a parameterized test by annotating your test method with @ParameterizedTest instead of @Test. You must also provide a data source, which is essentially a list of data rows. For each data row, JUnit calls the test method with data from the row as parameters.

The parameterized test method for the RomanNumberConverter needs two pieces of information: the Arabic number to be passed to the toRoman method and the expected Roman equivalent to be used in an assertEquals statement. You can use a @CsvSource to provide data rows for the test; each row is a CSV (comma-separated values) string.

Here's a parameterized test for the RomanNumberConverter:

utj3-junit/01/src/test/java/util/ARomanNumberConverter.java
```
@ParameterizedTest
@CsvSource({
    "1,    I",
    "2,    II",
    "3,    III",
    "10,   X",
    "20,   XX",
    "11,   XI",
    "200,  CC",
    "732,  DCCXXXII",
    "2275, MMCCLXXV",
    "999,  CMXCIX",
    "444,  CDXLIVI", // failure
})
void convertAll(int arabic, String roman) {
    assertEquals(roman, converter.toRoman(arabic));
}
```

The first data row in the @CsvSource (highlighted) contains the CSV string "1,   I".
JUnit splits this string on the comma and trims the resulting values. It passes
these values—the number 1 and the string "I"—to the convertAll test method
(highlighted).

JUnit takes the CSV values and uses them, left to right, as arguments to the
test method. So when the test method is executed, 1 gets assigned to the int
arabic parameter (with JUnit converting the string to an int), and "I" gets assigned
to the String roman parameter.

Since the above example shows eleven CSV data rows, JUnit will run convertAll
eleven times. IntelliJ shows the parameters for each of the eleven cases:

Note how JUnit indicates the failing (incorrectly specified) case.

The JUnit documentation[2] goes into considerable detail about the various
data source mechanisms available.

---

2.   https://junit.org/junit5/docs/current/user-guide/#writing-tests-parameterized-tests-sources

Here's a quick summary:

@ValueSource	A single array of values. Useful only if your test takes one parameter (which implies that the expected outcome is the same for every source value)
@EnumSource	Iterates all the possible enum values, with some options for inclusion/exclusion and regex matching
@MethodSource	Expects the name of a method, which must return all data rows in a stream
@CsvFileSource	Mostly the same thing as @CsvSource, except that you specify a filename containing the CSV rows
@ArgumentsSource	Allows you to create a custom, reusable data source in a class that extends an interface named ArgumentsProvider

While parameterized tests in JUnit are sophisticated and flexible beasts, @CsvSource will suit most of your needs. I've never needed another data source variant (though I don't frequently use parameterized tests).

In summary, parameterized tests are great when you need to demonstrate data (not behavioral) variants. These are a couple of pervasive needs:

- Code that conditionally executes if a parameter is null *or* an empty string. A parameterized test with two inputs (null and "") lets you avoid test duplication.

- Code around border conditions, particularly because such code often breeds defects. For example, for code that conditionally executes if n <= 0, use a parameterized test with the values n - 1 and n.

Otherwise, create a new @Test that describes a distinct behavior.

Summary

On most systems, you'll end up with many hundreds or thousands of unit tests. You'll want to keep your maintenance costs low by taking advantage of a few JUnit features, including lifecycle methods, nested classes, and parameterized tests. These features allow you to reduce redundant code and make it easy to run a related set of tests.

Now that you've learned how to best organize your tests, in the next chapter, you'll dig into topics that relate to executing tests using JUnit. You'll pick up some good habits for deciding how many tests to run (and when to not run tests). You'll learn how to run subsets of tests as well as how to temporarily disable tests.

CHAPTER 7

Executing JUnit Tests

You learned about assertions, test organization, and the JUnit lifecycle of execution earlier in this part of the book.

Having all the tests in the world is useless if you never run them. You'll want to run tests often as you build software on your own machine like you've been doing so far. But you'll also want to run them as part of the process of vetting integrated software before deploying it, perhaps as part of a continuous build process.

In this chapter, you'll learn "when," "what," and more of the "how" of running tests:

- What set of unit tests you'll want to run when executing JUnit

- Grouping tests using the JUnit @Tag annotation, which allows you to execute arbitrary groups of tests

- Temporarily *not* running your tests using the @Disabled annotation

Testing Habits: What Tests to Run

Full-fledged Java IDEs (for example, IntelliJ IDEA or Eclipse) have built-in support for JUnit. Out of the box, you can load a project, click on its test directory, and execute tests without having to configure anything. You saw in Chapter 1, Building Your First JUnit Test, on page 3 at least a couple of ways to run JUnit tests from within IntelliJ IDEA. In the following sections, you'll see how the number of tests you run affects your results.

Run All the Tests

If your tests are fast (see Fast Tests, on page 66), it's possible to run thousands of unit tests within a few seconds. When you have fast tests, you can run all of them with every tiny change. If you broke something elsewhere in the codebase, you'll know it immediately. Fast tests provide an awe-inspiring power-up.

Run as Many Tests as You Can Stand

IDEA and other IDEs make it easy to choose the opposite of running everything, which is to run only one test at a time. IDEA, for example, provides a small "play" icon button to the left of each test method.

Suppose you're adding a test named issuesSMSAlertOnWithdrawal to the test class AFundedAccount. The problem with running only issuesSMSAlertOnWithdrawal is that it's surrounded by a number of other tests in AFundedAccount that verify potentially related behaviors in the Account production class. As you start changing Account to support the new SMS alert behavior, it's possible to break these other Account behaviors.

You want to know the moment you break other code. In general, the longer you go without feedback that you've broken things, the longer it will take you to find and fix things. Piling more code around defective code starts to obscure problems and can also make it harder to fix due to the amount of entanglement.

A key value of your unit tests is fast feedback. The only way to get that feedback, though, is to actually run the darn things.

Fortunately, you're learning to design your tests to be fast. It might not be reasonable to run all your tests because they take more than a few seconds, but it had better be reasonable to run all the tests in, say, AFundedAccount. Your IDE should make it easy to run all tests in a single class. With JUnit, you can also group subsets of related tests using nested classes (see Organizing Related Tests into Nested Classes, on page 126).

If running all of a class's tests takes too long, fix the problem before it gets worse and wastes even more time. The fix might involve some redesign. You might extract some slower, integration-style tests from an otherwise fast test class. Or, you might introduce mock objects (see Chapter 3, Using Test Doubles, on page 53) to transform slow tests into fast tests. Or, more dramatically, you might fix the unfortunate dependencies in your production class that foster slow tests.

It's possible for changes in one class to break tests for other classes. Behavior in Account, for example, is verified by tests in AnAccount *and* AFundedAccount. If all potentially impacted test classes are in the same package, take a step up and run all the tests within that package. If it's too slow to run all the tests in a package, I have the same blunt advice: fix the problem.

 Run as many tests as you can stand, as often as you can stand.

If you habituate to running one test at a time, you'll eventually discover defects elsewhere later than you should. About the only time you should run a single test is if you're struggling to get it to pass and find yourself in debugging mode or using System.out.println statements to trace what's going on. At that point, running multiple tests will make it difficult to focus on the problematic one.

Creating Arbitrary Test Groups Using Tags

JUnit 5 lets you mark a test class or a test method with the @Tag annotation. You can use these tags as the basis for running arbitrary sets of tests with JUnit. This is known as *filtering* your tests.

Let's take a look at an example. When making changes to the Account class, you should run all tests in *both* AnAccount and AFundedAccount. You could run all the tests in the package containing both these classes, but you can also use tags to be precise about the subset of tests to run.

Mark both two classes with the @Tag annotation:

utj3-junit/01/src/test/java/tags/AnAccount.java

```java
import org.junit.jupiter.api.Tag;
import org.junit.jupiter.api.Test;
// ...

@Tag("account")
class AnAccount {
    // ...

    @Test
    void withdrawalReducesAccountBalance() {
        // ...
    }
    // ...
}
```

utj3-junit/01/src/test/java/tags/AnUnfundedAccount.java

```java
import org.junit.jupiter.api.Tag;
import org.junit.jupiter.api.Test;
// ...
```

```
@Tag("account")
class AnUnfundedAccount {
    // ...

    @Test
    void hasPositiveBalanceAfterInitialDeposit() {
        // ...
    }

    // ...
}
```

To run the tests in these two tagged classes, you must provide a filter to JUnit. Your IDE might allow you to do this directly when you run tests. If you're using Maven or Gradle, both of these tools provide direct support for specifying filters. In the worst case, you can run JUnit as a standalone command and provide the filter at that time.

Visit JUnit's documentation for running tests for further information[1] on using tags with Maven, Gradle, or command-line JUnit.

Using Tags in IntelliJ IDEA

With IntelliJ IDEA, you configure how tests are run in the Run/Debug Configurations dialog.

From IDEA's main menu, access the Run/Debug Configurations dialog by selecting Run ▶ Edit Configurations. From within the Run/Debug Configurations dialog, add a new configuration by clicking the + button. IDEA provides a dropdown titled Add New Configuration; select JUnit from its long list of options.

The dialog defaults to running tests within a single test class; you will need to change this to tell JUnit to run a tag instead. Within the dialog's Build and run section, you should see a dropdown with Class currently selected. Select instead Tags from this dropdown. In the input field to the right of the dropdown, type in the text account as the tag to execute. This text should match the "account" string you specified in your @Tag declarations.

Your dialog should look similar to the figure on page 139.

 Specifying utj3-junit as the classpath (-cp) may generate errors. Ensure you've chosen utj3-junit.test.

---

1.   https://junit.org/junit5/docs/current/user-guide/#running-tests

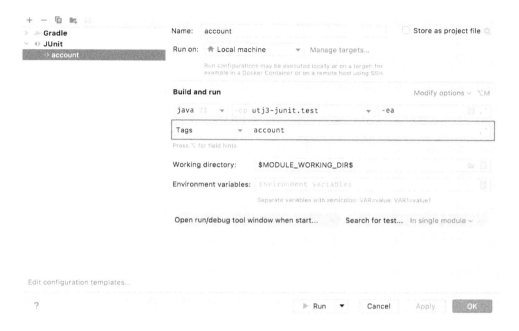

You can now click on Apply and then Run to execute only tests marked with the "account" tag.

Tag Expressions

IDEA supports *tag expressions*, which are Boolean expressions that allow more sophisticated filtering.

In addition to tagging the two account-related test classes, suppose you also want to run the set of tests related to hot-fixes for discovered defects. You might have tagged a single test method:

utj3-junit/01/src/test/java/tags/AnInMemoryDatabase.java
```java
import org.junit.jupiter.api.Tag;
import org.junit.jupiter.api.Test;

class AnInMemoryDatabase {
   // ...
   @Tag("v11.1_defects")
   @Test
   void objectCopiedWhenAddedToDatabaseFailing() {
     // ...
   }
   // ...
}
```

When specifying tags within your run configuration, you can enter the following tag expression:

```
account | v11.1_defects
```

The | (or) operator indicates that JUnit should run the union of tests tagged with "account" and tests tagged with "v11_defects." Specifically, JUnit will run tests in AnAccount and AnUnfundedAccount, as well as the test named objectCopiedWhenAddedToDatabaseFailing.

Tag expressions support inverting a filter using the ! (not) operator and running the intersection of two tags using the & (and) operator. They also allow the use of parentheses to clarify or force the precedence of the operators.

Overusing Tags

As with anything, heavy use of the tags feature may be a sign that something else is amiss.

If you find you've used more-or-less permanent tag names (like *account*), try reorganizing your production and/or test code to eliminate the need for the tag. You might extract a new package, move classes around, move test methods to other classes, and so on. Within a single test class, use a @Nested class to collect a focused set of tests related to a single concept ("withdrawal").

Temporarily Disabling Tests with @Disabled

Occasionally, you'll want to keep a specific test from getting executed, usually because it's failing. Maybe you don't have the time to fix it at the moment and want to focus on getting other tests to pass first—during which time, other test failures will be a distraction.

You might have other legitimate reasons to avoid running a certain test. Maybe you're waiting on an answer from the business about a specific unit behavior.

You can temporarily comment out tests, of course, but the better answer is to mark the test methods in question with the @Disabled annotation. JUnit will bypass executing any such marked test methods. You can similarly mark a test class as @Disabled, in which case JUnit will run none of its test methods.

Using @Disabled is a better way of bypassing tests because JUnit can remind you that some tests await your revisit. JUnit can't remind you if you comment out tests, in which case your tests may remain forever in limbo. (That's one way to break a test's back.)

utj3-junit/01/src/test/java/scratch/AnUnfundedAccount.java

```
import org.junit.jupiter.api.Disabled;
import org.junit.jupiter.api.Test;

class AnUnfundedAccount {
    @Disabled
    @Test
    void disallowsWithdrawals() {
        // ...
    }

    @Test
    void doesNotAccrueInterest() {
        // ... uh oh we need to focus on this test
    }
}
```

The informational string provided to the @Disabled annotation is optional. You should probably use it to describe why you disabled the test unless you're going to remove that annotation in the next few minutes or so.

To be honest, few reasons exist to push up a @Disabled test. One legitimate reason (been there): "Midnight emergency fix resulted in broken tests. Revisit tomorrow!" In which case, the following reason might suffice:

```
@Disabled("broken after emergency fix")
```

Allowing disabled tests in your integrated codebase is otherwise a bad, bad process smell.

The JUnit test runner you use, whether it's built into your IDE or your build automation tool (Gradle or Maven, for example), should make it clear that some of your tests are disabled. In the following IntelliJ IDEA test runner, the test disallowsWithdrawals is marked with a grey "no symbol" (⊘) to indicate it is disabled:

You'll appreciate the reminder that you've left a test in limbo.

Unfortunately, by default, running your tests at the command line with Gradle only tells you there are disabled tests if at least one test fails. And you only see that if you scroll upward through the Gradle output.

Gradle is a great way to build and run tests within a continuous build environment. But don't use Gradle for interactive unit testing unless you customize its output to remind you of disabled tests. Have it fail the test run if any disabled tests exist or show their count as the last line of output.

Disabled tests should not really exist other than on your own machine. Avoid integrating disabled tests—they usually represent big questions about the health of your system, such as these: Is the test really needed? Can we just delete it? What do we currently understand about why we couldn't immediately get this to pass?

Exploring More Features

JUnit has grown over its past 20-something years into a fairly large and sophisticated tool. It's likely that the features you've learned in this chapter will be enough for your needs for years to come. However, it's also possible that one of JUnit's other features[2] might be useful for your special circumstances. Here's a quick summary:

assumptions	Abort execution of a test if an assumption is not met (but don't count it as failed).
conditional test execution	Enable or disable tests conditionally. Conditions can reference the OS, architecture, Java version, value of a system property/environment variable, or custom-coded predicates.
display names	Rather than show the (typically) camel-cased test name during a test run, show the contents of a string.
display name generators	Generate more human-readable test names by transforming the test method names. For example, transform underscores in test names into spaces.
dynamic tests	Generate tests at runtime.
parallel execution	Run tests concurrently to speed up their execution.
repeated tests	Run a test a specified number of times.
suites	Programmatically declare a filtered collection of tests to execute.
temp dir context	Write a file-dependent test that executes in the context of a temporary directory.
timeouts	Fail a test (or lifecycle method) if its execution time exceeds a specific duration.

---

2.   https://junit.org/junit5/docs/current/user-guide/

Summary

In this and the prior two chapters that dig into JUnit, you learned the bulk of what you'll need to know about writing assertions, organizing your tests, and running your tests.

With this solid foundation for JUnit, you can move on to more important concerns. In the next part of the book, you'll focus on tests and their relationship to your system's design. You'll refactor your code "in the small" because you have tests that give you the confidence to do so. You'll touch on larger design concepts as well, and you'll also learn how to design your tests to increase the return on your investment in them.

Part III

Increasing ROI: Unit Testing and Design

*Elevate your unit tests beyond mere logic validation.
In this part, learn how to use your tests to maintain
clean code—both "in the small" and "in the large"—
and document your system's unit capabilities.*

CHAPTER 8

Refactoring to Cleaner Code

In Parts I and II, you dug deep into how to write unit tests and take advantage of JUnit. In this part, you'll learn to take advantage of unit tests to help shape the design of your system, as well as document the numerous unit-level behavioral choices you've made. Your ability to keep your system simpler and your tests clearer can reduce your development costs considerably.

You'll start by focusing on design "in the small," addressing the lack of clarity and excessive complexity that's commonplace in most systems. You'll accomplish this by learning to *refactor*—making small, frequent edits to the code you write. Your design improvements will help reduce the cost of change.

In a clear, well-designed system, it might take seconds to locate a point of change and understand the surrounding code. In a more typically convoluted system, the navigation and comprehension tasks often require minutes instead. Once you've understood the code well enough to change it, a well-designed system might accommodate your change readily. In the convoluted system, weaving in your changes might take hours.

 Convoluted systems can increase your maintenance costs by an order of magnitude or more.

You can, with relative ease, create systems that embody *clean code*. In brief, this describes clean code:

- Concise: It imparts the solution without unnecessary code.

- Clear: It can be directly understood.

- Cohesive: It groups related concepts together and apart from unrelated concepts.

- Confirmable: It can be easily verified with tests.

Your unit tests provide you with that last facet of clean code.

A Little Bit o' Refactor

Refactoring is a fancy way to indicate that you're transforming the underlying structure of your code—its implementation details—while retaining its existing functional behavior. Since refactoring involves reshaping and moving code, you must ensure your system still works after such manipulations. Unit tests are the cheapest, fastest way to do so.

Refactoring is to coding as editing is to writing. Even the best (expository) writers edit most sentences they write to make them immediately clear to readers. Coding is no different. Once you capture a solution in an editor, your code is often harder to follow than necessary.

Writers follow the mindset to write first for themselves and then for others. To do so as a programmer, first, code your solution in a way that makes sense to you. Then, consider your teammates who must revisit your code at some point in the future. Rework your code to provide a clearer solution now while it still makes sense to you.

 Code in two steps: first, capture your thoughts in a correct solution. Second, clarify your solution for others.

Confidence is the key consideration when it comes to refactoring. Without the confidence that good unit tests provide, you'd want to be extremely cautious about "fixing" code that's already working. In fact, without unit tests, you might think, "it ain't broke. Don't fix it." Your code would start its life unedited—with deficiencies—and would get a little worse with each change.

If you've followed the recommendations in this book, however, you can make changes willy-nilly. Did you think of a new name for a method, one that makes more sense? Rename it (ten seconds in a good IDE; perhaps minutes otherwise), run your tests, and know seconds later that nothing broke. Method too long and hard to follow? Extract a chunk of it to a new method, and run your tests. Method in the wrong place? Move it, run tests. You can make small improvements to your codebase all day long, each making it incrementally easier (cheaper) to work with.

An Opportunity for Refactoring

The code you'll clean up comes from iloveyouboss (albeit a different version of it). See Exacerbating a Threading Issue, on page 80 for an overview of the application. Take a look at the Profile class in iloveyouboss:

utj3-refactor/01/src/main/java/iloveyouboss/Profile.java
```java
import java.util.*;
import static iloveyouboss.Weight.*;

public class Profile {
    private final Map<String,Answer> answers = new HashMap<>();
    private final String name;
    private int score;

    public Profile(String name) { this.name = name; }

    public void add(Answer... newAnswers) {
        for (var answer: newAnswers)
            answers.put(answer.questionText(), answer);
    }

    public boolean matches(Criteria criteria) {
        score = 0;

        var kill = false;
        var anyMatches = false;
        for (var criterion: criteria) {
            var answer = answers.get(criterion.answer().questionText());
            var match = criterion.weight() == IRRELEVANT ||
                        answer.match(criterion.answer());
            if (!match && criterion.weight() == REQUIRED) {
                kill = true;
            }
            if (match) {
                score += criterion.weight().value();
            }
            anyMatches |= match;
        }
        if (kill) {
            return false;
        }
        return anyMatches;
    }

    public int score() { return score; }

    @Override
    public String toString() { return name; }
}
```

This class provides the beginnings of the core matching functionality. A Profile is comprised of answers to questions that prospective employees might ask about a company: Do you provide bonuses? Do you hire remote workers? Will you wash my dog for me? It exposes the core matching functionality through its matches method. The matches method takes on a Criteria object containing the preferred answers that a would-be employee has specified.

The matches method isn't particularly long, weighing in at around a dozen total lines of expressions and/or statements. Yet it's reasonably dense, requiring attentive, stepwise reading. Spend a little time looking at matches to see if you can pin down what it does.

Testing the class's behavior sufficiently required seven unit tests:

utj3-refactor/01/src/test/java/iloveyouboss/AProfile.java
```java
import org.junit.jupiter.api.*;
import static iloveyouboss.Weight.*;
import static iloveyouboss.YesNo.*;
import static org.junit.jupiter.api.Assertions.*;

class AProfile {
    Profile profile = new Profile("Geeks Inc.");
    Criteria criteria;

    Question freeLunch;
    Answer freeLunchYes;
    Answer freeLunchNo;

    Question bonus;
    Answer bonusYes;
    Answer bonusNo;

    Question hasGym;
    Answer hasGymNo;
    Answer hasGymYes;

    String[] NO_YES = {NO.toString(), YES.toString()};

    @BeforeEach
    void createQuestionsAndAnswers() {
        bonus = new Question("Bonus?", NO_YES, 1);
        bonusYes = new Answer(bonus, YES);
        bonusNo = new Answer(bonus, NO);

        freeLunch = new Question("Free lunch?", NO_YES, 1);
        freeLunchYes = new Answer(freeLunch, YES);
        freeLunchNo = new Answer(freeLunch, NO);

        hasGym = new Question("Gym?", NO_YES, 1);
        hasGymYes = new Answer(hasGym, YES);
        hasGymNo = new Answer(hasGym, NO);
    }
```

```java
@Nested
class DoesNotMatch {
    @Test
    void whenAnyRequiredCriteriaNotMet() {
        profile.add(freeLunchNo, bonusYes);
        criteria = new Criteria(
                new Criterion(freeLunchYes, REQUIRED),
                new Criterion(bonusYes, IMPORTANT));

        var matches = profile.matches(criteria);

        assertFalse(matches);
    }

    @Test
    void whenNoneOfMultipleCriteriaMatch() {
        profile.add(bonusNo, freeLunchNo);
        criteria = new Criteria(
            new Criterion(bonusYes, IMPORTANT),
            new Criterion(freeLunchYes, IMPORTANT));

        var matches = profile.matches(criteria);

        assertFalse(matches);
    }
}

@Nested
class Matches {
    @Test
    void whenCriteriaIrrelevant() {
        profile.add(freeLunchNo);
        criteria = new Criteria(
            new Criterion(freeLunchYes, IRRELEVANT));

        var matches = profile.matches(criteria);

        assertTrue(matches);
    }

    @Test
    void whenAnyOfMultipleCriteriaMatch() {
        profile.add(bonusYes, freeLunchNo);
        criteria = new Criteria(
            new Criterion(bonusYes, IMPORTANT),
            new Criterion(freeLunchYes, IMPORTANT));

        var matches = profile.matches(criteria);

        assertTrue(matches);
    }
}
```

```
@Nested
class Score {
    @Test
    void isZeroWhenThereAreNoMatches() {
        profile.add(bonusNo);
        criteria = new Criteria(
            new Criterion(bonusYes, IMPORTANT));

        profile.matches(criteria);

        assertEquals(0, profile.score());
    }

    @Test
    void doesNotIncludeUnmetRequiredCriteria() {
        profile.add(bonusNo, freeLunchYes);
        criteria = new Criteria(
            new Criterion(bonusYes, REQUIRED),
            new Criterion(freeLunchYes, IMPORTANT));

        profile.matches(criteria);

        assertEquals(IMPORTANT.value(), profile.score());
    }

    @Test
    void equalsCriterionValueForSingleMatch() {
        profile.add(bonusYes);
        criteria = new Criteria(
            new Criterion(bonusYes, IMPORTANT));

        profile.matches(criteria);

        assertEquals(IMPORTANT.value(), profile.score());
    }

    @Test
    void sumsCriterionValuesForMatches() {
        profile.add(bonusYes, freeLunchYes, hasGymNo);
        criteria = new Criteria(
            new Criterion(bonusYes, IMPORTANT),
            new Criterion(freeLunchYes, NICE_TO_HAVE),
            new Criterion(hasGymYes, VERY_IMPORTANT));

        profile.matches(criteria);

        assertEquals(IMPORTANT.value() + NICE_TO_HAVE.value(),
            profile.score());
    }
}
}
```

The tests' examples should help you understand the Profile class.

Extract Method: Your Second-Best Refactoring Friend

Before this section's heading sends you digging in the index, your *best* refactoring friend is *rename*, whether it be a class, method, or variable of any sort. Clarity is largely about declaration of intent, and good names are what impart clarity best in code.

Your goal: reduce complexity in matches so you can readily understand what it's responsible for. The method is currently a jumble of code that obscures the overall set of steps required—its *algorithm* or *policy*. You'll shift the code from "implementation detail" to "clear declarations" by *extracting* detailed bits of logic to new, separate methods.

Conditional expressions often read poorly, particularly when they are complex. An example is the assignment to match that appears atop the for loop in matches:

```
utj3-refactor/01/src/main/java/iloveyouboss/Profile.java
public boolean matches(Criteria criteria) {
    // ...
    for (var criterion: criteria) {
        var answer = answers.get(criterion.answer().questionText());
➤       var match = criterion.weight() == IRRELEVANT ||
➤                   answer.match(criterion.answer());
        // ...
    }
}
```

The right-hand side of the assignment seemingly defines when there's a match. Specifically, it says there's a match either when the criterion is irrelevant *or* when the criterion's answer matches the corresponding answer in the profile. Isolate this complexity by extracting it to a separate method named isMatch. In IntelliJ IDEA, extract methods by following these mouse-heavy steps:

1. Highlight the appropriate code.
2. Open the context menu (via right-click).
3. Select Refactor ▶ Extract Method from the menu.
4. Type a name for the new method (or accept the one suggested).
5. Press Enter.

IntelliJ creates a method containing the highlighted code and then replaces the highlighted code with a call to the new method.

After extracting isMatches, you're left with a simple declaration in matches and a short helper method in the Profile class:

utj3-refactor/02/src/main/java/iloveyouboss/Profile.java
```java
for (var criterion: criteria) {
    var answer = answers.get(criterion.answer().questionText());
    var match = isMatch(criterion, answer);
    // ...
}
```

utj3-refactor/02/src/main/java/iloveyouboss/Profile.java
```java
private boolean isMatch(Criterion criterion, Answer answer) {
    return criterion.weight() == IRRELEVANT ||
            answer.match(criterion.answer());
}
```

The loop's code is one step closer to showing only high-level policy and de-emphasizing lower-level details. The isMatch method provides the specifics about whether an individual criterion is a match for an answer.

It's too easy to break behavior when moving code about, sometimes, even when your IDE moves it for you. After making this change, run all the tests to ensure they still pass. Good tests provide confidence to make countless small changes. You'll know the moment you introduce a sneaky little defect.

 With each small change, run your fast set of tests for confidence. It's cheap, easy, and gratifying.

The ability to move code about safely is one of the most important benefits of unit testing. You can add new features safely as well as shape the code toward a better design. In the absence of sufficient tests, you'll tend to make fewer changes or changes that are highly risky.

Finding Better Homes for Your Methods

Your loop is a bit easier to read—great! But code in the newly extracted isMatch method has nothing to do with the Profile object itself—it interacts with Answer and Criterion objects. One of those two classes is probably a better place for the isMatch behavior.

Criterion objects already know about Answer objects, but Answer isn't dependent on Criterion. As such, *move* the newly extracted matches method to the Criterion record. Moving it to Answer would create a bidirectional dependency with Answer and Criterion objects depending on each other. Such a tight coupling would mean that changes to either type could propagate to the other, which in turn could create other problems.

In IntelliJ IDEA, move the method by following these steps:

1. Click its name.
2. Open the context menu (via right-click).
3. Select Refactor ▶ Move Instance Method from the menu.
4. Select the instance expression Criterion criterion.
5. Press Enter.

Here's isMatch in its new home:

utj3-refactor/03/src/main/java/iloveyouboss/Criterion.java
```java
import static iloveyouboss.Weight.IRRELEVANT;

public record Criterion(Answer answer, Weight weight) {
    boolean isMatch(Answer answer) {
        return weight() == IRRELEVANT || answer.match(answer());
    }
}
```

And here's what the loop looks like after the move:

utj3-refactor/03/src/main/java/iloveyouboss/Profile.java
```java
for (var criterion: criteria) {
    var answer = answers.get(criterion.answer().questionText());
    var match = criterion.isMatch(answer);
    if (!match && criterion.weight() == REQUIRED) {
        kill = true;
    }
    if (match) {
        score += criterion.weight().value();
    }
    anyMatches |= match;
}
```

The expression assigned to the answer local variable is hard to read because of the method chaining:

utj3-refactor/03/src/main/java/iloveyouboss/Profile.java
```java
var answer = answers.get(criterion.answer().questionText());
```

The code asks criterion for its answer object and then asks the answer for its question text. Better: ask the criterion to directly return the question text. As the first step toward that goal, extract the expression criterion.answer().questionText() to a new method named questionText:

utj3-refactor/04/src/main/java/iloveyouboss/Profile.java
```java
public boolean matches(Criteria criteria) {
    // ...
```

```
    for (var criterion: criteria) {
➤       var answer = answers.get(questionText(criterion));
        // ...
    }
    // ...
}

➤ private String questionText(Criterion criterion) {
    return criterion.answer().questionText();
}
```

Now move questionText to the Criterion class. If you move it via IDEA's automated refactoring support, select Criterion criterion as the instance expression.

The method disappears from Profile. The expression assigned to the answer local variable no longer involves method chaining:

utj3-refactor/05/src/main/java/iloveyouboss/Profile.java

```
public boolean matches(Criteria criteria) {
    // ...
    for (var criterion: criteria) {
➤       var answer = answers.get(criterion.questionText());
        // ...
    }
    // ...
}
```

Criterion is now responsible for retrieving and returning the question text:

utj3-refactor/05/src/main/java/iloveyouboss/Criterion.java

```
import static iloveyouboss.Weight.IRRELEVANT;

public record Criterion(Answer answer, Weight weight) {
    // ...
    String questionText() {
        return answer().questionText();
    }
}
```

Next, extract the whole right-hand side of the answer assignment to a method that helps explain what the answer represents:

utj3-refactor/06/src/main/java/iloveyouboss/Profile.java

```
public boolean matches(Criteria criteria) {
    // ...
    for (var criterion: criteria) {
➤       var answer = profileAnswerMatching(criterion);
        var match = criterion.isMatch(answer);
        // ...
    }
    // ...
}
```

```
➤   private Answer profileAnswerMatching(Criterion criterion) {
        return answers.get(criterion.questionText());
    }
```

Each extract method you do increases the conciseness of matches bit by bit. Using intention-revealing names for the new methods also increases the clarity of matches. The new methods also represent opportunities to move responsibilities to where they belong. Profile gets simpler while the previously barren Criterion builds up its usefulness.

Removing Temporaries of Little Value

Temporary variables ("temps") have a number of uses. They can cache the value of an expensive computation or collect things that change throughout the body of a method. A temp can also clarify the intent of code—a valid choice even if it's used only once.

In matches, the answer local variable provides none of those three benefits. You can *inline* such a pointless variable by replacing any occurrences of it with the answerMatching(criterion) expression. In IntelliJ IDEA, inline a variable by following these steps:

1. Click its name.
2. Open the context menu (via right-click).
3. Select Refactor ▶ Inline Variable from the menu.

Any references to the variable are replaced with the right-hand side of the assignment. The assignment statement disappears:

utj3-refactor/07/src/main/java/iloveyouboss/Profile.java
```
public boolean matches(Criteria criteria) {
    // ...
    for (var criterion: criteria) {
➤       var match = criterion.isMatch(profileAnswerMatching(criterion));
        // ...
    }
    // ...
}
```

The true intent for match can be understood directly. Paraphrasing: a match exists when the criterion is a match for the corresponding profile answer.

Speeding Up with Automated Refactoring

You can, of course, do this or any other refactoring manually, cutting and pasting little bits of code until you reach the same outcome. But once you've learned that a good IDE can do the job at least ten times as fast, it makes little sense not to take advantage of that power.

More importantly, you can trust that (in Java, at least) an automated refactoring generally will not break code. You're far more likely to mess up along the way through a manual refactoring. Java automated refactorings are code transformations that have been proven in all senses of the word.

You can further speed up by using the keyboard shortcuts for each automated refactoring rather than click through menus and dialogs. Throughout your development day, you'll find heavy use for a small number of core automated refactorings: introduce variable/constant/field/parameter, extract method, inline method, inline variable, move method, and change signature. It won't take long to ingrain the corresponding shortcuts. You can reduce most refactoring operations to about three to four seconds from 10 seconds or more (clicking through the UI) or from several minutes (manually).

Lucky you: 20 years ago, most Java programmers manually moved code about in highly unsafe ways. Thirty years ago, automated refactoring tools didn't exist. Today, the power and speed they grant can't be overstated. You can watch the computer do the dirty work and know that your code still works.

Amplifying the Core Intent of Code

Let's re-examine the slightly improved matches method:

```
utj3-refactor/07/src/main/java/iloveyouboss/Profile.java
public boolean matches(Criteria criteria) {
    score = 0;

    var kill = false;
    var anyMatches = false;
    for (var criterion: criteria) {
        var match = criterion.isMatch(profileAnswerMatching(criterion));
        if (!match && criterion.weight() == REQUIRED) {
            kill = true;
        }
        if (match) {
            score += criterion.weight().value();
        }
        anyMatches |= match;
    }
    if (kill)
        return false;

    return anyMatches;
}
```

Careful reading reveals the following outcomes:

- Return true if any criterion matches, false if none do.
- Calculate the score by summing the weights of matching criteria.
- Return false when any required criterion does not match the corresponding profile answer.

Let's restructure matches to directly emphasize these three core concepts.

Extract Concept: Any Matches Exist?

The determination of whether any matches exist is scattered through the method. It involves both the anyMatches and matches local variables:

utj3-refactor/08/src/main/java/iloveyouboss/Profile.java
```java
public boolean matches(Criteria criteria) {
    score = 0;

    var kill = false;
    var anyMatches = false;
    for (var criterion: criteria) {
        var match = criterion.isMatch(profileAnswerMatching(criterion));
        if (!match && criterion.weight() == REQUIRED) {
            kill = true;
        }
        if (match) {
            score += criterion.weight().value();
        }
        anyMatches |= match;
    }
    if (kill)
        return false;

    return anyMatches;
}
```

Your goal: move all the logic related to making that determination to its own method. Here are the steps:

1. Change the return statement to return the result of calling a new method, anyMatches().

2. Create a new method, anyMatches, that returns a Boolean value.

3. *Copy* (don't cut) the relevant logic into the new method.

The result:

utj3-refactor/09/src/main/java/iloveyouboss/Profile.java
```java
public boolean matches(Criteria criteria) {
    score = 0;
```

```java
    var kill = false;
    var anyMatches = false;
    for (var criterion: criteria) {
        var match = criterion.isMatch(profileAnswerMatching(criterion));
        if (!match && criterion.weight() == REQUIRED) {
            kill = true;
        }
        if (match) {
            score += criterion.weight().value();
        }
        anyMatches |= match;
    }
    if (kill)
        return false;

➤   return anyMatches(criteria);
}

➤ private boolean anyMatches(Criteria criteria) {
    var anyMatches = false;
    for (var criterion: criteria) {
        var match = criterion.isMatch(profileAnswerMatching(criterion));
        anyMatches |= match;
    }
    return anyMatches;
}
```

There's no automated refactoring for this change. You're making riskier manual changes, so run your tests! Once they pass, remove the two lines of code in matches that reference the anyMatches variable:

utj3-refactor/10/src/main/java/iloveyouboss/Profile.java
```java
public boolean matches(Criteria criteria) {
    score = 0;

    var kill = false;
    for (var criterion: criteria) {
        var match = criterion.isMatch(profileAnswerMatching(criterion));
        if (!match && criterion.weight() == REQUIRED) {
            kill = true;
        }
        if (match) {
            score += criterion.weight().value();
        }
    }
    if (kill)
        return false;

    return anyMatches(criteria);
}
```

The loop, of course, must remain and so must the line of code that assigns to the match variable.

You might be concerned about that method extraction and its performance implications. We'll discuss.

Extract Concept: Calculate Score for Matches

Now that you've isolated the anyMatches logic by extracting it to a new method, you can do the same for the code that calculates the score. If you put the call to calculateScore below if (kill) return false, however, the tests break. (The score needs to be calculated before any unmet required criterion results in an aborted method.)

utj3-refactor/11/src/main/java/iloveyouboss/Profile.java
```java
public boolean matches(Criteria criteria) {
    calculateScore(criteria);

    var kill = false;
    for (var criterion: criteria) {
        var match = criterion.isMatch(profileAnswerMatching(criterion));
        if (!match && criterion.weight() == REQUIRED) {
            kill = true;
        }
    }
    if (kill)
        return false;

    return anyMatches(criteria);
}

private void calculateScore(Criteria criteria) {
    score = 0;
    for (var criterion: criteria) {
        var match = criterion.isMatch(profileAnswerMatching(criterion));
        if (match) {
            score += criterion.weight().value();
        }
    }
}
```

Hmmm. You might be wondering if you're creating performance problems.

Extract Concept: Return False When Required Criterion Not Met

The code remaining in the loop aborts method execution if the profile doesn't match a required criterion, returning false. Similarly, extract this logic to a new method, anyRequiredCriteriaNotMet:

utj3-refactor/12/src/main/java/iloveyouboss/Profile.java

```java
public boolean matches(Criteria criteria) {
    calculateScore(criteria);

    var kill = anyRequiredCriteriaNotMet(criteria);
    if (kill)
        return false;

    return anyMatches(criteria);
}

private boolean anyRequiredCriteriaNotMet(Criteria criteria) {
    var kill = false;
    for (var criterion: criteria) {
        var match = criterion.isMatch(profileAnswerMatching(criterion));
        if (!match && criterion.weight() == REQUIRED) {
            kill = true;
        }
    }
    return kill;
}
```

Matches is now five lines of code and fairly easy to follow! But some cleanup work remains, particularly in the three newly extracted methods. For one, the loops are all old-school for-each loops. You'll clean up these problems after we address the performance elephant in the room.

The implementation for matches now involves three loops spread across three methods instead of a single loop through the criteria. That might seem horrifying to you. We'll come back to discuss the performance implications; for now, let's talk about the benefits you gain with the new design.

Earlier, you invested some time in carefully reading the original code in order to glean its three intents. The Boolean logic throughout created opportunities for confusion along the way. Now, matches (almost) directly states the method's high-level goals.

The implementation details for each of the three steps in the algorithm are hidden in the corresponding helper methods calculateScore, anyRequiredCriteriaNotMet, and anyMatches. Each helper method allows the necessary behavior to be expressed in a concise, isolated fashion, not cluttered with other concerns.

Are You Kidding Me? Addressing Concerns over Performance

At this point, you might be feeling a little perturbed. After refactoring the matches method, each of anyMatches, calculateScore, and anyRequiredCriteriaNotMet iterates through the criterion collection. Your code now loops three times instead of one. You've potentially tripled the time to execute matches.

Do you have a real performance problem relevant to the real requirements, or do you only suspect one exists? Many programmers speculate about where performance problems might lie and about what the best resolution might be. Unfortunately, such speculations can be quite wrong.

Base all performance optimization attempts on real data, not speculation.

The first answer to any potential performance problem is to measure. If understanding performance characteristics is a pervasive and critical application concern, you want to do that analysis from the perspective of end-to-end functionality—more holistically—rather than at the level of individual unit or method performance. (You'll still ultimately be narrowing down to a hopefully small number of methods that need to be fixed.) For such needs, you'll want a tool like JMeter.[1] You can also incorporate JUnitPerf,[2] which allows you to write performance tests using JUnit.

If you have an occasional concern about the performance of an individual unit, you can create a few "roll your own" performance probes. As long as you're careful with your conclusions, they'll be adequate for your needs.

The following code runs in the context of a JUnit test (though it has no assertions and is currently not a test) and displays the number of milliseconds elapsed. The probe code creates a Criteria object with answers to 20 questions. It then loops a million times. Each loop creates a new Profile, adds randomized answers to the 20 questions, and then determines whether or not the profile matches the criteria.

utj3-refactor/12/src/test/java/iloveyouboss/AProfilePerformance.java
```java
import org.junit.jupiter.api.Test;
import java.util.List;
import java.util.Random;
import java.util.concurrent.atomic.AtomicInteger;
import java.util.function.Consumer;
import static iloveyouboss.YesNo.*;
import static java.util.stream.IntStream.range;

class AProfilePerformance {
    int questionCount = 20;
    Random random = new Random();
```

---

1.   http://jmeter.apache.org/
2.   https://github.com/noconnor/JUnitPerf

```java
    @Test
➤   void executionTime() {
        var questions = createQuestions();
        var criteria = new Criteria(createCriteria(questions));

        var iterations = 1_000_000;
        var matchCount = new AtomicInteger(0);
        var elapsedMs = time(iterations, i -> {
            var profile = new Profile("");
            profile.add(createAnswers(questions));
            if (profile.matches(criteria))
                matchCount.incrementAndGet();
        });
        System.out.println("elapsed: " + elapsedMs);
        System.out.println("matches: " + matchCount.get());
    }

    long time(int times, Consumer<Integer> func) {
        var start = System.nanoTime();
        range(0, times).forEach(i -> func.accept(i + 1));
        return (System.nanoTime() - start) / 1_000_000;
    }

    int numberOfWeights = Weight.values().length;

    Weight randomWeight() {
        if (isOneInTenTimesRandomly()) return Weight.REQUIRED;

        var nonRequiredWeightIndex =
            random.nextInt(numberOfWeights - 1) + 1;
        return Weight.values()[nonRequiredWeightIndex];
    }

    private boolean isOneInTenTimesRandomly() {
        return random.nextInt(10) == 0;
    }

    YesNo randomAnswer() {
        return random.nextInt() % 2 == 0 ? NO : YES;
    }

    Answer[] createAnswers(List<Question> questions) {
        return range(0, questionCount)
            .mapToObj(i -> new Answer(questions.get(i), randomAnswer()))
            .toArray(Answer[]::new);
    }

    List<Question> createQuestions() {
        String[] noYes = {NO.toString(), YES.toString()};
        return range(0, questionCount)
            .mapToObj(i -> new Question("" + i, noYes, i))
            .toList();
    }
```

```
    List<Criterion> createCriteria(List<Question> questions) {
        return range(0, questionCount)
            .mapToObj(i -> new Criterion(new Answer(
                questions.get(i), randomAnswer()), randomWeight()))
            .toList();
    }
}
```

I ran the probe on an old laptop five times to shake out any issues around timing and the clock cycle. Execution time averaged at 1470ms.

The iterations (1,000,000) and data size (20 questions) are arbitrary choices. You might choose numbers with some real-world credibility using actual production characteristics, but that's not critical. Mostly, you want a sense of whether or not the degradation is significant enough to be concerned about.

I also ran the probe against version 8 of the profile, which represents the code right before you started factoring into multiple loops. Execution time averaged at 1318ms (with a low standard deviation, under 3 percent).

Execution time for the cleaner design represents an 11.5 percent increase for the new solution. It's a sizeable amount, percentage-wise, but it's not anywhere near three times worse due to the triple looping. For most people, it's a non-issue, but you must decide if the degradation will create a real problem regarding end-user impact.

Take care when doing this kind of probe. It's possible to craft a probe that mischaracterizes reality. For example, Java can, at times, optimize out parts of the code you're profiling.

If you process very high volumes, performance may indeed be critical to the point where the degradation is too much. Ensure you measure after each optimization attempt and validate whether or not the optimization made enough of a difference.

Optimized code can easily increase the cost of both understanding and changing a solution by an order of magnitude. A clean design can reveal intent in a handful of seconds, as opposed to a minute or more with an optimized design. Always derive a clean design and then optimize your code only if necessary.

A clean design can provide more flexibility and opportunities for optimizing the code. Caching, for example, is a lot easier if the things being cached are isolated from other bits of code.

A clean design is your best starting point for optimization.

Note: this probe is intended to be throw-away code. However, you might need to elevate it to your integration test suite, where it would fail if someone pushed a solution that violated the execution time threshold. To do so, you'd add an assertion that the probe finished in under x milliseconds. The challenge is determining what x should be, given likely varying execution contexts (differing machines and differing loads, for example). One approach would involve calculating the threshold dynamically as part of test execution, using a baseline measurement of a simple, stable operation.

Next up, you'll change the for-each loops to use the Java streams interface. This refactoring, afforded by the tests, would allow you to parallelize the execution of a stream as one way to improve performance.

Final Cleanup

Let's return to the fun and see how tight you can make the code.

First, replace the old-school loops with Java streams. Start with anyMatches:

utj3-refactor/13/src/main/java/iloveyouboss/Profile.java
```
private boolean anyMatches(Criteria criteria) {
    return criteria.stream()
        .anyMatch(criterion ->
            criterion.isMatch(profileAnswerMatching(criterion)));
}
```

To get that compiling and passing, you'll need to add a stream method to the Criteria record:

utj3-refactor/13/src/main/java/iloveyouboss/Criteria.java
```
public Stream<Criterion> stream() {
    return criteria.stream();
}
```

Next, rework the calculateScore method:

utj3-refactor/13/src/main/java/iloveyouboss/Profile.java
```
private void calculateScore(Criteria criteria) {
    score = criteria.stream()
        .filter(criterion ->
            criterion.isMatch(profileAnswerMatching(criterion)))
        .mapToInt(criterion -> criterion.weight().value())
        .sum();
}
```

After cleaning up anyRequiredCriteriaNotMet similarly, it's much simpler to follow without the (horribly named) kill temporary variable:

utj3-refactor/13/src/main/java/iloveyouboss/Profile.java
```java
private boolean anyRequiredCriteriaNotMet(Criteria criteria) {
    return criteria.stream()
        .filter(criterion ->
            !criterion.isMatch(profileAnswerMatching(criterion)))
        .anyMatch(criterion -> criterion.weight() == REQUIRED);
}
```

You've supplanted all three loops. Delete the iterator method in the Criteria record.

Finally, inline kill in the core matches method:

utj3-refactor/13/src/main/java/iloveyouboss/Profile.java
```java
public boolean matches(Criteria criteria) {
    calculateScore(criteria);

    if (anyRequiredCriteriaNotMet(criteria)) return false;

    return anyMatches(criteria);
}
```

You can capture that core four-line policy in a few other ways, but this approach reads fine.

Summary

It's easy to write a lot of code quickly. It's just as easy to let that code get dirty to the point where it becomes difficult to comprehend and navigate. Unit tests provide the safeguards you need to clean up messy code without breaking things.

In this chapter, you learned techniques for keeping your system clean continually to help you keep your system from degrading into a frustrating mess. You renamed variables and methods, you extracted smaller methods, you inlined variables, and you replaced older Java constructs with newer ones. You might call this very incremental method-level cleanup "micro" refactoring—a programmer's version of the continuous editing that a writer performs.

Don't let your code get to the point of the convoluted matches methods. Do recognize that difficult code like matches is rampant in most systems, and it doesn't take long for developers to create it.

As you begin to sweep away the small bits of dust in your system, you'll start to see larger design concerns—problems related to the overall structure of the system and how its responsibilities are organized. Next up, you'll learn how to lean on unit tests again to address these larger design concerns through "macro" refactoring.

Right now, the code you refactored in matches clearly states what's going on. But it also poses some concerns about the bigger design picture. The Profile class, for example, might be doing too much.

In the next chapter, you'll explore where your design falls flat. You'll take advantage of your tests to support getting things back on track.

CHAPTER 9

Refactoring Your Code's Structure

In the last chapter, you focused on refactoring the matches method into a number of more composed methods. You also focused on the clarity and conciseness of each method. This continual editing of small bits of code is a fundamental piece of design—you are making choices about how to implement a solution in a manner that keeps code comprehension and maintenance costs low.

These are examples of "micro" design concerns:

- How you capture state in fields
- How you organize code into methods
- How those methods interact with each other
- How those methods interact with the external world

To many developers, a software system's design is mostly a "macro" concern:

- How you organize classes into packages
- How you organize methods into classes
- How those classes interact with each other

Both sets of concerns are relevant to the long-term maintainability of a system. One or both can be impacted any time you make a decision about how to organize and implement your code.

A software system's design is the combined collection of choices made at both macro and micro levels.

You might be thinking, "This is a unit testing book. Why is this guy talking about design so much?"

It turns out that writing unit tests isn't an exercise that occurs in a vacuum. Your system's design impacts your ability to write tests and vice versa. You might even consider the tests themselves a piece of the larger, continually shifting puzzle we call design. They provide confidence that your system's design exhibits the most important aspect of design—that it supports a *correct* solution, working as intended.

 The most important aspect of a system's design is that it works as intended.

In this chapter, you'll focus on bigger design concerns:

- The Single Responsibility Principle (SRP) guides you to small classes that do *one* core thing to increase flexibility and ease of testing, among other things.

- The command-query separation (CQS) principle says to design methods that do *one* of creating a side effect or returning a value but never both

- Refactoring the production code toward a better design. When refactoring, change *one* of either production code or tests at a time and never both.

Perhaps you noticed a focus on the notion of "one" in that list. It's not a coincidence; it's a core mentality in incremental software development.

 One Thing At A Time (OTAAT).

You'll apply these principles by refactoring code in the Profile class.

The Profile Class and the SRP

Take a look at the Profile class:

utj3-refactor/13/src/main/java/iloveyouboss/Profile.java
```java
import java.util.HashMap;
import java.util.Map;
import static iloveyouboss.Weight.REQUIRED;

public class Profile {
    private final Map<String,Answer> answers = new HashMap<>();
    private final String name;
    private int score;

    public Profile(String name) { this.name = name; }

    public void add(Answer... newAnswers) {
        for (var answer: newAnswers)
            answers.put(answer.questionText(), answer);
    }
```

```java
public boolean matches(Criteria criteria) {
    calculateScore(criteria);

    if (anyRequiredCriteriaNotMet(criteria)) return false;

    return anyMatches(criteria);
}
private boolean anyRequiredCriteriaNotMet(Criteria criteria) {
    return criteria.stream()
        .filter(criterion ->
            !criterion.isMatch(profileAnswerMatching(criterion)))
        .anyMatch(criterion -> criterion.weight() == REQUIRED);
}

private void calculateScore(Criteria criteria) {
    score = criteria.stream()
        .filter(criterion ->
            criterion.isMatch(profileAnswerMatching(criterion)))
        .mapToInt(criterion -> criterion.weight().value())
        .sum();
}

private boolean anyMatches(Criteria criteria) {
    return criteria.stream()
        .anyMatch(criterion ->
            criterion.isMatch(profileAnswerMatching(criterion)));
}

private Answer profileAnswerMatching(Criterion criterion) {
    return answers.get(criterion.questionText());
}

public int score() { return score; }

@Override
public String toString() { return name; }
}
```

At under seventy source lines, Profile doesn't seem inordinately large or excessively complex. But it hints at less-than-ideal design.

Profile tracks and manages information for a company or person, including a name and a collection of answers to questions. This set of information that Profile captures will need to change over time—more information will need to be added, and some might need to be removed or altered.

As a secondary responsibility, Profile calculates a score to indicate if—and to what extent—a set of criteria matches the profile. With the refactoring you accomplished in the previous chapter, you ended up with a number of methods that directly support the matches method. Changes to the Profile class are thus probable for a second reason: you'll undoubtedly change the sophistication of your matching algorithm over time.

The Profile class violates the Single Responsibility Principle (SRP) of object-oriented class design, which says classes should have only one reason to change. (The SRP is one of a set of class design principles—see the following sidebar.) Focusing on the SRP decreases the risk of change. The more responsibilities a class has, the easier it is to break other existing behaviors when changing code within the class.

SOLID Class-Design Principles

In the mid-1990s, Robert C. Martin gathered five principles for object-oriented class design, presenting them as the best guidelines for building a maintainable object-oriented system. Michael Feathers attached the acronym SOLID to these principles in the early 2000s.[a]

- Single Responsibility Principle (SRP). Classes should have one reason to change. Keep your classes small and single-purposed.

- Open-Closed Principle (OCP). Design classes to be open for extension but closed for modification. Minimize the need to make changes to existing classes.

- Liskov Substitution Principle (LSP). Subtypes should be substitutable for their base types. Method overrides shouldn't break a client's expectations for behavior.

- Interface Segregation Principle (ISP). Clients shouldn't have to depend on methods they don't use. Split a larger interface into a number of smaller interfaces.

- Dependency Inversion Principle (DIP). High-level modules should not depend on low-level modules; both should depend on abstractions. Abstractions should not depend on details; details should depend on abstractions.

---

a.   http://en.wikipedia.org/wiki/SOLID_(object-oriented_design)

Smaller, more focused classes more readily provide value in another context—re-use! In contrast, a very large class with lots of responsibilities cannot possibly be used in other contexts.

Underlying the SOLID principles are the concepts of cohesion and coupling. Classes in your systems should exhibit high cohesion and low coupling. Such systems make change easier, and they also make unit testing easier.

The concepts of SOLID, low coupling, and high cohesion are not new, but they're also not "outdated." Despite some post-modern ideas about software design, these principles remain valid. They're not absolutes: all choices in software systems represent tradeoffs. You must balance the principles with each other, with other considerations (like performance), and with other circumstances or constraints of your reality.

Extracting a New Class

The Profile class defines two responsibilities:

- Track information about a profile.
- Determine whether and to what extent a set of criteria matches a profile.

To improve your system's design, you'll split responsibilities into two classes, each small and adherent to the SRP. To do so, you'll extract the code related to the profile-matching behavior to another class, Matcher. As with all refactoring, you'll take an incremental path—make a small change and then run the tests to make sure they still pass.

For your first change, move the calculateScore logic into Matcher. Start by changing the code in matches to declare your intent: rather than call calculateScore directly from matches, construct a new Matcher object with the information it needs—the hash map of answers and the criteria—and ask it for the score. Assign that returned score to the score field:

utj3-refactor/14/src/main/java/iloveyouboss/Profile.java
```java
public boolean matches(Criteria criteria) {
    score = new Matcher(criteria, answers).score();

    if (anyRequiredCriteriaNotMet(criteria)) return false;

    return anyMatches(criteria);
}
```

Copy (don't cut it just yet) the calculateScore method from Profile into Matcher. In the constructor of Matcher, first, store the answers argument in a field. Then, call the calculateStore method, passing it the Criteria object that was passed to the constructor.

Add a score field and a score() accessor method to return it.

Compilation at this point reveals that calculateScore() needs to call profileAnswerMatching(). Copy over that method.

Your Matcher class should now look like the following:

utj3-refactor/14/src/main/java/iloveyouboss/Matcher.java
```java
import java.util.Map;

public class Matcher {
    private final Map<String, Answer> answers;
    private int score;
```

```java
    public Matcher(Criteria criteria, Map<String, Answer> answers) {
        this.answers = answers;
        calculateScore(criteria);
    }

    private void calculateScore(Criteria criteria) {
        score = criteria.stream()
            .filter(criterion ->
                criterion.isMatch(profileAnswerMatching(criterion)))
            .mapToInt(criterion -> criterion.weight().value())
            .sum();
    }

    private Answer profileAnswerMatching(Criterion criterion) {
        return answers.get(criterion.questionText());
    }

    public int score() {
        return score;
    }
}
```

Both Profile and Matcher now compile. Your tests should run successfully.

The code in Profile no longer uses the calculateScore private method. Delete it. The profileAnswerMatching method is still used by code in Profile. Indicate that it's duplicated elsewhere with a comment. If profileAnswerMatching is still needed by both classes after you finish moving code about, you'll want to factor that code to a single place.

Moving Matches Functionality to Matcher

You've delegated the scoring responsibility to Matcher and invoked it from matches. The other code in matches represents the second goal of the method—to answer true or false depending on whether the criteria match the set of answers.

Matcher represents a more appropriate home for that matches logic. Let's similarly delegate the matching responsibility to the Matcher class.

You can tackle this refactoring in many ways. Let's take one small step at a time.

utj3-refactor/15/src/main/java/iloveyouboss/Profile.java
```java
public boolean matches(Criteria criteria) {
    score = new Matcher(criteria, answers).score();

➤   if (anyRequiredCriteriaNotMet(criteria)) return false;
➤
➤   return anyMatches(criteria);
}
```

Extract the two highlighted lines to a method with a name other than matches, which is already used. How about isMatchFor?

utj3-refactor/16/src/main/java/iloveyouboss/Profile.java
```java
public boolean matches(Criteria criteria) {
    score = new Matcher(criteria, answers).score();

    return isMatchFor(criteria);
}

private boolean isMatchFor(Criteria criteria) {
    if (anyRequiredCriteriaNotMet(criteria)) return false;
    return anyMatches(criteria);
}
```

Move isMatchFor to Matcher. Your IDE should let you know that the two methods called by isMatchFor—anyRequiredCriteriaNotMet and anyMatches—must come along for the ride. Move them too.

Here is isMatchFor in its new home, along with the related methods:

utj3-refactor/17/src/main/java/iloveyouboss/Matcher.java
```java
public class Matcher {
    // ...
    public boolean isMatchFor(Criteria criteria) {
        if (anyRequiredCriteriaNotMet(criteria))
            return false;
        return anyMatches(criteria);
    }

    private boolean anyMatches(Criteria criteria) {
        return criteria.stream()
            .anyMatch(criterion ->
                criterion.isMatch(profileAnswerMatching(criterion)));
    }

    private boolean anyRequiredCriteriaNotMet(Criteria criteria) {
        return criteria.stream()
            .filter(criterion ->
                !criterion.isMatch(profileAnswerMatching(criterion)))
            .anyMatch(criterion -> criterion.weight() == REQUIRED);
    }

    Answer profileAnswerMatching(Criterion criterion) {
        return answers.get(criterion.questionText());
    }
    // ...
}
```

The matches method in Profile should be down to two statements:

utj3-refactor/17/src/main/java/iloveyouboss/Profile.java

```java
public boolean matches(Criteria criteria) {
    score = new Matcher(criteria, answers).score();

    return new Matcher(criteria, answers).isMatchFor(criteria);
}
```

Tests still pass? Good. Extract the common initialization of Matcher in matches to a local variable:

utj3-refactor/18/src/main/java/iloveyouboss/Profile.java

```java
public boolean matches(Criteria criteria) {
    var matcher = new Matcher(criteria, answers);
    score = matcher.score();
    return matcher.isMatchFor(criteria);
}
```

Moving all the matching logic into Matcher trims the Profile class nicely:

utj3-refactor/18/src/main/java/iloveyouboss/Profile.java

```java
import java.util.HashMap;
import java.util.Map;

public class Profile {
    private final Map<String,Answer> answers = new HashMap<>();
    private final String name;
    private int score;

    public Profile(String name) {
        this.name = name;
    }

    public void add(Answer... newAnswers) {
        for (var answer: newAnswers)
            answers.put(answer.questionText(), answer);
    }

    public boolean matches(Criteria criteria) {
        var matcher = new Matcher(criteria, answers);
        score = matcher.score();
        return matcher.isMatchFor(criteria);
    }

    public int score() {
        return score;
    }

    @Override
    public String toString() {
        return name;
    }
}
```

The Profile class now appears to adhere to the SRP. Its methods are all small and straightforward—you can gather a sense of everything that's going on in each of them at a glance.

Profile is also fairly cohesive: changes to matching or scoring logic will be made in Matcher. Changes to the Profile class itself (for example, it needs to store additional attributes) will not be triggered by changes to matching/scoring logic and will unlikely require changes to Matcher.

Cleaning Up After a Move

Shift your focus back to Matcher, into which you moved a bunch of methods. Any time you move a method, you'll want to determine if opportunities exist for improving the code in its new home.

The moved anyRequiredCriteriaNotMet and anyMatches methods both require access to the criteria instance. Alter the constructor in Matcher to store criteria as a new field. Once criteria is available as a field, there's no reason to pass criteria around to the calculateScore, anyRequiredCriteriaNotMet, and anyMatches methods.

The removal of the criteria argument from the matches method requires you to change the calling code in Profile. After you make that change, note that without the criteria argument, return matcher.isMatchFor() reads poorly. Rename the isMatchFor method back to matches:

utj3-refactor/19/src/main/java/iloveyouboss/Profile.java
```java
public boolean matches(Criteria criteria) {
    var matcher = new Matcher(criteria, answers);
    score = matcher.score();
    return matcher.matches();
}
```

Here's the cleaned-up Matcher class:

utj3-refactor/19/src/main/java/iloveyouboss/Matcher.java
```java
public class Matcher {
    private final Criteria criteria;
    private final Map<String, Answer> answers;
    private int score;

    public Matcher(Criteria criteria, Map<String, Answer> answers) {
        this.criteria = criteria;
        this.answers = answers;
        calculateScore();
    }
```

```
➤      private void calculateScore() {
           score = criteria.stream()
               .filter(criterion ->
                   criterion.isMatch(profileAnswerMatching(criterion)))
               .mapToInt(criterion -> criterion.weight().value())
               .sum();
       }

       public boolean matches() {
➤          if (anyRequiredCriteriaNotMet()) return false;
➤          return anyMatches();
       }

➤      private boolean anyMatches() {
           return criteria.stream()
               .anyMatch(criterion ->
                   criterion.isMatch(profileAnswerMatching(criterion)));
       }

➤      private boolean anyRequiredCriteriaNotMet() {
           return criteria.stream()
               .filter(criterion ->
                   !criterion.isMatch(profileAnswerMatching(criterion)))
               .anyMatch(criterion -> criterion.weight() == REQUIRED);
       }

       private Answer profileAnswerMatching(Criterion criterion) {
           return answers.get(criterion.questionText());
       }

       public int score() {
           return score;
       }
   }
```

A couple more tasks and then you can consider the class sufficiently cleaned up...for now. You can improve the matches method in Matcher, and you can tighten up the scoring logic.

First, the matches method in Matcher requires three lines to express what could be phrased as a single complex conditional:

```
utj3-refactor/19/src/main/java/iloveyouboss/Matcher.java
public boolean matches() {
➤      if (anyRequiredCriteriaNotMet()) return false;
➤      return anyMatches();
   }
```

As short as this method is, it remains stepwise rather than declarative. It requires readers to think about how to piece together three elements.

Combine these separate conditionals into a single expression. Invert the result of anyRequiredCriteriaNotMet and combine it with the result of anyMatches using the *and* (&&) operator:

utj3-refactor/20/src/main/java/iloveyouboss/Matcher.java
```java
public boolean matches() {
    return !anyRequiredCriteriaNotMet() && anyMatches();
}
```

But double-negatives read poorly. (Boolean logic, in general, is tough for many of us; you want to avoid making things worse.) Eliminate the double-negative by doing the following:

1. Flip the logic in anyRequiredCriteriaNotMet to return true if all required criteria *are* met.

2. Invert the name of anyRequiredCriteriaNotMet to allRequiredCriteriaMet.

3. Remove the *not* (!) operator.

utj3-refactor/21/src/main/java/iloveyouboss/Matcher.java
```java
public boolean matches() {
➤    return allRequiredCriteriaMet() && anyMatches();
}

private boolean allRequiredCriteriaMet() {
    return criteria.stream()
➤        .filter(criterion -> criterion.weight() == REQUIRED)
➤        .allMatch(criterion ->
➤            criterion.isMatch(profileAnswerMatching(criterion)));
}
```

That should make a lot more immediate sense to virtually all readers of the code. You might also change the order of the expression to first ask if there are any matches and then ensure that all required criteria are met—it logically flows a little better.

For your second final bit of cleanup, the scoring logic is unnecessarily split across the class. Move the calculateScore logic into the score accessor and then remove calculateScore and the now-unused score field. Your change also carries the benefit of not incurring the score calculation cost if it is not used by the client.

utj3-refactor/21/src/main/java/iloveyouboss/Matcher.java
```java
public int score() {
    return criteria.stream()
        .filter(criterion ->
            criterion.isMatch(profileAnswerMatching(criterion)))
        .mapToInt(criterion -> criterion.weight().value())
        .sum();
}
```

When you first learned about object-oriented design, you might have picked up a recommendation to design your classes like "the real world." It's an okay starting point, particularly for folks new to OO design, but don't take it too far. Dogmatically "real-world" designs may seem appealing, but they create systems that are more difficult to maintain.

The Profile class could be construed as a "real-world" entity. A simplistic real-world implementation would result in the Profile class containing all the logic related to matching on criteria. The version of Profile that you saw at the start of the refactoring exercises is such a real-world implementation. A system full of such larger, overly responsible classes will be hard to understand and change. It will provide virtually no opportunities for re-use and contain considerable duplication,

Create classes that map to concepts, not concrete notions. The Matcher concept allows you to isolate the code related to matching, which keeps its code simpler. The Profile code from which it came gets simpler as well.

Every code change you make alters the design of a system. Some of those changes can have negative impacts on behavior elsewhere in the system. So far, in this chapter, you've focused on such macro design considerations.

As you start to correct design flaws, whether micro or macro, you'll more readily spot additional problems. For example, sometimes extracting a small amount of code to a new method will highlight a glaringly obvious deficiency—one that was not so obvious when surrounded by a lot of other code.

The methods in Profile are now all very small, and one of them indeed exposes a design flaw. Let's return to the micro design space and discuss the concept of command-query separation.

Command-Query Separation

The only remaining oddity in Profile is how it handles scoring logic. Examine its matches method:

```
utj3-refactor/21/src/main/java/iloveyouboss/Profile.java
public boolean matches(Criteria criteria) {
    var matcher = new Matcher(criteria, answers);
    score = matcher.score();
    return matcher.matches();
}
```

As a side effect, Profile stores a score. But a profile doesn't have a single fixed score. It only references a calculated score that's associated with an attempt to match on criteria.

The score side effect causes another problem, which is that a client can't separate one interest from the other. If a client wants (only) the score for a set of criteria, it must first call the matches() method. This sort of *temporal coupling* is not going to be immediately obvious to a developer and demands clear documentation. The client would ignore the boolean value returned by matches (awkward!) and then call the score accessor. Conversely, for a client interested in determining whether a set of criteria matches, the call to matches ends up altering the Profile's score attribute.

A method that both returns a value and generates a side effect (changes the state of the class or some other entity in the system) violates the principle known as *command-query separation* (CQS): A method should either be a *command*, creating a side effect, or a *query* that returns a value. It should not be both.

Lack of CQS can create potential pain for client code. If a query method alters the state of an object, it might not work to call that method again. You might not get the same answer a second time, and it might cause trouble to trigger the side effect a second time.

Lack of CQS also violates expectations for developers using the query method. Without careful reading of the code and its tests, it's possible for a developer to completely overlook the side effect and thus create a problem.

Fixing the CQS Problem in Profile

A client of Profile should be free to call a method without having to know they must first call another. Make clients happy by moving all the score-related logic into the score accessor. It's not much work, particularly since you'd moved the bulk of the logic into Matcher.

```
utj3-refactor/22/src/main/java/iloveyouboss/Profile.java
public boolean matches(Criteria criteria) {
    return new Matcher(criteria, answers).matches();
}

public int score(Criteria criteria) {
    return new Matcher(criteria, answers).score();
}
```

Most significantly, the score method is no longer a raw accessor. It now takes on a Criteria instance as an argument and then delegates to a new Matcher that calculates and retrieves the score.

Don't forget to delete the score field from Profile; it is no longer needed.

As a result of the change to Profile, three tests in AProfile no longer compile. Calls to the score method on a Profile instance now require a criteria object as an argument. Here's an example of one fixed test showing the changed assertion statement:

```
utj3-refactor/22/src/test/java/iloveyouboss/AProfile.java
@Test
void isZeroWhenThereAreNoMatches() {
    profile.add(bonusNo);
    criteria = new Criteria(
        new Criterion(bonusYes, IMPORTANT));
    var score = profile.score(criteria);
    assertEquals(0, score);
}
```

The Costs of Maintaining Unit Tests

Refactoring—changing the implementation of a solution without changing its behavior—should not normally break tests. Here, however, you *did* make a behavioral change due to a deficiency in the Profile interface. Your updated design now exposes the score method's behavior in a different manner than before, hence the broken tests. You might consider that your refactoring "pushed out a change to the interface."

Sure, you must spend time to fix the tests. In this case, having tests in the first place enabled you to recognize and fix a faulty design.

You've learned throughout this book the potential benefits of unit tests:

- Releasing fewer defects
- Changing your code at will with high confidence
- Knowing exactly and rapidly what behaviors the system embodies

This book can help you attain those benefits and increase your ROI.

 The return on investment from well-designed tests outweighs their cost.

Moving forward, when your tests break as you refactor, think about it as a design smell. The more tests that break simultaneously, the bigger the chance you missed an opportunity to improve the design, whether of the tests or production code.

Refocusing Tests

After moving behavior from Profile to Matcher, the tests in AProfile now have nothing to do with Profile. You'll want to move the tests to a new class—AMatcher—and then adapt them to interact with Matcher, not Profile.

Currently, Matcher's constructor requires a Map<String,Answer> (where the String key represents a question's text) as its second parameter. The tests in AProfile involve adding a list of Answer objects to a profile, however:

```
utj3-refactor/21/src/test/java/iloveyouboss/AProfile.java
@Test
void whenNoneOfMultipleCriteriaMatch() {
    profile.add(bonusNo, freeLunchNo);
    criteria = new Criteria(
        new Criterion(bonusYes, IMPORTANT),
        new Criterion(freeLunchYes, IMPORTANT));

    var matches = profile.matches(criteria);

    assertFalse(matches);
}
```

It'd be nice to only have to minimally change the tests. Right now, however, they'd need to convert each list of answers into a Map<String,Answer> before constructing the Matcher.

Instead, think about the most concise way to express your tests. Here's what you'd like Matcher's tests to look like—very similar to the tests in AProfile:

```
utj3-refactor/22/src/test/java/iloveyouboss/AMatcher.java
@Test
void whenNoneOfMultipleCriteriaMatch() {
    criteria = new Criteria(
        new Criterion(bonusYes, IMPORTANT),
        new Criterion(freeLunchYes, IMPORTANT));
    matcher = new Matcher(criteria, bonusNo, freeLunchNo);

    var matches = matcher.matches();

    assertFalse(matches);
}
```

Note that the test necessarily creates a matcher object *after* the criteria. Also, the call to matches no longer requires any arguments.

The test assumes it can create a Matcher object using the same list of answers added to a profile by tests in AProfile. Make that happen by adding a constructor and helper method to Matcher, letting it do the dirty work:

```
utj3-refactor/22/src/main/java/iloveyouboss/Matcher.java
public Matcher(Criteria criteria, Answer... matcherAnswers) {
    this.criteria = criteria;
    this.answers = toMap(matcherAnswers);
}

private Map<String, Answer> toMap(Answer[] answers) {
    return Stream.of(answers).collect(
        Collectors.toMap(Answer::questionText, answer -> answer));
}
```

Getting all of the tests to that adapted shape is maybe 15-20 minutes of work. You'll need to:

- Declare a Matcher field named matcher.
- Eliminate the profile field.
- For each test:
  - Assign a new Matcher instance to matcher. Create it using the test's criteria plus the list of answers previously provided to the profile's add method. Ensure this assignment statement appears *after* the line that creates the Criteria.

  - Remove the statement that adds answers to the profile (for example, profile.add(freeLunch, bonusYes);).

If you get stuck—or just want to give up—go ahead and copy in the code from the distribution for this book.

You can now revisit and clean up the tests in AProfile.

Revisiting the Profile Class: Delegation Tests

Someone created nice, exhaustive tests for the Profile class. (Hey...that was me. You're welcome.) But you copied them over to AMatcher, without really changing the essence of the logic they verify. You also removed all that interesting logic from Profile.

The Profile class still contains three methods with logic. Out of these, the matches and score methods do nothing but delegate to Matcher. Still, you should feel compelled to provide tests for these methods. They'll probably never break, but would at least help describe what's going on.

Were you to test the score and matches methods, you'd have at least a couple of options. You could introduce mock objects (see Chapter 3, Using Test Doubles, on page 53) to verify that the work was delegated to the Matcher in each case. You could also choose a simple, representative case involving the scoring and matching. Both have their merits and demerits.

Would, should, could. Maybe you're sensing I'm not going to have you write tests for these methods. You'll instead push out the work of interacting with the Matcher directly to the client of Profile—a service class, perhaps—as a simplifying design choice. The service class can handle the coordination between the profile, matcher, and criteria. That code might look like this:

utj3-refactor/23/src/main/java/iloveyouboss/MatcherService.java
```java
public class MatcherService {
    public boolean matches(int profileId, int criteriaId) {
        var profile = profileData.retrieve(profileId);
        var criteria = criteriaData.retrieve(criteriaId);
        return new Matcher(criteria, profile.answers()).matches();
    }

    public int score(int profileId, int criteriaId) {
        var profile = profileData.retrieve(profileId);
        var criteria = criteriaData.retrieve(criteriaId);
        return new Matcher(criteria, profile.answers()).score();
    }
    // ...
}
```

You'll want to (and have to) make a few more changes, but everything is now a little simpler in the other three classes impacted.

After pushing out the matches and score methods, the only logic remaining in the Profile class appears in its add(Answer) method. Since no code in Profile cares about the answers, you can simplify the class to store a list of Answer objects rather than create a Map. Here's the cleaned-up version of Profile:

utj3-refactor/23/src/main/java/iloveyouboss/Profile.java
```java
import java.util.ArrayList;
import java.util.List;

public class Profile {
    private final List<Answer> answers = new ArrayList<>();
    private final String name;

    public Profile(String name) {
        this.name = name;
    }

    public void add(Answer... newAnswers) {
        for (var answer: newAnswers)
            answers.add(answer);
    }

    public List<Answer> answers() {
        return answers;
    }
```

```java
public String name() {
    return name;
}
```

And here's a simple test to add:

utj3-refactor/23/src/test/java/iloveyouboss/AProfile.java
```java
import org.junit.jupiter.api.Test;
import java.util.List;
import static org.junit.jupiter.api.Assertions.assertEquals;

class AProfile {
    Question question = new Question("?", new String[] {"Y","N"}, 1);
    Profile profile = new Profile("x");

    @Test
    void supportsAddingIndividualAnswers() {
        var answer = new Answer(question, "Y");

        profile.add(answer);

        assertEquals(List.of(answer), profile.answers());
    }
}
```

Your changes impact the constructors in Matcher again. While updating the class, you can also change Matcher to be a Java record instead of a class. Here's the final code (minus imports):

utj3-refactor/23/src/main/java/iloveyouboss/Matcher.java
```java
public record Matcher(Criteria criteria, Map<String, Answer> answers) {
    public Matcher(Criteria criteria, List<Answer> matcherAnswers) {
        this(criteria, asMap(matcherAnswers));
    }

    public Matcher(Criteria criteria, Answer... matcherAnswers) {
        this(criteria, asList(matcherAnswers));
    }

    private static Map<String, Answer> asMap(List<Answer> answers) {
        return answers.stream().collect(
            Collectors.toMap(Answer::questionText, answer -> answer));
    }

    public boolean matches() {
        return allRequiredCriteriaMet() && anyMatches();
    }

    private boolean allRequiredCriteriaMet() {
        return criteria.stream()
            .filter(criterion -> criterion.weight() == REQUIRED)
            .allMatch(criterion ->
                criterion.isMatch(profileAnswerMatching(criterion)));
    }
```

```
    private boolean anyMatches() {
        return criteria.stream()
            .anyMatch(criterion ->
                criterion.isMatch(profileAnswerMatching(criterion)));
    }

    private Answer profileAnswerMatching(Criterion criterion) {
        return answers.get(criterion.questionText());
    }

    public int score() {
        return criteria.stream()
            .filter(criterion ->
                criterion.isMatch(profileAnswerMatching(criterion)))
            .mapToInt(criterion -> criterion.weight().value())
            .sum();
    }
}
```

Left to you, dear reader: combining both matching logic and scoring logic in Matcher decreases cohesion. Your mission: split off the scoring logic into a new class, Scorer. It should take at most 15 minutes. Don't forget to split off the tests!

Summary

In this chapter, you improved the design of iloveyouboss, leaning mostly on a couple of simple design concepts for guidance: the SRP and command-query separation. You owe it to yourself to know as much as possible about these and other concepts in design. (Take a look at *Clean Code [Mar08]*, for example, but keep reading.) And don't forget what you learned in Chapter 8, Refactoring to Cleaner Code, on page 147: small, continual code edits make a big difference. Armed with a stockpile of design smarts, your unit tests will allow you to reshape your system so that it more easily supports the inevitable changes coming.

Your system's design quality also inversely correlates to your pain and frustration level. The worse your design, the longer it will take to understand the code and make changes. Keeping the design incrementally clean will keep costs to a small fraction of what they'll become otherwise.

Be flexible. Be willing to create new, smaller classes and methods. Automated refactoring tools make doing so easy. Even without such tools, it takes only minutes. It's worth the modest effort. Design flexibility starts with smaller, more composed building blocks.

Now that you've learned to continually address your system's micro and macro-level design *because your unit tests allow you to do so with high confidence*, it's time to take a look at those tests themselves. Next up, you'll see how streamlining your tests lets them pay off even more as concise, clear, and correct documentation on all the unit capabilities you've built into your system.

CHAPTER 10

Streamlining Your Tests

You've wrapped up a couple of chapters that teach you how to use tests to keep your code clean. Now, it's time to focus on the tests themselves.

Your tests represent a significant investment. They'll pay off by minimizing defects and allowing you to keep your production system clean through refactoring. But, they also represent a continual cost. You need to continually revisit your tests as your system changes. At times, you'll want to make sweeping changes and might end up having to fix numerous broken tests as a result.

In this chapter, you'll learn to refactor your tests, much like you would refactor your production system, to maximize understanding and minimize maintenance costs. You'll accomplish this by learning to identify a series of "smells" in your tests that make it harder to quickly understand them. You'll work through an example or two of how you can transform each smell into de-odorized code.

The deodorization process is quick. In reading through the chapter, you might think it would take a long time to clean a test similar to the example in the chapter. In reality, it's often well under fifteen minutes of real work once you learn how to spot the problems.

Tests as Documentation

Your unit tests should provide lasting and trustworthy documentation of the capabilities of the classes you build. Tests provide opportunities to explain things that the code itself can't do as easily. Well-designed tests can supplant a lot of the comments you might otherwise feel compelled to write.

Documenting Your Tests with Consistent Names

The more you combine cases into a single test, the more generic and meaningless the test name becomes. A test named matches doesn't tell anyone squat about what it demonstrates.

As you move toward more granular tests, each focused on a distinct behavior, you have the opportunity to impart more meaning in each of your test names. Instead of suggesting what *context* you're going to test, you can suggest what *happens* as a result of invoking some behavior against a certain context.

You're probably thinking, "Real examples, please, Jeff, and not so much babble." Here you go:

not-so-hot name	cooler, more descriptive name
makeSingleWithdrawal	withdrawalReducesBalanceByWithdrawnAmount
attemptToWithdrawTooMuch	withdrawalOfMoreThanAvailableFundsGeneratesError
multipleDeposits	multipleDepositsIncreaseBalanceBySumOfDeposits

That last test name seems kind of an obvious statement, but that's because you already understand the ATM domain and the concept of deposits. Often, you're in unfamiliar territory, where the code and business rules are unfamiliar. A precise test name can provide you with extremely useful context.

You can go too far. Reasonable test names probably consist of up to seven (plus or minus two) words. Longer names quickly become dense sentences that take time to digest. If test names are typically long, your design may be amiss.

Seek a consistent form for your test names to reduce the friction that others experience when perusing your tests. Most of the test examples in this book are named to complete a sentence that starts with the test class name. For example:

```
class APortfolio {
  @Test
  void increasesSizeWhenPurchasingNewSymbol() {
    // ...
  }
}
```

Concatenate each test name to the class name: "a portfolio increases size when purchasing a new symbol."

Another possible form:

doingSomeOperationGeneratesSomeResult

And another:

someResultOccursUnderSomeCondition

Or you might decide to go with the *given-when-then* naming pattern, which derives from a process known as behavior-driven development:[1]

givenSomeContextWhenDoingSomeBehaviorThenSomeResultOccurs

Given-when-then test names can be a mouthful, though you can usually drop the *givenSomeContext* portion without creating too much additional work for your test reader:

whenDoingSomeBehaviorThenSomeResultOccurs

...which is about the same as *doingSomeOperationGeneratesSomeResult.*

JUnit 5's support for nested test classes allows you to structure your test class to directly support given-when-then:

```
utj3-refactor-tests/01/src/test/java/portfolio/ANonEmptyPortfolio.java
class ANonEmptyPortfolio {
    Portfolio portfolio = new Portfolio();
    int initialSize;

    @BeforeEach
    void purchaseASymbol() {
        portfolio.purchase("LSFT", 20);
        initialSize = portfolio.size();
    }

    @Nested
    class WhenPurchasingAnotherSymbol {
        @BeforeEach
        void purchaseAnotherSymbol() {
            portfolio.purchase("AAPL", 10);
        }

        @Test
        void increasesSize() {
            assertEquals(initialSize + 1, portfolio.size());
        }
    }
}
```

Which form you choose isn't as important as being consistent. Your main goal: create easy-to-read test names that clearly impart meaning.

---

1. http://en.wikipedia.org/wiki/Behavior-driven_development

Keeping Your Tests Meaningful

If others (or you yourself) have a tough time understanding what a test is doing, don't add comments. That's like adding footnotes to describe poorly written text. Improve the test instead, starting with its name. These are other things you can do:

- Improve any local variable names.
- Introduce meaningful constants.
- Prefer matcher-based assertions (for example, those from AssertJ).
- Split larger tests into smaller, more focused tests.
- Move test clutter to helper methods and @Before methods.

 Rework test names and code to tell stories instead of introducing explanatory comments.

Searching for an Understanding

You're tasked with enhancing the search capabilities of an application. You know you must change the util.Search class, but you're not at all familiar with it. You turn to the tests. Well, *a* test—there's only one. You roll your eyes in annoyance and then begin struggling to figure out what this test is trying to prove:

```
utj3-refactor-tests/01/src/test/java/util/SearchTest.java
public class SearchTest {
  @Test
  public void testSearch() {
    try {
      String pageContent = "There are certain queer times and occasions "
        + "in this strange mixed affair we call life when a man takes "
        + "this whole universe for a vast practical joke, though "
        + "the wit thereof he but dimly discerns, and more than "
        + "suspects that the joke is at nobody's expense but his own.";
      byte[] bytes = pageContent.getBytes();
      ByteArrayInputStream stream = new ByteArrayInputStream(bytes);
      // search
      Search search = new Search(stream, "practical joke", "1");
      Search.LOGGER.setLevel(Level.OFF);
      search.setSurroundingCharacterCount(10);
      search.execute();
      assertFalse(search.errored());
      List<Match> matches = search.getMatches();
      assertNotNull(matches);
      assertTrue(matches.size() >= 1);
```

```
Match match = matches.get(0);
assertEquals("practical joke", match.searchString());
assertEquals("or a vast practical joke, though t",
    match.surroundingContext());
stream.close();

// negative
URLConnection connection =
    new URL("http://bit.ly/15sYPA7").openConnection();
InputStream inputStream = connection.getInputStream();
search = new Search(
    inputStream, "smelt", "http://bit.ly/15sYPA7");
search.execute();
assertEquals(0, search.getMatches().size());
stream.close();
} catch (Exception e) {
e.printStackTrace();
fail("exception thrown in test" + e.getMessage());
}
}
}
```

(Text in pageContent by Herman Melville from *Moby Dick*.)

Match is only a Java record with the three String fields: searchTitle, searchString, and surroundingContext.

The test name, testSearch, doesn't tell you anything useful. A couple of comments don't add much value either. To fully understand what's going on, you'll have to read the test line by line and try to piece its steps together.

(You won't see the Search class itself in this chapter since your focus will solely be on cleaning up the tests for better understanding. Visit the source distribution if you're curious about the Search class.)

You decide to refactor testSearch while you work through understanding it, with the goal of shaping it into one or more clear, expressive tests. You look for various *test smells*—nuggets of code that emanate an odor. Odors aren't necessarily foul, though they can greatly diminish the readability of your tests.

Test Smell: Legacy Code Constructs

You'll be making several passes through the test, each with a different intent.

A quick scan of the test reveals old-school Java and JUnit, evidenced by the lack of local variable type inferencing and the unnecessary use of public for the class and test method. One of the best things about the newer versions of both Java and JUnit is their ability to simplify your code.

First, make a couple of quick cleanup passes:

1. Remove public from the test class and test methods. They are clutter.
2. Replace local variable type names with the var type.

Here's a snippet:

utj3-refactor-tests/02/src/test/java/util/SearchTest.java

```
class SearchTest {
    @Test
    void testSearch() {
        try {
            var pageContent = "There are certain queer times and occasions "
                // ...
            var bytes = pageContent.getBytes();
            var stream = new ByteArrayInputStream(bytes);
            //...
```

The elimination of a few unnecessary tokens will begin to help you focus more on what's relevant.

Test Smell: Unnecessary Test Code

The test testSearch() contains a few assertions, none expecting exceptions themselves. If the test code throws an exception, a try/catch block catches it, spews a stack trace onto System.out, and explicitly fails the test.

Unless your test expects an exception to be thrown—because you've explicitly designed it to set the stage for throwing an exception—you can let other exceptions fly. Don't worry, JUnit traps any exceptions that explode out of your test. When JUnit catches an unexpected exception, it marks the test as an *error*, and displays the stack trace in its output.

The try/catch block surrounding all the test code adds no value. Remove it. Modify the signature of testSearch() to indicate that it can throw an IOException:

utj3-refactor-tests/03/src/test/java/util/SearchTest.java

```
@Test
void testSearch() throws IOException {
    var pageContent = "There are certain queer times and occasions "
        // ...
    var bytes = pageContent.getBytes();
    var stream = new ByteArrayInputStream(bytes);
    // ...
    stream.close();
}
```

Careful editing helps your tests tell a clear story about system behaviors. And as long as your tests pass, you can trust that story.

Comments represent a failure to let the code tell the story. For now, delete the two comments in testSearch.

Tests provide trustworthy documentation on the unit behaviors of your system.

About eight statements into the test method, you notice a not-null assert—an assertion that verifies that a value is not null:

```
utj3-refactor-tests/02/src/test/java/util/SearchTest.java
var matches = search.getMatches();
assertNotNull(matches);
assertTrue(matches.size() >= 1);
```

The first line assigns the result of search.getMatches() to the matches local variable. The second statement asserts that matches is not a null value. The final line verifies that the size of matches is at least 1.

Checking that a variable isn't null before dereferencing it is a good thing, right?

In production code, perhaps. In this test, the call to assertNotNull is again clutter. It adds no value: if matches *is* actually null, the call to matches.size() generates a NullPointerException. JUnit traps this exception and errors the test. You're notified of the error, and it's no harder to figure out what the problem is.

Like the try/catch block, calling assertNotNull adds no value. Remove it:

```
utj3-refactor-tests/03/src/test/java/util/SearchTest.java
var matches = search.getMatches();
assertTrue(matches.size() >= 1);
```

That's one fewer line of test to wade through!

Test Smells: Generalized and Stepwise Assertions

A well-structured test distills the interaction with the system to three steps: arranging the data, acting on the system, and asserting on the results (see Scannability: Arrange—Act—Assert, on page 18). Although the test requires detailed code to accomplish each of these steps, you can improve understanding by organizing those details into *abstractions*—code elements that maximize the essential concepts and hide the unnecessary details.

Good tests provide examples of how clients interact with the system.

The following part of the test starts with a statement that appears to be the act step—a call to search.getMatches():

```
utj3-refactor-tests/03/src/test/java/util/SearchTest.java
var matches = search.getMatches();
assertTrue(matches.size() >= 1);
var match = matches.get(0);
assertEquals("practical joke", match.searchString());
assertEquals("or a vast practical joke, though t",
    match.surroundingContext());
```

The hint that search.getMatches represents the act step is that it's followed immediately by four lines of assertion-related code that appears to check the list of matches returned by search.getMatches(). These lines require stepwise reading. Here is a quick attempt at paraphrasing them:

- Ensure there's at least one match
- Get the first match
- Ensure that its search string is "practical joke"
- Ensure that its surrounding context is some longer string

The first statement—assertTrue(matches.size() >= 1—appears to be an unnecessarily generalized assertion. A quick scan of the Melville content (declared in the arrange step) reveals that the search string "practical joke" appears once and exactly once in the test.

Most tests should make precise assertions, usually with assertEquals. *You* are creating the tests—you can set them up to be precise. To test a one-based case (search results find a single match), create content with exactly one match for the given search string and then assert that the one match exists.

In this case, you don't need to use >=. You could replace that with a precise comparison: assertEquals(1, matches.size()). But you have an even better resolution.

The test tediously takes four lines to verify what seems to be a single concept: that the list of matches contains a single match object, initialized with a specific search string and surrounding context. Java supports declaring an initialized list, which lets you simplify the test to a single-statement assert:

```
utj3-refactor-tests/04/src/test/java/util/SearchTest.java
var matches = search.getMatches();
assertEquals(List.of(
    new Match("1",
        "practical joke",
        "or a vast practical joke, though t")),
    matches);
```

Anywhere you find two or more lines of stepwise assertion code that asserts a single concept, distill them to a single, clear statement in the test. Sometimes a short helper method is all it takes. If you use AssertJ, you can create a custom matcher that provides a concise assertion.

Amplify abstractions in your test. Hide the implementation specifics elsewhere.

In the second chunk of test code, near the end of the method, you spot another small opportunity for introducing an abstraction. The final assertion (highlighted) compares the size of search matches to 0:

```
utj3-refactor-tests/04/src/test/java/util/SearchTest.java
@Test
void testSearch() throws IOException {
    // ...
    search.execute();
➤   assertEquals(0, search.getMatches().size());
    stream.close();
}
```

The missing abstraction is the concept of emptiness. Altering the assertion reduces the extra mental overhead needed to understand the size comparison:

```
utj3-refactor-tests/05/src/test/java/util/SearchTest.java
search.execute();
➤ assertTrue(search.getMatches().isEmpty());
stream.close();
```

Every small amount of mental clutter adds up. A system with never-ending clutter wears you down, much as road noise builds to create further fatigue on a long car trip.

Test Smell: Missing Abstractions

A well-abstracted test emphasizes everything that's important to understanding it and de-emphasizes anything that's not. Any data used in a test should help tell its story.

Sometimes, you're forced to supply data to get code to compile, even though that data is irrelevant to the test at hand. For example, a method might take additional arguments that have no impact on the test.

Your test contains some *magic literals* that aren't at all clear:

```
utj3-refactor-tests/05/src/test/java/util/SearchTest.java
var search = new Search(stream, "practical joke", "1");
```

And:

```
utj3-refactor-tests/05/src/test/java/util/SearchTest.java
assertEquals(List.of(
    new Match("1",
      "practical joke",
      "or a vast practical joke, though t")),
  matches);
```

Perhaps these were magically conjured by a wizard who chose to keep their meanings arcane.

You're not sure what the "1" string represents, so you navigate into the constructors for Search and Match. You discover that "1" is a search title, a field whose value appears irrelevant right now.

Including the "1" literal raises unnecessary questions. What does it represent? How, if at all, is it relevant to the results of the test?

At least one other magic literal exists. The second call to the Search constructor contains a URL as the title argument:

```
utj3-refactor-tests/05/src/test/java/util/SearchTest.java
var connection =
    new URL("http://bit.ly/15sYPA7").openConnection();
var inputStream = connection.getInputStream();
search = new Search(
➤    inputStream, "smelt", "http://bit.ly/15sYPA7");
```

At first glance, it appears that the URL has a correlation with the URL passed to the URL constructor two statements earlier. But digging reveals that no real correlation exists.

Developers waste time when they must dig around to find answers. You'll help them by introducing an intention-revealing constant. Replace the confusing URL and the "1" magic literal with the A_TITLE constant, which suggests a title with any value.

Here's the latest version of the test, highlighting lines with the new abstraction:

```
utj3-refactor-tests/06/src/test/java/util/SearchTest.java
class SearchTest {
➤    static final String A_TITLE = "1";

    @Test
    void testSearch() throws IOException {
        var pageContent = "There are certain queer times and occasions "
            + "in this strange mixed affair we call life when a man takes "
            + "this whole universe for a vast practical joke, though "
            + "the wit thereof he but dimly discerns, and more than "
            + "suspects that the joke is at nobody's expense but his own.";
```

```
        var bytes = pageContent.getBytes();
        var stream = new ByteArrayInputStream(bytes);
➤       var search = new Search(stream, "practical joke", A_TITLE);
        Search.LOGGER.setLevel(Level.OFF);
        search.setSurroundingCharacterCount(10);
        search.execute();
        assertFalse(search.errored());
        var matches = search.getMatches();
        assertEquals(List.of(
➤           new Match(A_TITLE,
               "practical joke",
               "or a vast practical joke, though t")),
           matches);
        stream.close();

        var connection =
           new URL("http://bit.ly/15sYPA7").openConnection();
        var inputStream = connection.getInputStream();
➤       search = new Search(
           inputStream, "smelt", A_TITLE);
        search.execute();
        assertTrue(search.getMatches().isEmpty());
        stream.close();
    }
}
```

You could have named the constant ANY_TITLE or ARBITRARY_TITLE. Or, you might have used an empty string, which suggests data that you don't care about (though sometimes the distinction between an empty string and a nonempty string *is* relevant).

Test Smell: Bloated Construction

The Search class requires you to pass an InputStream on a Search object through its constructor. Your test builds an InputStream in two places. The first construction requires three statements:

utj3-refactor-tests/06/src/test/java/util/SearchTest.java
```
var pageContent = "There are certain queer times and occasions "
    + "in this strange mixed affair we call life when a man takes "
    + "this whole universe for a vast practical joke, though "
    + "the wit thereof he but dimly discerns, and more than "
    + "suspects that the joke is at nobody's expense but his own.";
var bytes = pageContent.getBytes();
var stream = new ByteArrayInputStream(bytes);
```

The test contains implementation detail specifics involving extracting bytes from a string and then creating a ByteArrayInputStream. That's stuff you don't need to see to understand the test, and it represents a missing abstraction. Introduce a helper method that creates an InputStream on a provided string of text:

utj3-refactor-tests/07/src/test/java/util/SearchTest.java
```
class SearchTest {
    // ...
    @Test
    void testSearch() throws IOException {
        var stream = streamOn("There are certain queer times and occasions "
            + "in this strange mixed affair we call life when a man "
            + "takes this whole universe for a vast practical joke, "
            + "though the wit thereof he but dimly discerns, and more "
            + "than suspects that the joke is at nobody's expense but his own.");
        var search = new Search(stream, "practical joke", A_TITLE);
        // ...
    }

    private ByteArrayInputStream streamOn(String text) {
        return new ByteArrayInputStream(text.getBytes());
    }
}
```

Morphing arbitrary detail into clear declarations is gradually improving the test.

Test Smell: Multiple Assertions

Your long test appears to represent two distinct cases. The first demonstrates finding a search result, and the second represents finding no match. The blank line provides a clear dividing point:

utj3-refactor-tests/07/src/test/java/util/SearchTest.java
```
@Test
void testSearch() throws IOException {
    var stream = streamOn("There are certain queer times and occasions "
    // ...
    var search = new Search(stream, "practical joke", A_TITLE);
    Search.LOGGER.setLevel(Level.OFF);
    search.setSurroundingCharacterCount(10);
    search.execute();
    assertFalse(search.errored());
    var matches = search.getMatches();
    assertEquals(List.of(
        new Match(A_TITLE,
            "practical joke",
            "or a vast practical joke, though t")),
        matches);
    stream.close();

    var connection =
        new URL("http://bit.ly/15sYPA7").openConnection();
    var inputStream = connection.getInputStream();
```

```
search = new Search(
    inputStream, "smelt", A_TITLE);
search.execute();
assertTrue(search.getMatches().isEmpty());
stream.close();
}
```

Split the test into two test methods, coming up with a better name for each (the code won't compile until both test names are distinct). Also, take a moment to rename the test class to ASearch.

 Verifying only one behavior per test facilitates concise test naming.

The resulting two test methods:

```
utj3-refactor-tests/08/src/test/java/util/ASearch.java
@Test
void returnsMatchesWithSurroundingContext() throws IOException {
    var stream = streamOn("There are certain queer times and occasions "
        // ...
    var search = new Search(stream, "practical joke", A_TITLE);
    Search.LOGGER.setLevel(Level.OFF);
    search.setSurroundingCharacterCount(10);
    search.execute();
    assertFalse(search.errored());
    var matches = search.getMatches();
    assertEquals(List.of(
            new Match(A_TITLE,
                "practical joke",
                "or a vast practical joke, though t")),
        matches);
    stream.close(); // delete me
}

@Test
void returnsNoMatchesWhenSearchTextNotFound() throws IOException {
    var connection =
        new URL("http://bit.ly/15sYPA7").openConnection();
    var inputStream = connection.getInputStream();
    var search = new Search(inputStream, "smelt", A_TITLE);
    search.execute();
    assertTrue(search.getMatches().isEmpty());
    inputStream.close();
}
```

The listing shows fixes to two compile failures that occurred when splitting. First, since the search variable was re-used in the original test, its use in the second test now needs a type declaration. The var type will suffice.

Also, the second test's last line (which closes the stream) wasn't compiling. Amusingly, it turns out that the combined mess of a single test was calling close twice on stream, and not at all on inputStream. Changing the last line to inputStream.close() fixed the problem.

You can delete the line that closes stream in the first test. There's no need to close a ByteArrayInputStream (least of all in a test). (The other close needs to occur to avoid connection and resource issues for other tests or for itself if run multiple times.)

Next, use Java's try-with-resources feature to ensure that inputStream gets closed. You can then delete the inputStream.close() statement for good:

```
utj3-refactor-tests/09/src/test/java/util/ASearch.java
@Test
void returnsNoMatchesWhenSearchTextNotFound() throws IOException {
    var connection =
        new URL("http://bit.ly/15sYPA7").openConnection();
    try (var inputStream = connection.getInputStream()) {
        var search = new Search(inputStream, "smelt", A_TITLE);

        search.execute();
        assertTrue(search.getMatches().isEmpty());
    }
}
```

Test Smell: Irrelevant Details in a Test

Your tests should execute cleanly, showing only a summary with the passing and failing tests. Don't allow your test run to be littered with dozens or perhaps hundreds and more lines of log messages, "expected" exception stack traces, and System.out.println clutter.

Ensure test execution does not pollute console output.

When your test summary is clean, any new exceptions will stand out like a sore thumb rather than get lost in a sea of stack traces. You'll also easily spot any new console output that you've temporarily added.

In the prior section, you split one larger test into two. Now, when you run your tests, you'll notice some logging output:

```
Mar 29, 2024 1:35:50 PM util.Search search
INFO: searching matches for pattern:smelt
```

The first test contains the following line, but the second test does not:

```
Search.LOGGER.setLevel(Level.OFF);
```

Suppressing logger output when the second test runs would be as easy as adding the setLevel call to the second test. But that's the wrong place for it.

While only a single line, the code needed to suppress logging is a distraction that adds no meaning to any test. De-emphasize the setLevel call by moving it to a @BeforeEach method.

```
utj3-refactor-tests/09/src/test/java/util/ASearch.java
@BeforeEach
void suppressLogging() {
    Search.LOGGER.setLevel(Level.OFF);
}
// ...
```

Looking for further irrelevant details, you ponder the assertion in the first test that ensures the search has not errored:

```
utj3-refactor-tests/09/src/test/java/util/ASearch.java
var search = new Search(stream, "practical joke", A_TITLE);
search.setSurroundingCharacterCount(10);
search.execute();
assertFalse(search.errored());
var matches = search.getMatches();
assertEquals(List.of(
    // ...
```

The assertion appears valid—a second postcondition of running a search. But it hints at a missing test case: if there's an assertFalse, an assertTrue should exist. For now, delete the assertion and add it to your "todo" test list (see Covering Other Cases: Creating a Test List, on page 24). You'll return to add a couple of new tests once you've streamlined all the test code.

Take care when moving details to @BeforeEach or helper methods. Don't remove information from a test that's essential to understanding it.

 Good tests contain all the information needed to understand them. Poor tests send you on scavenger hunts.

Test Smell: Misleading Organization

Speed up cognition by making the act, arrange, and assert parts of a test (see Scannability: Arrange—Act—Assert, on page 18) explicit. Arrows in the following listing show the blank lines to insert around the act step:

```
utj3-refactor-tests/10/src/test/java/util/ASearch.java
@Test
void returnsMatchesWithSurroundingContext() {
   var stream = streamOn("There are certain queer times and occasions "
        // ...
   var search = new Search(stream, "practical joke", A_TITLE);
   search.setSurroundingCharacterCount(10);

   search.execute();

   var matches = search.getMatches();
   assertEquals(List.of(
        new Match(A_TITLE,
            "practical joke",
            "or a vast practical joke, though t")),
      matches);
}

@Test
void returnsNoMatchesWhenSearchTextNotFound() throws IOException {
   var connection =
      new URL("http://bit.ly/15sYPA7").openConnection();
   try (var inputStream = connection.getInputStream()) {
      var search = new Search(inputStream, "smelt", A_TITLE);

      search.execute();

      assertTrue(search.getMatches().isEmpty());
   }
}
```

You're getting close. Time for a final pass against the two tests!

Test Smell: Implicit Meaning

The big question every test must clearly answer: why does it expect the result it does? Developers must be able to correlate any assertions with the arrange step. Unclear correlation forces developers to wade through code for meaning.

The returnsMatchesWithSurroundingContext test searches for practical joke in a long string, expecting one match. A patient reader could determine where practical joke appears and then figure out that ten characters before it and ten characters after it represent the string:

```
"or a vast practical joke, though t"
```

But making developers dig for understanding is rude. Make things explicit by choosing better test data. Change the input stream to contain a small amount of text. Then, change the content so that the surrounding context information doesn't need to be explicitly counted:

```
utj3-refactor-tests/11/src/test/java/util/ASearch.java
@Test
void returnsMatchesWithSurroundingContext() {
➤    var stream = streamOn("""
➤        rest of text here
➤        1234567890search term1234567890
➤        more rest of text""");
➤    var search = new Search(stream, "search term", A_TITLE);
     search.setSurroundingCharacterCount(10);

     search.execute();

     var matches = search.getMatches();
     assertEquals(List.of(
             new Match(A_TITLE,
➤                "search term",
➤                "1234567890search term1234567890")),
         matches);
}
```

Now, it's fairly easy to see why a surrounding character count of 10 produces the corresponding context results in the Match object.

You have no end of ways to improve the correlation across a test. Meaningful constants, better variable names, better data, and sometimes even doing small calculations in the test can help. Use your creativity here!

Diversion: Speeding Up Your Tests

As you incrementally shape the design of your tests, you'll be distracted by other opportunities to improve them. You can divert to address those opportunities, or you can add a reminder to do so.

Let's use returnsNoMatchesWhenSearchTextNotFound to take a quick detour and speed up the second test. It works against a live URL's input stream, making it slow. Since your first test is a fast unit test that verifies the happy path case, you want a similarly fast test to cover the unhappy path case. (You might want to retain the live test for integration testing purposes.)

Initialize the stream field to contain a small bit of arbitrary text. To help make the test's circumstance clear, search for "text that ain't gonna match":

```
utj3-refactor-tests/11/src/test/java/util/ASearch.java
@Test
➤ void returnsNoMatchesWhenSearchTextNotFound() {
➤    var stream = streamOn("text that ain't gonna match");
➤    var search = new Search(stream, "missing search term", A_TITLE);
```

```
    search.execute();
    assertTrue(search.getMatches().isEmpty());
}
```

Your test no longer throws a checked exception. Remove the throws clause from the test's signature.

Adding Tests from Your Test List

In Test Smell: Irrelevant Details in a Test, on page 202, you added a couple of needed tests to your test list. Now that you've whittled down your messy initial test into two sleek, clear tests, you should find it relatively easy to add a couple of new tests.

First, write a test that demonstrates how a completed search returns false for the errored() query:

utj3-refactor-tests/11/src/test/java/util/ASearch.java
```
@Test
void erroredReturnsFalseWhenReadSucceeds() {
    var stream = streamOn("");
    var search = new Search(stream, "", "");

    search.execute();

    assertFalse(search.errored());
}
```

Then, test the case where accessing the input stream throws an exception:

utj3-refactor-tests/11/src/test/java/util/ASearch.java
```
@Test
public void erroredReturnsTrueWhenUnableToReadStream() {
    var stream = createStreamThrowingErrorWhenRead();
    var search = new Search(stream, "", "");

    search.execute();

    assertTrue(search.errored());
}

private InputStream createStreamThrowingErrorWhenRead() {
    return new InputStream() {
        @Override
        public int read() throws IOException { throw new IOException(); }
    };
}
```

Time spent to add the new tests: less than a few minutes each.

Summary

You ended up with four sleek, refactored tests. A developer can understand the goal of each test through its name, which provides a generalized summary of behavior. They can see how that behavior plays out by reading the example within the test. Arrange—Act—Assert (AAA) guides them immediately to the act step so that they can see how the code being verified gets executed. They can reconcile the asserts against the test name's description of behavior. Finally, if needed, they can review the arrange step to understand how it puts the system in the proper state to be tested.

The tests are scannable. A developer can rapidly find and digest each test element (name, arrange, act, and assert) they're interested in. The needed comprehension can happen in seconds rather than minutes. Remember also that readily understood tests—descriptions of unit behavior—can save even hours of time required to understand production code.

Seeking to understand your system through its tests motivates you to keep them as clean as they should be.

It only takes minutes to clean up tests enough to save extensive future amounts of comprehension time.

You now have a complete picture of what you must do in the name of design: refactor your production code for clarity and conciseness, refactor your production code to support more flexibility in design, design your system to support mocking of dependency challenges, and refactor your tests to minimize maintenance and maximize understanding.

You're ready to move on to the final part of this book, a smorgasbord of additional topics related to unit testing.

Part IV

Bigger Topics Around Unit Testing

Writing tests is but a part of a larger experience. Explore unit testing in various modern and relevant contexts: test-driven development (TDD), project teams, and AI-driven development.

CHAPTER 11

Advancing with Test-Driven Development (TDD)

You're now armed with what you'll need to know about straight-up unit testing in Java. In this part, you'll learn about three significant topics:

- Using TDD to flip the concept of unit testing from test-after to test-driven
- Considerations for unit testing within a project team
- Using AI tooling to drive development, assisted by unit tests

You'll start with a meaty example of how to practice TDD.

It's hard to write unit tests for some code. Such "difficult" code grows partly from a lack of interest in unit testing. In contrast, the more you consider how to unit test the code you write, the more you'll end up with easier-to-test code. ("Well, duh!" responds our reluctant unit tester Joe.)

With TDD, you think first about the *outcome* you expect for the code you're going to write. Rather than slap out some code and then figure out how to test it (or even what it should do), you first capture the expected outcome in a test. You then code the behavior needed to meet that outcome. This reversed approach might seem bizarre or even impossible, but it's the core element in TDD.

With TDD, you wield unit tests as a tool to help you shape and control your systems. Rather than a haphazard practice where you sometimes write unit tests after you write code, and sometimes you don't, describing outcomes and verifying code through unit tests becomes your central focus.

You will probably find the practice of TDD dramatically different than anything you've experienced in software development. The way you build code and the shape that your code takes on will change considerably. You may well find TDD highly gratifying and ultimately liberating, strangely enough.

In this chapter, you'll test drive a small solution using TDD, unit by unit, and talk about the nuanced changes to the approach that TDD brings.

The Primary Benefit of TDD

With plain ol' after-the-fact unit testing, the obvious, most significant benefit you gain is increased confidence that the code you wrote works as expected—at least to the coverage that your unit tests provide. With TDD, you gain that same benefit and many more.

Systems degrade primarily because we don't strive often or hard enough to keep the code clean. We're good at quickly adding code into our systems, but on the first pass, it's more often not-so-great code than good code. We don't spend a lot of effort cleaning up that initially costly code for many reasons. Joe chimes in with his list:

- "We need to move on to the next task. We don't have time to gild the code."

- "I think the code reads just fine the way it is. I wrote it, I understand it. I can add some comments to the code if you think it's not clear."

- "We can refactor the code when we need to make further changes in that area."

- "It works. Why mess with a good thing? If it ain't broke, don't fix it. It's too easy to break something else when refactoring code."

Thanks, Joe, for that list of common rationalizations for letting code degrade.

With TDD, your fear about changing code can evaporate. Indeed, refactoring is a risky activity, and we've all made plenty of mistakes when making seemingly innocuous changes. But if you're following TDD well, you're writing unit tests for virtually all cases you implement in the system. Those unit tests give you the freedom you need to continually improve the code.

Starting Simple

TDD is a three-part cycle:

1. Write a test that fails.
2. Get the test to pass.
3. Clean up any code added or changed in the prior two steps.

The first step of the cycle tells you to write a test describing the behavior you want to build into the system. Seek to write a test representing the smallest possible—but useful—increment to the code that already exists.

For your exercise, you'll test-drive a small portfolio manager. Your requirements will be revealed to you incrementally as well, in batches, by your product owner Madhu. Imagine that each requirements batch was not previously considered. Your job is to deliver a solution for each incremental need to production.

You want to ensure that you can continue to accommodate new batches of requirements indefinitely. To meet that ongoing demand, your focus after getting each new test to pass—as part of the clean-up step in TDD—will be to distill the solution to employ the simplest possible design. You will seek maximally concise, clear, and cohesive code.

Each new TDD cycle starts with choosing the next behavior to implement. For the smoothest progression through building a solution, you'll seek a behavior that produces the smallest possible increment from the current solution.

In other words, you're trying to ensure each TDD cycle represents a tiny little step that requires only a tiny bit of new code or changed code.

You'll step through four increments of code. You'll be able to deliver each increment to production.

Increment 1: Deferring Complexity

For your first requirements batch, you're tasked with delivering very simple rudiments of a portfolio.

You'll be able to make purchases for the portfolio. For now, a purchase involves a stock symbol, such as SONO (Sonos) or AAPL (Apple), and a number of shares purchased for that symbol.

But your solution won't need to track the actual symbols or shares of each. Madhu tells you that all it needs to answer are the following two things:

- *Whether or not it is empty.* A portfolio is empty if no purchases have been made and not empty otherwise.

- *How many unique symbols have been purchased—the portfolio's size.* If you purchase AAPL once, you have one unique symbol. If you purchase AAPL a second time, you still have only the one unique symbol. If you purchase AAPL and then purchase SONO, you have two unique symbols.

The ZOM progression (see ZOM: Zero and One Done, Now Testing Many, on page 22) is a great place to start when practicing TDD. You'll employ it frequently as you try to derive the next-smallest increment.

You want to start with the absolute simplest requirement. Between the two concerns—emptiness and size—emptiness seems simplest. Your first test is a zero-based verification: the portfolio is empty when created (in other words, no purchases have been made).

```
utj3-tdd/01/src/test/java/app/APortfolio.java
import org.junit.jupiter.api.Test;
import static org.junit.jupiter.api.Assertions.assertTrue;

public class APortfolio {
    @Test
    void isEmptyWhenCreated() {
        var portfolio = new Portfolio();

        assertTrue(portfolio.isEmpty());
    }
}
```

In order to compile and run the test, you'll need to supply an implementation for the Portfolio class. You also want a test that fails (more on that as you go). Returning false from isEmpty will cause the call to assertTrue to fail:

```
utj3-tdd/01/src/main/java/app/Portfolio.java
public class Portfolio {
    public boolean isEmpty() {
        return false;
    }
}
```

Now, you can run JUnit. You expect a failure and receive it:

```
Expected :true
Actual   :false
```

All is well.

 Avoid costly, poor assumptions with TDD. Ensure each new test fails before you write the code to make it pass.

You seek the simplest code that will get the test to pass in order to avoid adding code until you have a test that demands its existence:

```
utj3-tdd/02/src/main/java/app/Portfolio.java
public boolean isEmpty() {
    return true;
}
```

As far as the cleanup step in the TDD cycle is concerned, that four-line solution is expressed about as concisely and clearly as it can get. Time to move on.

If you're using a capable source repository such as Git, now is the time to commit your code. Committing each new bit of behavior as you do TDD makes it easy to back up and change direction as needed.

You've written a test for a Boolean method that demonstrates when it returns true. A second test, demonstrating the conditions that produce a false return, is required. Creating a non-empty portfolio requires test code that makes a purchase:

```
utj3-tdd/03/src/test/java/app/APortfolio.java
@Test
void isNotEmptyAfterPurchase() {
    var portfolio = new Portfolio();

    portfolio.purchase("AAPL", 1);

    assertFalse(portfolio.isEmpty());
}
```

To appease the compiler, provide a purchase method:

```
utj3-tdd/03/src/main/java/app/Portfolio.java
public void purchase(String symbol, int shares) {
}
```

Run all of your Portfolio tests and ensure that (only) the newest one fails.

To get your tests passing, you could consider storing the symbol and shares in some sort of data structure, such as a HashMap. And that's probably your natural inclination as a developer. But it's a lot more than you need at this current moment. It speculates a need to be able to return the symbol and shares, a need that does not exist.

Your goal is to meet requirements and deliver. Yes, you probably will need to retain the symbol and shares in the portfolio. But TDD tells you to wait until that need exists. For now, your goal is to get the test passing in as straightforward and non-speculative a manner as possible.

If you need to retain a Boolean state, a Boolean field will unsurprisingly do the trick. On a purchase, update the Boolean to reflect that the portfolio is no longer empty.

utj3-tdd/04/src/main/java/app/Portfolio.java

```
public class Portfolio {
➤    private boolean isEmpty = true;

    public boolean isEmpty() {
➤        return isEmpty;
    }

    public void purchase(String symbol, int shares) {
➤        isEmpty = false;
    }
}
```

Your tests need love, too. They are no longer concise; both the tests you've written so far initialize a Portfolio object—a necessary thing to do, but not an interesting thing to do in the sense that it adds any meaning to either test. You can do the common initialization in a @BeforeEach method.

utj3-tdd/05/src/test/java/app/APortfolio.java

```
public class APortfolio {
    Portfolio portfolio;

➤    @BeforeEach
➤    void create() {
➤        portfolio = new Portfolio();
➤    }

    @Test
    void isEmptyWhenCreated() {
        assertTrue(portfolio.isEmpty());
    }

    @Test
    void isNotEmptyAfterPurchase() {
        portfolio.purchase("AAPL", 1);

        assertFalse(portfolio.isEmpty());
    }
}
```

For now, you've exhausted the Boolean. Two states/two behaviors/two tests. A Boolean won't support "many."

Go ahead and commit your code at this point. Going forward, you won't get any more reminders. Every time you get a test to pass and spend a bit of effort cleaning up the result, do a commit. You'll appreciate being able to revert to the previous increment of code.

The next of the two features to tackle for this batch is the notion of the portfolio's size, and...yes, you're right, a zero-based test.

```
utj3-tdd/06/src/test/java/app/APortfolio.java
@Test
void hasSize0WhenCreated() {
    assertEquals(0, portfolio.size());
}
```

To get this to compile but not pass the tests, return -1 from size. After observing the failure, hard-code a 0 to make it pass:

```
utj3-tdd/07/src/main/java/app/Portfolio.java
public int size() {
    return 0;
}
```

Hard-coding seems silly, but it is in keeping with the test-code-and-refactor rhythm of the TDD cycle. Your goal is to produce the simplest possible implementation for the latest test. More specifically, you want to only solve the current set of problems. By doing so, you avoid overengineering and premature speculation. Both will cost you in the long run.

You are learning to design for current need so that you can more easily take on new, never-before-considered requirements that you could never have predicted (or designed for).

Next test—make one purchase and have a portfolio with size one:

```
utj3-tdd/08/src/test/java/app/APortfolio.java
@Test
void hasSize1OnPurchase() {
    portfolio.purchase("AAPL", 1);
    assertEquals(1, portfolio.size());
}
```

Think for just a moment. Can you solve this problem given the current "data structure" (a Boolean)? Of course you can:

```
utj3-tdd/09/src/main/java/app/Portfolio.java
public int size() {
    return isEmpty ? 0 : 1;
}
```

Maybe a Boolean's two states can support more than you think.

It's possible that you're thinking *at this very moment* that TDD might be too pedantic to be useful. Hang in there. You're starting to use your brain to think differently about how to solve software problems. Specifically, you're focusing on what it means to find the next-smallest increment, probably something you've not done before.

One key benefit you might or might not have noticed: each of these increments is something you could get passing in no more than a couple minutes and in seconds-less-than-100 in many cases (unless you're a terrible typist, and that's okay too).

Ready for some real computing? The next test demands more than a two-state solution can support:

```
utj3-tdd/10/src/test/java/app/APortfolio.java
@Test
void incrementsSizeWithEachPurchaseDifferentSymbol() {
    portfolio.purchase("AAPL", 1);

    portfolio.purchase("SONO", 1);

    assertEquals(2, portfolio.size());
}
```

Your portfolio needs to track more than 0 and 1 values; it must be able to answer 2, and 3, and to infinity...and beyond. The two-state Boolean solution has reached its predictable end and must yield to the (short-to-live) future.

Introduce an int field named size, initialized to 0 and incremented on each purchase:

```
utj3-tdd/11/src/main/java/app/Portfolio.java
public class Portfolio {
    private boolean isEmpty = true;
    private int size = 0;

    public boolean isEmpty() {
        return isEmpty;
    }

    public void purchase(String symbol, int shares) {
        isEmpty = false;
        size++;
    }

    public int size() {
        return size;
    }
}
```

Note that you don't evict the Boolean-related code just yet. It can watch and continue to support current needs as progress, in the form of slightly more generalized code supporting new behavior, gets built next door.

Once you demonstrate that the generalization to an int works, you can take advantage of a refactoring step to purge all the old, limited behaviors:

utj3-tdd/12/src/main/java/app/Portfolio.java
```java
public class Portfolio {
    private int size = 0;

    public boolean isEmpty() {
        return size == 0;
    }

    public void purchase(String symbol, int shares) {
        size++;
    }

    public int size() {
        return size;
    }
}
```

Little pieces of code come and support a new initiative. Little pieces leave to ensure a clean, easy-to-navigate code neighborhood.

Maybe you're thinking, "this seems like a roundabout way to get to three lines of code." Two things are important to remember, however:

- You've created a handful of tests along with your solution. These tests will continue to provide protection.

- You're adopting a new mentality where someone could yell, "stop building!" at any time, and you'd be okay with that. With TDD, you constantly have the confidence to support releasing the system.

You've supported Zero, One, Many cases for the portfolio's size. Now, it's time to think about the interesting cases. Hearken back to the description of the requirements for this batch. One of them indicated that if you purchased Apple stock and then purchased more of Apple stock, you still only had one stock symbol and thus a portfolio size of one:

utj3-tdd/13/src/test/java/app/APortfolio.java
```java
@Test
void doesNotIncrementSizeWithPurchaseSameSymbol() {
    portfolio.purchase("AAPL", 1);
    portfolio.purchase("AAPL", 1);
    assertEquals(1, portfolio.size());
}
```

"*Now* is it time for the HashMap?" you might ask.

Not quite yet. Maybe half a hash map: A hash map is a collection of unique keys, each that maps to some value. You might remember from second grade that a collection of unique keys is known as a *set*.

Probably the easiest way to count the number of unique values is to throw them into a set and ask for its size.

You introduced "real computing" a few moments back in the form of incrementing an integer. Now, you'll get to use a "real data structure" in the form of a Java set object.

"Pedantic again?" you might ask. Maybe. "Why not just use a HashMap?" Because it's more complex than what you need right now.

utj3-tdd/14/src/main/java/app/Portfolio.java
```java
public class Portfolio {
    private int size = 0;
    private Set symbols = new HashSet<String>();

    public boolean isEmpty() {
        return symbols.isEmpty();
    }

    public void purchase(String symbol, int shares) {
        size++;
        symbols.add(symbol);
    }

    public int size() {
        return symbols.size();
    }
}
```

After verifying your updated solution, remove references to the size int:

utj3-tdd/15/src/main/java/app/Portfolio.java
```java
public class Portfolio {
    private Set symbols = new HashSet<String>();

    public boolean isEmpty() {
        return symbols.isEmpty();
    }

    public void purchase(String symbol, int shares) {
        symbols.add(symbol);
    }

    public int size() {
        return symbols.size();
    }
}
```

And...ship it! You've built support for tracking the size and emptiness of the portfolio. It has no extraneous, speculative moving parts and is as simple a solution as you could ask for. It's fully tested with six simple unit tests.

Increment 2: Generalizing the Implementation

Madhu's second batch of requirements for you is a batch of one: track the number of shares owned for a given symbol. A happy path test case:

```
utj3-tdd/16/src/test/java/app/APortfolio.java
@Test
void returnsSharesGivenSymbol() {
    portfolio.purchase("AAPL", 42);

    assertEquals(42, portfolio.sharesOf("AAPL"));
}
```

The tests to any point in time represent the set of assumptions you make. Currently, you are assuming there will only ever be a single purchase. As such, you can track the shares purchased using a single discrete field:

```
utj3-tdd/17/src/main/java/app/Portfolio.java
public class Portfolio {
    private Set symbols = new HashSet<String>();
➤   private int shares;

    // ...
    public void purchase(String symbol, int shares) {
        symbols.add(symbol);
➤       this.shares = shares;
    }

➤   public int sharesOf(String symbol) {
➤       return shares;
➤   }
}
```

You know that using a single field won't hold up to multiple purchases that are for differing symbols. That tells you that the next test you write—involve multiple purchases—will most certainly fail, keeping you in the TDD cycle:

```
utj3-tdd/18/src/test/java/app/APortfolio.java
@Test
void separatesSharesBySymbol() {
    portfolio.purchase("SONO", 42);

    portfolio.purchase("AAPL", 1);

    assertEquals(42, portfolio.sharesOf("SONO"));
}
```

"It's time, right?" you ask. Why yes, you can finally introduce the HashMap...if you must. There are other ways of solving the problem, but for now, the HashMap is the most direct.

utj3-tdd/19/src/main/java/app/Portfolio.java
```java
import java.util.HashMap;
import java.util.HashSet;
import java.util.Map;
import java.util.Set;

public class Portfolio {
    private Map<String, Integer> purchases = new HashMap<>();
    private Set symbols = new HashSet<String>();
    private int shares;

    public boolean isEmpty() {
        return purchases.isEmpty();
    }

    public void purchase(String symbol, int shares) {
        symbols.add(symbol);
        this.shares = shares;
        purchases.put(symbol, shares);
    }

    public int size() {
        return purchases.size();
    }

    public int sharesOf(String symbol) {
        return purchases.get(symbol);
    }
}
```

With your vaunted key-value data structure and supporting code in place, you can make a pass that eliminates the use of both symbols and shares fields:

utj3-tdd/20/src/main/java/app/Portfolio.java
```java
import java.util.HashMap;
import java.util.Map;

public class Portfolio {
    private Map<String, Integer> purchases = new HashMap<>();

    public boolean isEmpty() {
        return purchases.isEmpty();
    }

    public void purchase(String symbol, int shares) {
        purchases.put(symbol, shares);
    }

    public int size() {
        return purchases.size();
    }
```

```
    public int sharesOf(String symbol) {
        return purchases.get(symbol);
    }
}
```

Oops! You forgot about the zero-based test. Good habits take a while to ingrain, and it's still possible to temporarily forget even once ingrained.

utj3-tdd/21/src/test/java/app/APortfolio.java
```
@Test
void returns0SharesForSymbolNotPurchased() {
    assertEquals(0, portfolio.sharesOf("SONO"));
}
```

The failing test requires a single line of production code, a guard clause in the sharesOf method:

utj3-tdd/22/src/main/java/app/Portfolio.java
```
public int sharesOf(String symbol) {
    if (!purchases.containsKey(symbol)) return 0;

    return purchases.get(symbol);
}
```

With a quick refactoring pass and a bit of Java knowledge, you can simplify the two lines into one:

utj3-tdd/23/src/main/java/app/Portfolio.java
```
public int sharesOf(String symbol) {
    return purchases.getOrDefault(symbol, 0);
}
```

Next up—making sure that the portfolio returns the total number of shares across all purchases of the same symbol:

utj3-tdd/23/src/test/java/app/APortfolio.java
```
@Test
void accumulatesSharesOfSameSymbolPurchase() {
    portfolio.purchase("SONO", 42);

    portfolio.purchase("SONO", 100);

    assertEquals(142, portfolio.sharesOf("SONO"));
}
```

A small modification on an existing line of code is all you need:

utj3-tdd/24/src/main/java/app/Portfolio.java
```
public void purchase(String symbol, int shares) {
    purchases.put(symbol, sharesOf(symbol + shares)); // OOPS!
}
```

Except, oops. That's not quite the right implementation. A real mistake (by me), and the tests quickly caught it. The fix involves moving the parentheses:

utj3-tdd/25/src/main/java/app/Portfolio.java
```
public void purchase(String symbol, int shares) {
    purchases.put(symbol, sharesOf(symbol) + shares);
}
```

Increment 3: Factoring Out Redundancies

Your next challenge: support selling shares of a stock. There's not much point in buying stocks in the first place if you can't sell them.

Madhu discusses the requirements with you:

- Reduce shares of a holding when selling stocks.
- Throw an exception on attempts to sell more shares of a symbol than what is held.

Joe says, "okay," then pauses a moment and asks, "what happens if you sell all the shares of a stock? The portfolio's size—its count of unique symbols held—should come down by one, right?"

Madhu says, "Yes, a good thought, and let's make sure we test for that."

You both nod to Madhu and then turn to the monitor to code the first test:

utj3-tdd/26/src/test/java/app/APortfolio.java
```
@Test
void reducesSharesOnSell() {
    portfolio.purchase("AAPL", 100);

    portfolio.sell("AAPL", 25);

    assertEquals(75, portfolio.sharesOf("AAPL"));
}
```

The implementation of the new sell method looks exactly like the purchase method, with the exception of the minus sign:

utj3-tdd/26/src/main/java/app/Portfolio.java
```
public void purchase(String symbol, int shares) {
    purchases.put(symbol, sharesOf(symbol) + shares);
}

public void sell(String symbol, int shares) {
    purchases.put(symbol, sharesOf(symbol) - shares);
}
```

Both methods are heavy on implementation specifics and not abstractions. You can extract the commonality to a shared method named updateShares:

```
utj3-tdd/27/src/main/java/app/Portfolio.java
public void purchase(String symbol, int shares) {
    updateShares(symbol, shares);
}

public void sell(String symbol, int shares) {
    updateShares(symbol, -shares);
}

private void updateShares(String symbol, int shares) {
    purchases.put(symbol, sharesOf(symbol) + shares);
}
```

Without the safety control that TDD provides, you would be less likely to make small improvements to the codebase. It's part of the reason why most codebases steadily degrade over time with lots of crud building up everywhere—poorly expressed code, redundant code, overly complex solutions, and so on. The typical developer has little confidence to properly edit their code once they get their "first draft" working.

 TDD enables safe refactoring of virtually all of your code.

A second test, for the exceptional case:

```
utj3-tdd/28/src/test/java/app/APortfolio.java
@Test
void throwsWhenSellingMoreSharesThanHeld() {
    portfolio.purchase("AAPL", 10);

    assertThrows(InvalidTransactionException.class, () ->
        portfolio.sell("AAPL", 10 + 1));
}
```

The guard clause that gets it to pass:

```
utj3-tdd/28/src/main/java/app/Portfolio.java
public void sell(String symbol, int shares) {
    if (sharesOf(symbol) < shares)
        throw new InvalidTransactionException();

    updateShares(symbol, -shares);
}
```

You look at the implementation in sell, thinking it needs improvement. The first two lines smack of implementation specifics (even though there aren't a whole lot of other ways to implement that logic). It doesn't have the immediacy that the other line in sell has. You extract it to its own method:

```
utj3-tdd/29/src/main/java/app/Portfolio.java
public void sell(String symbol, int shares) {
    abortOnOversell(symbol, shares);

    updateShares(symbol, -shares);
}
private void abortOnOversell(String symbol, int shares) {
    if (sharesOf(symbol) < shares)
        throw new InvalidTransactionException();
}
```

Time to move on to the special case: when all shares of a stock are sold, ensure that the size of the portfolio reduces:

```
utj3-tdd/30/src/test/java/app/APortfolio.java
@Test
void reducesSizeWhenLiquidatingSymbol() {
    portfolio.purchase("AAPL", 50);

    portfolio.sell("AAPL", 50);

    assertEquals(0, portfolio.size());
}
```

The test fails, as expected. Your solution:

```
utj3-tdd/30/src/main/java/app/Portfolio.java
public void sell(String symbol, int shares) {
    abortOnOversell(symbol, shares);
    updateShares(symbol, -shares);
    removeSymbolIfSoldOut(symbol);
}
private void removeSymbolIfSoldOut(String symbol) {
    if (sharesOf(symbol) == 0)
        purchases.remove(symbol);
}
```

Increment 4: Introducing a Test Double

For the final increment, Madhu tells you that you'll need to capture and save a timestamp for each purchase or sale. He indicates that later requirements will need this information. These are the current requirements:

- Provide details about the last transaction (purchase or sale) made, including the timestamp.

- Produce a list of all transactions, ordered reverse-chronologically.

You choose to start with the requirement for the last transaction. Before you forget, you drop a zero-based test in place:

```
utj3-tdd/31/src/test/java/app/APortfolio.java
@Test
void returnsNullWhenNoPreviousTransactionMade() {
    assertNull(portfolio.lastTransaction());
}
```

The next test, a one-based test for the last transaction, will require you to be able to verify the timestamp of when the transaction was created. Time is an ever-changing quantity. If production code captures the instant in time when a transaction occurs, how can a test know what timestamp to expect?

Your solution uses a *test double* (see Chapter 3, Using Test Doubles, on page 53) that the Java class java.time.Clock provides for just this purpose. You use the static method fixed on the Clock class, providing it a java.time.Instant object. The clock object acts like a real-world broken clock, fixed to one point in time. Every subsequent time inquiry will return the test instant you gave it.

After creating a Clock object with a fixed instant, the test injects it into the portfolio via a setter:

```
utj3-tdd/31/src/test/java/app/APortfolio.java
@Nested
class LastTransaction {
    Instant now = Instant.now();

    @BeforeEach
    void injectFixedClock() {
        Clock clock = Clock.fixed(now, ZoneId.systemDefault());
        portfolio.setClock(clock);
    }

    @Test
    void returnsLastTransactionAfterPurchase() {
        portfolio.purchase("SONO", 20);

        assertEquals(portfolio.lastTransaction(),
            new Transaction("SONO", 20, BUY, now));
    }
}
```

The Portfolio class initializes its clock field to a working (production) clock. When run in production, the clock returns the actual instant in time. When run in the context of a unit test, the production clock gets overwritten with the injected "broken" clock. Portfolio code doesn't know or care about which context it's executing in.

The following listing introduces both the clock as well as the ability to track a "last transaction" object:

```
utj3-tdd/31/src/main/java/app/Portfolio.java
import java.time.Clock;
import static app.TransactionType.BUY;
import static java.lang.Math.abs;
// ...
public class Portfolio {
➤    private Transaction lastTransaction;
➤    private Clock clock = Clock.systemUTC();
     // ...
     public void purchase(String symbol, int shares) {
         updateShares(symbol, shares);
     }

     private void updateShares(String symbol, int shares) {
➤        lastTransaction =
➤            new Transaction(symbol, abs(shares), BUY, clock.instant());
         purchases.put(symbol, sharesOf(symbol) + shares);
     }

     // ...
     public void setClock(Clock clock) {
         this.clock = clock;
     }

➤    public Transaction lastTransaction() {
➤        return lastTransaction;
➤    }
}
```

Here are declarations for the supporting types TransactionType and Transaction:

```
utj3-tdd/31/src/main/java/app/TransactionType.java
public enum TransactionType {
    BUY, SELL;
}
```

```
utj3-tdd/31/src/main/java/app/Transaction.java
import java.time.Instant;

public record Transaction(
    String symbol, int shares, TransactionType type, Instant now) {}
```

In the prior increment, you factored out the redundancy between the sell and purchase methods, creating a new method, updateShares. It was the better design choice for at least a couple of reasons:

- It increased the abstraction level and, thus, the understandability of the code.
- It increased the conciseness of the solution, reducing future costs to understand both sell and update.

Here, the shared method allowed you to isolate the creation of the Transaction to a single method.

You add a second test so that the transaction type gets set appropriately for sell transactions:

```
utj3-tdd/32/src/test/java/app/APortfolio.java
@Test
void returnsLastTransactionAfterSale() {
    portfolio.purchase("SONO", 200);

    portfolio.sell("SONO", 40);

    assertEquals(portfolio.lastTransaction(),
        new Transaction("SONO", 40, SELL, now));
}
```

```
utj3-tdd/32/src/main/java/app/Portfolio.java
public void purchase(String symbol, int shares) {
    updateShares(symbol, shares, BUY);
}

public void sell(String symbol, int shares) {
    abortOnOversell(symbol, shares);
    updateShares(symbol, -shares, SELL);
    removeSymbolIfSoldOut(symbol);
}

private void updateShares(String symbol, int shares, TransactionType type) {
    lastTransaction =
        new Transaction(symbol, abs(shares), type, clock.instant());
    purchases.put(symbol, sharesOf(symbol) + shares);
}
```

Moving on to the transaction history requirement:

```
utj3-tdd/33/src/test/java/app/APortfolio.java
@Nested
class TransactionHistory {
    Instant now = Instant.now();

    @BeforeEach
    void injectFixedClock() {
        Clock clock = Clock.fixed(now, ZoneId.systemDefault());
        portfolio.setClock(clock);
    }

    @Test
    void returnsEmptyListWhenNoTransactionsMade() {
        assertTrue(portfolio.transactions().isEmpty());
    }
```

```java
    @Test
    void returnsListOfTransactionsReverseChronologically() {
        portfolio.purchase("A", 1);
        portfolio.purchase("B", 2);
        portfolio.purchase("C", 3);

        assertEquals(portfolio.transactions(), List.of(
            new Transaction("C", 3, BUY, now),
            new Transaction("B", 2, BUY, now),
            new Transaction("A", 1, BUY, now)
        ));
    }
}
```

Although two tests are shown here to simplify the presentation in this book, ensure you incrementally write each and develop the solution for each separately. Writing multiple tests at a time is improper TDD practice.

The implementation:

utj3-tdd/33/src/main/java/app/Portfolio.java

```java
import java.time.Clock;
import java.util.LinkedList;
import java.util.List;
// ...
public class Portfolio {
➤   private Transaction lastTransaction;
➤   private LinkedList transactions = new LinkedList();
    // ...
    private void updateShares(String symbol,
                             int shares,
                             TransactionType type) {
        lastTransaction =
            new Transaction(symbol, abs(shares), type, clock.instant());
➤       transactions.addFirst(lastTransaction);
        purchases.put(symbol, sharesOf(symbol) + shares);
    }

    public Transaction lastTransaction() {
        return lastTransaction;
    }

➤   public List<Transaction> transactions() {
➤       return transactions;
➤   }
    // ...
}
```

You no longer need the field lastTransaction, as you can extract the most recent transaction from the transaction list. You'll want to change both the updateShares and lastTransaction methods. Ensure you remove the field afterward.

```
utj3-tdd/34/src/main/java/app/Portfolio.java
private void updateShares(String symbol,
                         int shares,
                         TransactionType type) {
    var transaction =
        new Transaction(symbol, abs(shares), type, clock.instant());
    transactions.addFirst(transaction);
    purchases.put(symbol, sharesOf(symbol) + shares);
}

public Transaction lastTransaction() {
    return transactions.peekFirst();
}
```

You might consider the solution design at this point to be flawed. It uses two distinct data structures to manage information that could be represented with one. If you consider the list of transactions as the "document of record," all inquiries regarding the portfolio can be calculated from it. The information captured in the purchases HashMap is essentially an optimized calculation.

The dual data structure implementation is a recipe for later disaster, particularly as the solution increases in complexity. If new behaviors are added, it's possible that an oversight will lead to inconsistent data representations in each data structure.

The better solution would be to eliminate the hash map, replacing all inquiries of it with operations on the history stream instead. If you're curious what this looks like, visit versions 35 and 36 in the source distribution.

Test-Driven Development vs. Test-After Development

TDD centers on the simple cycle of test-code-refactor. "Significantly reduced defects" would seem to be the key benefit of practicing TDD, but it can accrue some even more valuable benefits. Most of them derive from describing *every* desired, incremental outcome before coding it into the system.

By definition, TDD gives you near-complete unit test coverage, which in turn gives you the following significant benefits:

- High confidence that the unit behaviors are correct
- The ability to continuously retain a high-quality design
- The ability to incorporate new changes safely and without fear
- Clear, trustworthy documentation on all intended behaviors

Your cost of change can reduce dramatically as a result.

You've been learning *test-after development* (TAD, as in "a tad too late") in this book. With TAD, testing is an afterthought—as in, "I thought about writing some unit tests after I developed my stellar code but decided not to."

You could absolutely achieve full coverage with TAD. There's no mechanical reason why you couldn't write TAD tests that cover every behavior in your system. The reality, though, is that almost no one ever does.

TAD can be harder than TDD. Determining all the behavioral intents of previously written code can be tough, even if it was written within the last hour. It seems simpler, in contrast, to first capture the desired outcome with a test.

Writing tests for code with private dependencies and myriad entanglements is also tough. It seems simpler to shape code to align with the needs of a test instead of the other way around.

Here's a short list of reasons we don't write enough tests when doing TAD:

1. We run out of time and are told to move on to the next thing. "We just need to ship."

2. Because it's often hard, we sometimes give up, particularly if we're told to move on.

3. We think our code doesn't stink. "I just wrote this, it looks great."

4. We avoid it because unit testing isn't as much fun as writing the production code.

5. Someone else told us we had to do it, which can be another discouragement for some of us.

Re-read How Much Coverage Is Enough?, on page 77 if you think there's little difference between 75% and 100% coverage. Minimally, remember that 75% coverage means that a quarter of the code in your system remains at risk.

The Rhythm of TDD

TDD cycles are short. Without all the chatter accompanying this chapter's example, each test-code-refactor cycle takes maybe a few minutes. Increments of code written or changed at each step in the cycle are likewise small.

Once you've established a short-cycle rhythm with TDD, it becomes obvious when you're heading down a rathole. Set a regular time limit of about ten minutes. If you haven't received any positive feedback (passing tests) in the last ten minutes, discard what you were working on and try again, taking even smaller steps. If you were committing after introducing (and cleaning) each new increment, reverting to the prior increment will be a trivial operation.

Yes, you heard right—throw away costly code. Treat each cycle of TDD as a time-boxed experiment whose test is the hypothesis. If the experiment is going awry, restarting the experiment and shrinking the scope of assumptions (taking smaller steps) can help you pinpoint where things went wrong. The fresh take can often help you derive a better solution in less time than you would have wasted on the mess you were making.

Summary

In this chapter, you toured the practice of TDD, which takes all the concepts you've learned about unit testing and puts them into a simple disciplined cycle: write a test, get it to pass, ensure the code is clean, and repeat. Adopting TDD may change the way you think about design.

Next, you'll learn about some topics relevant to unit testing as part of a development team.

CHAPTER 12

Adopting Team Practices

You last learned about TDD, a concept you can employ on your own. When you work in a team environment, shifting to TDD represents an effective way to take your unit testing practice to the next, more disciplined level. In this chapter, you'll learn a few other considerations for doing unit testing within a team environment.

If you're like most of us, you're working on a project with other team members. You want to be on the same page with them when it comes to unit testing. In this chapter, you'll learn about working agreements that your team must hash out to avoid wasting time on endless debates and code thrashing. Topics include test standards, code/test review, and continuous integration.

Coming up to Speed

Incorporating a new practice like unit testing requires continual vigilance. Even if you enjoy writing unit tests and are good about covering the new code you write, you'll sometimes face an uphill battle within your team. They might not be as vigilant, and they're probably producing code at a rate that far outpaces your ability to test it. You might also face a team that insists on tossing all safeguards, tests included, in order to meet a critical deadline.

"Unit testing isn't free," says Joe, "We've gotta deliver in two weeks. We're way behind and just need to slam out code."

Lucia responds to Joe, "The worst possible time to throw away unit tests is *while in crunch mode*. Squeezing lots of coding into a short time will guarantee a mess. It'll take longer to know if everything still works and to fix the defects that arise...and there'll be a lot more of those. One way or another, we'll pay dearly if we dispense with quality for short-term gains."

"Slapping out code with no tests only speeds us up for a very short period of time—maybe a couple of days or so. Invariably, we'll hit ugly defects requiring long debugging sessions. Maybe the worst of it is that we'll create chunks of legacy code that'll cost us forever. Sorry Joe, tossing unit tests isn't worth it."

Not much will allow you to escape last-minute crunches unscathed, no matter how good you are at development. Once you're there, all you can do is negotiate or work excessive hours. But if you insist on quality controls from day one, it won't happen nearly as often.

Unit testing is a part of those quality controls. Let's look at how to ensure that it becomes a habit within your team.

Getting on the Same Page with Your Team

Approaches to unit testing can vary dramatically from developer to developer. Some insist on TDD. Others resist unit testing at all costs, producing only tests they feel forced to write. Some prefer lumping multiple cases into a single test method. Some favor slower integration tests. Some will disagree with other recommendations you've learned from this book.

Your team must get on the same page, whether it's regarding unit testing standards or how you review code in the first place. Long debates or continual back-and-forth without resolution are wastes of everyone's time. You'll never agree on everything, but you can quickly discover what you do agree on and increase consensus over time.

Your team can establish initial working agreements as part of team chartering activities. *Liftoff [LN17]* is a great guide for facilitating effective chartering sessions.

Establishing Standards

You'll want to derive some standards around unit testing. Start minimally. Answer two questions:

- What code (and test) related elements are wasting our time?
- What simple standards can we quickly agree on?

Run a sub-hour discussion that results in a short list of standards, or better, in a code example that clearly embodies the standards. Over time, ensure that standards stay relevant and followed. Reference them when violated, review them when disagreement arises, and revise them as needed.

Here's a short, incomplete list of unit test practices to standardize on:

- Which tests developers should run prior to check-in
- How to name test classes and test methods
- Whether to use JUnit's assertions or an assertion library like AssertJ
- Whether to use AAA or not
- Which mock tool to prefer
- Whether to prohibit console output on test runs (please do)
- How to identify and discourage slow tests in the unit test suite

Your team should quickly adopt and adhere to most of these standards. Some will require continual vigilance, such as eliminating all console output from a test run. You might be able to automate solutions to ensure people comply; otherwise, you might find yourself continually pestering folks. You might also find that some standards just aren't worth the effort.

Increasing Quality with Post Facto Reviews

To ensure everyone adheres to standards, your team must exert collective peer pressure through some form of code review. Your team's investment in code and unit tests is too expensive to allow individuals to do anything they want to the codebase.

Many teams require *pull requests* (PRs)—a feature most closely associated with GitHub. A developer submits a pull request for a chunk of work deemed ready for integration into the main branch. GitHub notifies the rest of the team, who reviews and comments on changes made. Reviewers approve a request by *pulling* (merging) it into the main branch.

The PR process has become a preferred standard in many organizations. While it appears efficient, the PR process is the least effective of the review mechanisms. That's because it is the least agile—it attempts to streamline reviews by minimizing face-to-face human interaction.[1]

You might initiate review sessions where unit test producers solicit feedback from others on the team. Such post facto reviews can range from informal code walkthroughs to fairly formal processes like Fagan inspections, which are designed to streamline and standardize the review.[2]

When using Fagan inspections, the person creating the document—the thing to be reviewed (usually code)—is responsible for soliciting reviewers, much as when doing PRs. A meeting is typically held a couple of days later, which

---

1. https://medium.com/pragmatic-programmers/prs-shift-left-please-part-one-b0f8bb79ef2b
2. http://en.wikipedia.org/wiki/Fagan_inspection

allows time for reviewers to take a look at the changes. Prior to the meeting, reviewers make note of defects and categorize them based on severity.

The inspection meeting is designed to go fast. Only the most severe problems are described, and discussions are constrained to clarifications only. Expressly prohibited during the meeting is "solutioning" any problem.

The document producer takes away the list of all problems (including ones that aren't severe) and fixes them as appropriate. A follow-up meeting to discuss the resolution can be held if needed.

Fagan inspections seem similar to PRs in that both are designed to be streamlined. But they also involve face-to-face communication, which can help eliminate misunderstandings. The opportunity to interact also helps a team refine what's truly important to focus on when doing reviews.

The PR process, Fagan inspections, and things like code walkthroughs are all *post facto*—they occur after the code in question was produced. For that reason, they all suffer from a few challenges.

First, reviewers aren't usually familiar with the intimate details of the code product being reviewed. The best reviews—the ones that find problems before you ship them—come from people with a deep understanding of the code. The reality in most shops prevents this sort of time investment on the part of the reviewers—they're too busy working on their own thing.

As a result, post facto reviews find fewer defects than we'd like. Reviewers can discover many surface-level defects and style violations. But they often miss deeper-seated defects related to things you might only think of when you are deeply immersed in the challenge at hand. Such problems are often harder to fix after the fact, as they can be deeply intertwined with the existing solution.

Second, if there are serious problems, after-the-fact reviews come too late. Once the code is built and seemingly ready, teams are usually under too much pressure to ship it—by their peers, managers, and even themselves. They're not about to step back and significantly rework code that's purportedly already working. As a result, the team takes on problematic software that will cost them even more to maintain down the road.

In short, post facto reviews are too late and probably barely worth the time investment they require. Put another way, doing the work, reviewing it, reworking it, and re-reviewing it is an inefficient process.

Active Review via Pair Programming

A good review process would let a team review and reject a poor design before anyone tries to implement it. In the 1990s, much of software development was driven with design-up-front processes. A team typically invested 30 percent or more of a project producing *speculative* designs. Development work did not start until these designs were complete. The designs, based on exhaustively detailed requirements, were captured as heavy documents with copious diagrams and models. It worked...for a small number of situations.

Heavy up-front design doesn't work for most of us because it holds up poorly to that ever-present thing called *change*. Also, no matter the amount of up-front investment, speculative designs are often inadequate or flat-out wrong.

The intent of pair programming, or *pairing*, is to increase quality. To pair, two programmers work together side-by-side (or face-to-face remotely) to develop a two-heads-are-better-than-one solution. Pairing is an *active* form of review—its participants review each other's ideas and code as they code and fix any problems before moving on. Pair members help each other adhere to standards and practices like unit testing.

Few practices have drawn as much controversy in the software development world, however. The thought of working with other developers closely throughout the day sends many screaming for the exits. Even when practiced well, pairing incurs a number of overhead costs. It's also still possible for a pair to produce a solution that the rest of the team finds problematic.

Don't dismiss pairing out of hand, however. When done well, even active resisters can become converts, perhaps due to the increase in quality. Some find its highly interactive, collaborative aspect gratifying. The *PragPub* article "Pair Programming Benefits"[3] describes some potentials for its ROI. Another article, "Pair Programming in a Flash,"[4] lays out ground rules for successful pairing and points out a few pitfalls to avoid.

Pair swapping can be valuable. Before a task is considered complete, a new person replaces one of the starting pair's developers. This third party provides the perspective of someone not intimately involved in creating the current solution. They can help correct clarity and other issues not seen by the original pair. Recognize that to some extent, though, the process has reverted to work-review-rework—the new party is identifying and helping fix problems that might not have existed had they arrived sooner.

---

3.   https://langrsoft.com/ftp/pragpub-2011-07.pdf
4.   https://langrsoft.com/ftp/pragpub-2011-06.pdf

Active Review via Mob Programming

Maybe the answer is to have the *whole team* actively review everything related to delivering a feature—the design, tests, code, and anything else required—as that same team builds it all. This is the idea behind the nearly 15-year-old practice known as *mob programming* or *ensemble programming*.

While its name might suggest chaos, proper mob programming requires the team to work together in a structured manner in the same virtual or physical space. It's not "throw everyone in a room and see what happens."

When mob programming, one person acts as a *driver* whose job is to listen to the rest of the mob—the *navigators*—and translate their direction into code. Physically and in person, this means that the driver is the only one typing at a keyboard; the rest of the mob watches on a shared monitor.

After a short period of time— maybe a handful of minutes—the driver yields control to another mob member. A driver with a brilliant idea must relinquish their seat to step the next driver through their thinking.

These two simple rules maximize engagement and minimize domination and fear. Without structure, a mob usually devolves. A senior team member speeds off to their desired solution while the rest of the team watches confused and helpless from the back seat. But with short rotations and a driver who must follow direction, it becomes difficult for anyone to dominate.

The driver role is a short-lived experience, which can make it less intimidating, as can the fact that they're not responsible for knowing what to do. A good driver ramps up their listening and translating skills. They might start knowing nothing about a language, requiring detailed direction on its syntax ("type public static void main, then parentheses, then String[])"). It's rough at first, but most drivers quickly improve to the point where they can readily translate higher-level instruction ("write a method that filters the customer list down to active customers only") into code.

Mob programming seems to send fewer folks screaming for the exits than pairing. That's possibly because pairing demands continual attention and forces considerable intimacy between you and each of your teammates. Some pairs will just never click. In a mob, you're not "on point" for the entire development session, unlike when you're working in a pair.

Mob sessions can be highly effective. Mob programming eliminates a lot of the cost of splitting the work amongst sub-teams, whether they are pairs or individuals. Not only can you eliminate review sessions (everyone's there!), but ceremonies like standup meetings, iteration planning, and pull requests disappear or are greatly simplified. Since everyone is in the room, you find the problems sooner, you derive a better design that everyone can live with, you converge on a team coding standard, you have all the expertise available to use right now, and you write all the tests you need to write.

Most importantly (to me at least), mob sessions are usually a lot of fun, and I often feel like we got a lot more done.

If you choose to practice either mob or pair programming, you'll still end up with some individual work product. Make sure you use a post facto review process for this work.

Practicing Continuous Integration

"It works on my machine!" cries Joe. "Must be something wrong on *yours*," he says to Lucia.

Hearken to the call of the wild developer, heard ofttimes in olde shops that weren't practicing *continuous integration* (CI). With CI, all developers frequently *integrate* their changes with the centralized repository (commonly in GitHub). A tool known as a *CI server* monitors the repository. When the repository is updated, the CI server triggers a new build and runs one or more sets of tests prior to completion. The first of those test suites to execute is typically your team's unit tests.

 CI demands a solid suite of *fast* unit tests.

CI servers can be hosted internally or available in the cloud. The most common tools are Jenkins, GitHub Actions, and GitLab CI. Some alternative solutions include Azure DevOps, CircleCI, and TeamCity.[5] Some of the tools are free, some are licensed, and some are software as a service (SaaS).

The CI build's tests verify that the integrated codebase works as expected. If a developer pushes and any CI tests fail, the build fails and the team is notified of the problem. The unit tests running in CI thus establish a centralized, authoritative standard.

 Broken CI tests indicate a system that cannot be deployed. Resolve them before doing anything else.

---

5. https://blog.jetbrains.com/teamcity/2023/07/best-ci-tools/

Tools like Git can be configured to abort commit/push attempts when unit tests fail locally.

CI is a foundation for practicing *continuous deployment* (CD), wherein each successful build triggers a deployment to production. Amazon[6] and Netflix[7] are companies that deploy to production thousands of times daily using CD.

Conflicts and Merges

If two or more separate developers separately make changes to the same codebase, it's possible for their combined changes to break the system (even though the individual contributions worked prior to integration). In order for CI to work, each developer wishing to push must first pull the latest code from the central repository. They run their fantastic unit test suite to ensure nothing is broken and then push up what now becomes the latest version of the system. If they don't have a fantastic unit test suite, they must carefully review the combined code first. (Corollary: folks without a fantastic unit test suite or some other comprehensive test suite are not usually practicing CI.)

A healthy team that's created a trustworthy test suite integrates frequently. Some teams who practice TDD push up every TDD cycle, in other words, as often as every few minutes. Once they get a new behavior working and clean up the code, they integrate that new increment. This "continuous" aspect of CI helps make it work and be successful. Feedback comes sooner and in smaller increments. It's easier and faster to find and fix problems in such small increments.

In contrast, developers on less advanced teams defer integrating their changes until a feature is complete. They typically make their changes on code branches across the course of a day, a few days, and sometimes a few weeks. The amount of new code that must subsequently be integrated can be considerable, thus significantly likely to conflict with existing code.

Developers can spend hours, even days, managing a meticulous manual merge process to integrate a long-lived branch. The correct technical term for such a nightmare is "merge hell." The duration of the nightmare often increases proportionally with the age of the branch.

Better communication and division of labor can help minimize code conflicts and merge hell. But consider also mob programming (see Active Review via Mob Programming, on page 240).

---

6.   https://www.zdnet.com/article/how-amazon-handles-a-new-software-deployment-every-second/

7.   https://www.theserverside.com/feature/How-Netflix-built-tooling-for-multi-cloud-deployment

An Integration Process Checklist

Here's a summary of your steps as a developer for practicing continuous integration:

1. Pull from your central repo to get your local codebase up to date.
2. Change the code, running unit tests as you go.
3. Pull from the repo to integrate any new changes from teammates.
4. Manually review the incoming changes as appropriate.
5. Run your tests to ensure that the integrated code works.
6. Push your changes to the central repository.

Don't advance to the next step if any of your tests are failing.

A CI process fosters healthy peer pressure against costly code. Developers quickly habituate themselves to running their unit tests before check-in so as not to waste their teammates' time by causing the CI build process to fail.

 A CI server is a minimum for building a modern development team.

Summary

You and your team must be on the same page when it comes to unit testing. If it's new to your team, it'll take time to adopt and ingrain as a beneficial habit. If it's an existing practice, your team practices might need improvement.

In this chapter, you learned about establishing team-level standards for unit testing from both implementation and process perspectives. You also learned about the active review mechanisms that help ensure test quality—specifically, mob and pair programming. Finally, you discovered the key role that CI plays in unit testing.

Last up: times are changing rapidly. AI has dramatically made its way into the software development arena. Unlike previous attempts (anyone remember Prolog and 4GLs?), AI has made a ubiquitous impact not just in software development but in day-to-day life for many of us. AI's improvements are accelerating and there's little chance of its disappearance.

Yes, unit testing is quite relevant in the age of AI. Read on to discover how.

CHAPTER 13

Keeping AI Honest with Unit Tests

You've learned a number of benefits you can gain from writing unit tests: fewer defects, of course, but also trustworthy documentation, the ability to keep your code clean through refactoring, and a dramatic increase in confidence for shipping the system.

AI can generate code, creating increasingly dramatic implications for the software development industry and you. Yet, unit testing can and will provide tremendous value in your software development efforts. In this chapter, you'll take an approach involving AI generation of both production code *and* unit tests. You'll discover why unit tests remain essential, and you'll learn how to incorporate them into a workflow that will give you the confidence to ship.

AI Isn't Going Away

By the time you read this chapter, the capabilities of artificial intelligence (AI) will have advanced, perhaps significantly, from when I wrote it (January 2024). At some future point, very possibly within the span of your career, most (not all) software will be generated by AI.

You will still need to tell your AI assistant what to do.

Today, AI-generated code has limitations. It's of dubious quality, for one—very stepwise and highly concrete. Maybe when AI evolves to a point where the code always works as expected, its quality won't matter because, at that point, you might never have to read or write another word of code again. But today, AI-generated code may contain defects. ChatGPT, for example, perpetually admits that fact:

```
ChatGPT can make mistakes. Consider checking important information.
```

I've seen failures often occur when an LLM (Large Language Model) adds a new feature to an existing body of code, for example. You'll explore how to help your LLM do a better job with that challenge in this chapter. But left to its own devices, an LLM is increasingly likely to break existing functionality as it adds new increments.

 Do not trust any AI-generated code to be correct.

I've been pleasantly surprised, though: more often than not, the code LLMs (including ChatGPT, Meta.ai, and Claude) have produced for me has been correct. But I've also seen them generate enough wrong code to know that I could never fully depend on it.

From these limitations arises a critical need: if you're going to use AI tools to generate code, you'll need to create and run tests.

Fortunately, you've read the rest of this book (right?) and know how to do just that. Even better, AI will speed you up by coding the tests.

Give the benefit of the doubt to your pair programmer—whether artificial or human—but assume that you can both make mistakes. доверяй, но проверяй. ("Trust, but verify.")

Note: as I write this, you can also use tools like GitHub Copilot, JetBrains AI Assistant, and Duet to help you develop. These tools sit atop one or more LLMs and provide what can best be described as AI-assisted code completion. I highly recommend incorporating them into your regular code development process. In this chapter, however, you'll focus on using a test-driven process for generating code at the class level—with the intent of maximizing the amount of (verified) code that AI can generate for you.

Exploring a Simple Example with ChatGPT

Interaction with an LLM via prompting is a conversation. That conversation may play out very differently the next time I have it. As a result, it's probably best if this chapter reads as a story about my personal interaction with ChatGPT on a small example. Accordingly, unlike the rest of the book, this chapter is written in first-person past tense.

I held my conversation with OpenAI's chatbot, ChatGPT, which at the time was based on the GPT-4 LLM. My subsequent mentions of ChatGPT refer to this configuration. While other models may exist that have been trained to be optimized for programming tasks (Code Llama for example), the experience I relay in this chapter demonstrates an approach that will work—and will only get better with time—with virtually any current LLM.

I was responsible for producing an event check-in list. Given a list of attendees, I needed to write code that sorted them. Attendee names started with a first name, followed by zero or more "middle" names, followed by the surname or last name. Some examples:

```
Jeffrey John Langr
John Jacob Jingleheimer-Schmidt
John Yossarian
Arthur Ignatius Conan Doyle
```

The check-in list needed to show names in alphabetical order based on the *last* name, not the first name. I had to "normalize" each name, then, into the form "Last, First M. I.":

```
Langr, Jeffrey J.
Jingleheimer-Schmidt, John J.
Yossarian, John
Doyle, Arthur I. C.
```

Oh I. C. indeed: the middle names are transformed into initials. Other rules implicit in these examples include the obvious fact that names are separated by spaces and that a comma should appear after each last name.

I focused on the task of normalizing a single name, deferring the trivial task of *sorting* a list of names. First, however, I wanted to teach my LLM how to write code to help me and ChatGPT work better together.

Establishing a Java Standard

By default, ChatGPT generates stepwise code that requires too much time to fully comprehend. I wanted it to do better, so I supplied a prompt describing the kind of code I wanted:

> **YOU:** *I will be asking you to write Java code. Write all code as Jeff Langr. Jeff Langr (Jeff) has a specific coding standard. Here are the rules for your standard for Java language programming, which I will refer to as Jeff-Java when appropriate.*
>
> *1. Use 'var' when declaring local variables and the compiler allows it.*
>
> *2. Where possible, prefer use of the streams functionality and implement iterative operations using stream functions, such as 'map' and 'filter'.*
>
> *3. For any and all complex expressions—mathematics, complex conditionals, predicates, and so on—extract the code to a separate function. This should also hold true for lambdas within a chained stream expression.*

4. In general, create very short, intention-revealing functions for any complexity.

5. Avoid the use of temporaries in most cases unless there is a strong reason to use them (for example, to use them more than once within a single expression). Instead, extract the temporary's initialization to a separate function with the same name as the temporary, then inline the temporary to remove it.

ChatGPT affirmed my request:

CHAT-GPT: *Understood! Blah blah blah...*

You might wonder why I even bothered telling my LLM to improve the code. If an LLM can generate the code I need, I shouldn't have to read it.

However, hearken back to the earlier mentioned limitations of LLMs like ChatGPT. *They're gonna be wrong at times...*just like you and me. You'll have to read and manually update some amount of code. Even as that need likely diminishes over time, keeping your code organized (by predominantly creating small classes and methods) appears to increase the odds that the LLM-generated code is correct.

Providing Examples to ChatGPT

Incrementally test driving small, unit behaviors into a system remains the best choice for humans. For an LLM, maybe not.

I first tried getting ChatGPT to consume *all* my requirements for the name normalizer at once. The code was a mess, and it didn't work. I took the next-smaller step, which was to first give it a subset containing the four core cases it needed to cover. I helped ChatGPT focus on what I believe to be a proper design—one that, in general, is based on small classes and small methods. With such an improved design, I believe ChatGPT had a much better chance to correctly generate new increments.

One of the best ways to get good results from an LLM is to provide examples in your prompts. I followed that advice for the name normalizer after first describing in English what I wanted. My prompt provided five examples for four core cases:

YOU: *Write Java code for a feature known as the name normalizer. Given a person's name, the name normalizer should return the last name first, followed by a comma, then the first name.*

If there is one or more middle names, return the initial of each. The initial is the first letter followed by a period.

Assume that the name provided to the method is never empty or null.

Examples:

>   *input: Plato*
>   *output: Plato*
>
>   *input: Leonard Cohen*
>   *output: Cohen, Leonard*
>
>   *input: Samuel Leroy Jackson*
>   *output: Jackson, Samuel L.*
>
>   *input: George Raymond Richard Martin*
>   *output: Martin, George R. R.*
>
>   *input: Emma Azalia Smith Hackley*
>   *output: Hackley, Emma A. S.*

Unit tests and examples are birds of a feather—remember this tip from Chapter 10, Streamlining Your Tests, on page 189:

> Good tests provide examples of how clients interact with the system.

Accordingly, I told my LLM to translate the examples into tests:

YOU: *Also, provide JUnit tests for the core cases.*

I took a few seconds to vet the tests that ChatGPT generated to ensure that they correctly aligned with my examples. ChatGPT did a decent job, generating tests that used the same data as the examples I provided:

```
utj3-ai/01/src/test/java/util/NameNormalizerTest.java
import org.junit.jupiter.api.Test;
import static org.junit.jupiter.api.Assertions.assertEquals;

public class NameNormalizerTest {

    @Test
    public void testSingleName() {
        assertEquals("Plato",
            NameNormalizer.normalizeName("Plato"));
    }

    @Test
    public void testFirstNameLastName() {
        assertEquals("Cohen, Leonard",
            NameNormalizer.normalizeName("Leonard Cohen"));
    }
```

```
@Test
public void testMultipleMiddleNames() {
    assertEquals("Jackson, Samuel L.",
        NameNormalizer.normalizeName("Samuel Leroy Jackson"));
    assertEquals("Martin, George R. R.",
        NameNormalizer.normalizeName("George Raymond Richard Martin"));
}

@Test
public void testLongName() {
    assertEquals("Hackley, Emma A. S.",
        NameNormalizer.normalizeName("Emma Azalia Smith Hackley"));
}
}
```

ChatGPT got a little confused regarding the tests testMultipleMiddleNames and testLongName. I had ChatGPT fix this later (as I also did with the unnecessary test prefix for each test).

ChatGPT did a job (in other words, not a fine one) generating the corresponding normalizer implementation:

utj3-ai/01/src/main/java/util/NameNormalizer.java
```java
import java.util.Arrays;
import java.util.stream.Collectors;

public class NameNormalizer {

    public static String normalizeName(String name) {
        var nameParts = name.split(" ");
        if (nameParts.length == 1) {
            return name;
        }

        var lastName = nameParts[nameParts.length - 1];
        var firstName = nameParts[0];
        var middleNames =
            Arrays.copyOfRange(nameParts, 1, nameParts.length - 1);

        return formatLastNameFirst(lastName, firstName, middleNames);
    }

    private static String formatLastNameFirst(
        String lastName, String firstName, String[] middleNames) {
        var middleInitials = Arrays.stream(middleNames)
            .map(NameNormalizer::extractInitial)
            .collect(Collectors.joining(" "));

        return middleInitials.isEmpty() ?
            String.format("%s, %s", lastName, firstName) :
            String.format("%s, %s %s", lastName, firstName, middleInitials);
    }
```

```java
    private static String extractInitial(String name) {
        return name.charAt(0) + ".";
    }
}
```

Telling Your LLM to Clean Up Its Act

The LLM's solution passed the tests, and it wasn't bad, actually, but there were a few wrinkles to iron out. First, it didn't include a package name, which forced me to copy only part of its solution rather than wholesale copy-and-replace the generated code, which is a lot faster. (I'm imagining a near future where integration with IDEs is a lot better, and, in fact, I've begun building such a plugin myself.)

Here's my prompt to tell the LLM to add the package name, as well as smooth out the aforementioned wrinkles:

> **YOU:**   *The code should live in a Java package named util.*
>
> *The Jeff-Java standard indicates that you should avoid the use of temporaries in methods, but normalizeName has three temps that should be eliminated.*
>
> *Do not include the word test in the test name; it is redundant.*
>
> *Do not use static methods for the implementation. Prefer using instance methods for generated code.*
>
> *Update the Jeff-Java standard where appropriate to fix these problems for any code generated going forward.*

ChatGPT did a good job of delivering:

utj3-ai/02/src/test/java/util/NameNormalizerTest.java
```java
import org.junit.jupiter.api.Test;
import static org.junit.jupiter.api.Assertions.assertEquals;

public class NameNormalizerTest {

    private final NameNormalizer normalizer = new NameNormalizer();

    @Test
    public void singleName() {
        assertEquals("Plato", normalizer.normalizeName("Plato"));
    }

    @Test
    public void firstNameLastName() {
        assertEquals("Cohen, Leonard",
            normalizer.normalizeName("Leonard Cohen"));
    }
```

```java
    @Test
    public void multipleMiddleNames() {
        assertEquals("Jackson, Samuel L.",
            normalizer.normalizeName("Samuel Leroy Jackson"));
        assertEquals("Martin, George R. R.",
            normalizer.normalizeName("George Raymond Richard Martin"));
    }

    @Test
    public void longName() {
        assertEquals("Hackley, Emma A. S.",
            normalizer.normalizeName("Emma Azalia Smith Hackley"));
    }
}
```

utj3-ai/02/src/main/java/util/NameNormalizer.java
```java
import java.util.Arrays;
import java.util.stream.Collectors;

public class NameNormalizer {

    public String normalizeName(String name) {
        var nameParts = name.split(" ");
        if (nameParts.length == 1) {
            return name;
        }

        return formatLastNameFirst(nameParts[0],
            nameParts[nameParts.length - 1],
            Arrays.copyOfRange(
                nameParts, 1, nameParts.length - 1));
    }

    private String formatLastNameFirst(
        String firstName, String lastName, String[] middleNames) {
        var middleInitials = Arrays.stream(middleNames)
            .map(this::extractInitial)
            .collect(Collectors.joining(" "));

        return middleInitials.isEmpty() ?
            String.format("%s, %s", lastName, firstName) :
            String.format("%s, %s %s", lastName, firstName, middleInitials);
    }

    private String extractInitial(String name) {
        return name.charAt(0) + ".";
    }
}
```

And once again, all tests passed.

I disliked a few of its choices, but found the code fairly easy to follow and... almost good enough. I complained immediately:

YOU: *The arguments to formatLastNameFirst should have first been extracted to new functions, perhaps named firstName, middleNames, and lastName respectively.*

Update the Jeff-Java standard to indicate that the right-hand side of an assignment should first be extracted to a new function before inlining, if it is anything that involves "implementation-specific details," i.e., anything that might need to be explained.

Now we were talking! ChatGPT was doing a pretty good job of listening.

utj3-ai/03/src/main/java/util/NameNormalizer.java

```java
import java.util.Arrays;
import java.util.stream.Collectors;

public class NameNormalizer {

    public String normalizeName(String name) {
        var nameParts = name.split(" ");
        if (nameParts.length == 1) {
            return name;
        }

        return formatLastNameFirst(
            firstName(nameParts),
            lastName(nameParts),
            middleNames(nameParts));
    }

    private String firstName(String[] nameParts) {
        return nameParts[0];
    }

    private String lastName(String[] nameParts) {
        return nameParts[nameParts.length - 1];
    }

    private String[] middleNames(String[] nameParts) {
        return Arrays.copyOfRange(
            nameParts, 1, nameParts.length - 1);
    }

    private String formatLastNameFirst(
        String firstName, String lastName, String[] middleNames) {
        var middleInitials = Arrays.stream(middleNames)
            .map(this::extractInitial)
            .collect(Collectors.joining(" "));

        return middleInitials.isEmpty() ?
            String.format("%s, %s", lastName, firstName) :
            String.format("%s, %s %s", lastName, firstName, middleInitials);
    }

    private String extractInitial(String name) {
        return name.charAt(0) + ".";
    }
}
```

The code was at the point where I could easily reason about exactly what was going on. It took only a moment to understand any one method and trust that it did what it said.

I prompted ChatGPT to fix a few more things:

> **YOU:** *Simplify the method named extractInitial to initial.*
>
> *Move the assertion for "Samuel Leroy Jackson" to a new test initializesMiddleName.*
>
> *Move the assertion for "Emma Azalia Smith Hackley" to the test multipleMiddleNames.*
>
> *Eliminate the arguments to formatLastNameFirst. Instead, have its code directly access the functions firstName, lastName, and middleNames.*

ChatGPT complied:

utj3-ai/04/src/test/java/util/NameNormalizerTest.java

```java
@Test
public void initializesMiddleName() {
    assertEquals("Jackson, Samuel L.",
        normalizer.normalizeName("Samuel Leroy Jackson"));
}

@Test
public void multipleMiddleNames() {
    assertEquals("Martin, George R. R.",
        normalizer.normalizeName("George Raymond Richard Martin"));
    assertEquals("Hackley, Emma A. S.",
        normalizer.normalizeName("Emma Azalia Smith Hackley"));
}
```

utj3-ai/04/src/main/java/util/NameNormalizer.java

```java
public String normalizeName(String name) {
    this.nameParts = name.split(" ");
    if (nameParts.length == 1) {
        return name;
    }

    return formatLastNameFirst();
}
// ...
private String formatLastNameFirst() {
    var middleInitials = Arrays.stream(middleNames())
        .map(this::initial)
        .collect(Collectors.joining(" "));
    return middleInitials.isEmpty() ?
        String.format("%s, %s", lastName(), firstName()) :
        String.format("%s, %s %s", lastName(), firstName(), middleInitials);
}

private String initial(String name) {
    return name.charAt(0) + ".";
}
```

Adding a New Feature: Suffixes

I moved on to the next code increment, again providing an example for the LLM to translate into a test.

> YOU: *Alter both the code and the tests to support suffixes. A suffix appears after a comma at the end of a name.*
>
> *Examples*
>
> *input: Martin Luther King, Jr.*
>
> *output: King, Martin L., Jr.*

Here's what ChatGPT spewed out:

utj3-ai/05/src/test/java/util/NameNormalizerTest.java
```java
@Test
public void nameWithSuffix() {
    assertEquals("King, Martin L., Jr.",
        normalizer.normalizeName("Martin Luther King, Jr."));
}
```

utj3-ai/05/src/main/java/util/NameNormalizer.java
```java
public class NameNormalizer {

    private String[] nameParts;
    private String suffix = "";

    public String normalizeName(String name) {
        if (name.contains(",")) {
            var parts = name.split(", ");
            this.nameParts = parts[0].split(" ");
            this.suffix = ", " + parts[1];
        } else {
            this.nameParts = name.split(" ");
        }

        if (nameParts.length == 1) {
            return name;
        }

        return formatLastNameFirst() + suffix;
    }
    // ...
}
```

That went to pot pretty quickly. It did work, at least for the test case I gave it, but the code was back to stepwise, intertwined logic that was hard to follow. Also, ChatGPT seemed to have forgotten my Jeff-Java style rules.

Letting Your LLM Discover Missing Tests

Before I asked ChatGPT to fix the code, I took a little detour. I thought it might be useful to ask ChatGPT to *generate* test cases for its own code but in a new conversation. It produced this:

```
utj3-ai/05/src/test/java/util/NameNormalizerAITest.java
public class NameNormalizerAITest {
    private NameNormalizer normalizer = new NameNormalizer();

    @Test
    public void testSimpleTwoPartName() {
        assertEquals("Doe, John", normalizer.normalizeName("John Doe"));
    }

    @Test
    public void testNameWithMiddleInitial() {
        assertEquals("Doe, John A.",
            normalizer.normalizeName("John A. Doe"));
    }

    @Test
    public void testNameWithSuffix() {
        assertEquals("Doe, John Jr.",
            normalizer.normalizeName("John Doe, Jr."));
    }

    @Test
    public void testSingleName() {
        assertEquals("John", normalizer.normalizeName("John"));
    }

    @Test
    public void testNameWithMiddleNames() {
        assertEquals("Doe, John A. B.",
            normalizer.normalizeName("John Adam Bernard Doe"));
    }

    @Test
    public void testEmptyString() {
        assertEquals("", normalizer.normalizeName(""));
    }

    // Optional: If handling null is expected
    @Test
    public void testNullInput() {
        assertEquals(null, normalizer.normalizeName(null));
    }
}
```

The generated test cases were decent, though again, they ignored the Jeff-Java rule around test names. When I ran them, I discovered two test failures:

testNameWithSuffix and testNullInput. I ignored testNullInput since I'd decided the input to normalizeName couldn't ever be null.

The other failing test, testNameWithSuffix, involved a two-part name, whereas I'd only provided a three-part name to ChatGPT as an example. When I copied the test code for testNameWithSuffix into NameNormalizerTest, it still failed.

ChatGPT indeed had discerned the need for a test case that I'd missed! The failing test didn't point out a problem with the code, though—its expected output for "John Doe, Jr." was incorrect (it should have been "Doe, John, Jr.", with a comma after the first name).

I considered what I knew about iterating via ZOM (see ZOM: Zero and One Done, Now Testing Many, on page 22) and gave ChatGPT a one-two-three set of examples.

> **YOU:**   *Try again with the following changes.*
>
> *Alter both the code and the tests to support suffixes. A suffix appears after a comma at the end of a name.*
>
> *Examples*
>
> > *input: Madonna, Esq.*
> > *output: Madonna, Esq.*
> >
> > *input: John Doe, Sr.*
> > *output: Doe, John, Sr.*
> >
> > *input: Martin Luther King, Jr.*
> > *output: King, Martin L., Jr.*
>
> *Ensure you use the Jeff-Java standard. Most importantly, find a way to keep the suffix code isolated from as much of the existing code within NameNormalizer as possible.*
>
> *Do not include any tests around a null name.*

At first glance, the result looked promising:

utj3-ai/06/src/test/java/util/NameNormalizerTest.java
```java
@Test
public void nameWithSuffix() {
    assertEquals("King, Martin L., Jr.",
        normalizer.normalizeName("Martin Luther King, Jr."));
    assertEquals("Doe, John, Sr.",
        normalizer.normalizeName("John Doe, Sr."));
}
```

```java
@Test
public void singleNameWithSuffix() {
    assertEquals("Madonna, Esq.",
        normalizer.normalizeName("Madonna, Esq."));
}
```

utj3-ai/06/src/main/java/util/NameNormalizer.java

```java
public class NameNormalizer {

    private String[] nameParts;
    private String suffix = "";

    public String normalizeName(String name) {
        extractSuffix(name);
        if (nameParts.length == 1 && suffix.isEmpty()) {
            return name;
        }

        return formatLastNameFirst() + suffix;
    }

    private void extractSuffix(String name) {
        if (name.contains(",")) {
            var parts = name.split(", ", 2);
            this.nameParts = parts[0].split(" ");
            this.suffix = ", " + parts[1];
        } else {
            this.nameParts = name.split(" ");
        }
    }
    // ...
}
```

The AI solution was awkward. The method extractSuffix did extract the suffix, but it also set a value into nameParts, making the logic much harder to follow. A better solution would involve a pure function named extractSuffix that does *only* that—given a name, return the suffix or empty string.

I ignored the deficiency. ChatGPT was teaching me not to sweat the small stuff as much—unlike building my own code, where tending to all the small things speeds me up over time.

It had also become apparent that nitpicking every nuance of what the LLM produced seemed like it would take hours. I decided I'd prompt ChatGPT to fix the problem if I needed to revisit the extractSuffix method.

From AI, "good enough to have an easy conversation about" is good enough.

ChatGPT Breaks the Code

On the surface, the code ChatGPT produced was *reasonable*, except for the way it had designed extractSuffix. Alas, I now had a test failure involving poor Madonna.

```
Expected :Madonna, Esq.
Actual   :Madonna, Madonna, Esq.
```

"Madonna, Madonna, Esquire?" Sounds like a potential song, maybe a blatant ripoff of "Vogue." Maybe I should get ChatGPT to write some lyrics. (I did.)[1]

I went with the lazy flow—I asked ChatGPT to fix its mistake. (*It* broke stuff, so why should *I* fix it?) ChatGPT has had the effect of making me lazy, but maybe that's the good kind of lazy.

> **YOU:** *Expected :Madonna, Esq.*
> *Actual :Madonna, Madonna, Esq.*
>
> *See if you can fix the problem.*

The LLM had a sense of what was going on and how to fix it:

> **CHAT-GPT:** *The issue with the Madonna-based test case failing is due to how the normalization logic is applied even when there's only a single name part before the suffix, leading to the repetition of the name. To fix this, we need to adjust the logic to correctly handle cases where there's only a single name part (i.e., no first and last name separation, but potentially a suffix).*

The fix offered did pass the tests:

```
utj3-ai/07/src/main/java/util/NameNormalizer.java
public String normalizeName(String name) {
    extractSuffix(name);
    // Handle case for 1 name w/ no middle names but possible a suffix
➤   if (nameParts.length == 1) {
➤       return nameParts[0] + suffix;
➤   }
    return formatLastNameFirst() + suffix;
}
```

Defects in code are often good at hiding themselves—broken things may look reasonable. But reasonable isn't correct.

 Don't ship code just because it looks good.

---

1. https://langrsoft.com/2024/01/23/madonna/

Getting the LLM to Do Final Design Cleanup

The last thing to tackle was some final code cleanup.

> **YOU:** *The solution works. The method extractSuffix should be reworked, however, into a pure function (i.e., with no side effects). The side effects, if needed, should occur in normalizeName.*
>
> *Also, I just noticed the silliness in formatLastNameFirst. Inline the temporaries, please.*

Oh my. I don't want to show you the abomination it produced, but I suppose I must. Here's a small piece of it:

utj3-ai/08/src/main/java/util/NameNormalizer.java
```java
public String normalizeName(String name) {
   var extractedResult = extractSuffix(name);
   var nameParts = extractedResult[0].split(" ");
   var suffix = extractedResult[1];

   if (nameParts.length == 1) {
      return nameParts[0] + suffix;
   }

   var middleInitials = Arrays.stream(middleNames(nameParts))
      .map(this::initial)
      .collect(Collectors.joining(" "));

   return (nameParts[nameParts.length - 1] + ", " + nameParts[0] +
      (middleInitials.isEmpty() ? "" : " " + middleInitials)) + suffix;
}
```

I was a little upset at this point. My message to ChatGPT wasn't very pleasant.

> **YOU:** *Undo that last change. It's horrible. You inlined the helper functions like last(). Show me the prior version.*

Thankfully, ChatGPT only undid the inlining mess. It retained the conversion of extractSuffix to a functional method:

utj3-ai/09/src/main/java/util/NameNormalizer.java
```java
public String normalizeName(String name) {
   var result = extractSuffix(name);
   this.nameParts = result[0].split(" ");
   this.suffix = result[1];

   if (nameParts.length == 1) {
      return nameParts[0] + suffix;
   }

   return formatLastNameFirst() + suffix;
}
```

```java
    private String[] extractSuffix(String name) {
        if (name.contains(",")) {
            var parts = name.split(", ", 2);
            return new String[] {parts[0], ", " + parts[1]};
        } else {
            return new String[] {name, ""};
        }
    }

    private String formatLastNameFirst() {
        return lastName() + ", " + firstName() + middleInitialsString();
    }

    private String firstName() {
        return nameParts[0];
    }

    private String lastName() {
        return nameParts[nameParts.length - 1];
    }

    private String middleInitialsString() {
        if (nameParts.length > 2) {
            return " " + Arrays.stream(middleNames())
                .map(this::initial)
                .collect(Collectors.joining(" "));
        }
        return "";
    }

    private String[] middleNames() {
        if (nameParts.length > 2) {
            return Arrays.copyOfRange(nameParts, 1, nameParts.length - 1);
        }
        return new String[]{};
    }

    private String initial(String name) {
        return name.charAt(0) + ".";
    }
}
```

Its new solution clarified to me what ChatGPT was trying to do all along, but I hadn't noticed. The extractSuffix method was now returning a tuple—or Java's code-heavy version of one—a two-dimensional array containing the base name and suffix. With modern Java, using a record seemed a better choice.

> **YOU:** *Replace the tuple returned by extractSuffix with a version that uses a Java record, defined as a nested class within NameNormalizer.*

ChatGPT did the job:

```
utj3-ai/10/src/main/java/util/NameNormalizer.java
private record ExtractedNameParts(String[] nameParts, String suffix) {}

public String normalizeName(String name) {
    var extractedNameParts = extractSuffix(name);
    this.nameParts = extractedNameParts.nameParts();
    this.suffix = extractedNameParts.suffix();

    if (nameParts.length == 1) {
        return nameParts[0] + suffix;
    }

    return formatLastNameFirst() + suffix;
}

private ExtractedNameParts extractSuffix(String name) {
    if (name.contains(",")) {
        var parts = name.split(", ", 2);
        return new ExtractedNameParts(parts[0].split(" "), ", " + parts[1]);
    } else {
        return new ExtractedNameParts(name.split(" "), "");
    }
}
```

I'll take it. I felt that the code still had numerous little problems, particularly some bits where the code didn't declare well what was going on. For example, what's nameParts[0]? What's parts[0]?

But maybe that's okay. I reminded myself that *I wasn't trying to create "perfect" code.* (As if there was such a thing.)

It *is* important that an AI solution is composed of focused *units.* (Huh!) Small, single-purpose methods allow ChatGPT to employ intention-revealing, accurate method and variable names. In turn, those small, accurately named concepts allow both the LLM and you (or me) to continue with a sensible conversation as you add more increments and fix problems.

For Extra Credit

Start a similar conversation with your LLM of choice to build the name normalizer. Then, see how effective a solution it can produce by prompting a couple more features.

1. Harry Truman had a single-letter middle name, sort of, implying that it should not be abbreviated with a period.

   input: Harry S Truman

   output: Truman, Harry S

2. If a person has a salutation, it should precede the first name in the result. Known salutations include Dr, Mr, Mrs, Ms, Sir, Miss, Lord, and Esq. Each salutation may optionally be terminated by a period. Retain the period if it exists.

input: Dr. Martin Luther King, Jr.
output: King, Jr., Dr. Martin L.

input: Sir Patrick Stewart
output: Stewart, Sir Patrick

If you really want to get wild, a version supporting non-Western names would no doubt involve numerous additional rules.

Increasing Odds of Success with AI-Generated Code

The most important thing to remember when developing software with an LLM is you can't trust the code it generates. The skills you obtained in *Pragmatic Unit Testing in Java with JUnit,* however, provide you with a basis for verifying the code. Consider always following the *CAX* cycle, as demonstrated in this chapter, for generating code:

- Create both production code and tests when prompting the LLM, using (ZOM-inclusive) examples as the basis for the tests.

- Assess the fidelity of the generated tests with the examples you provided.

- e*Xecute the tests. Repeat the cycle (with alterations) if they don't all pass.

Also, provide a small set of programming style guidelines to your LLM to improve the solution's design and potentially increase the likelihood of a correct solution. Jeff-Java style represents a good starting point.

Will I Go Faster?

AI tools are only now emerging from their infancy, but they show a lot of promise. As with human toddlers, they thrive when you provide them with some direction and safeguards, but they can also surprise you with their cleverness, particularly when you let them explore.

Good design makes so many things easier: writing tests around code, understanding code, extending code, and so on. Generating code via an LLM is also easier when you direct it to follow a small set of guidelines for design that promote small, focused methods and intention-revealing names.

Will using an LLM speed you up? I believe the answer will be increasingly *yes*. For now, it will speed you up at least as much as any auto-code-complete mechanisms speed you up. You're typing far less, for one.

Personally, I can go considerably faster than an LLM for some pieces of producing a solution, particularly around small adjustments to the way I want the code expressed. But there are many operations that LLMs can do faster than me. For example, it was quicker to change the array-based tuple to a record than it would have been by hand. It's also a lot faster to have the LLM generate tests from examples.

Maybe my biggest speed-up is that I can take larger steps with an LLM than with TDD, where I do one small thing at a time. Sure, AI will get some things wrong as a result of the larger steps, but it's a lot quicker to revert and try something different when it does.

Summary

In *Pragmatic Unit Testing in Java with JUnit*, you've learned a wealth of approaches, skills, practices, and design tips. You can apply these skills immediately to your work and start to reap the multiple benefits of unit testing.

Whether or not you use AI to generate code, unit testing will remain an important tool in your development toolbox. Without good unit tests, you will always proceed with considerable risk. Done properly, unit tests will allow you to go faster and ship with high confidence.

Bibliography

[Bec02]   Kent Beck. *Test-Driven Development: By Example*. Addison-Wesley, Boston, MA, 2002.

[HT03]   Andy Hunt and Dave Thomas. *Pragmatic Unit Testing in Java with JUnit (out of print)*. The Pragmatic Bookshelf, Dallas, TX, 2003.

[LN17]   Diana Larsen and Ainsley Nies. *Liftoff, Second Edition (audio book)*. The Pragmatic Bookshelf, Dallas, TX, 2017.

[Mar08]   Robert C. Martin. *Clean Code: A Handbook of Agile Software Craftsmanship*. Prentice Hall, Englewood Cliffs, NJ, 2008.

Index

Thank you!

We hope you enjoyed this book and that you're already thinking about what you want to learn next. To help make that decision easier, we're offering you this gift.

Head on over to https://pragprog.com right now, and use the coupon code BUYANOTHER2024 to save 30% on your next ebook. Offer is void where prohibited or restricted. This offer does not apply to any edition of *The Pragmatic Programmer* ebook.

And if you'd like to share your own expertise with the world, why not propose a writing idea to us? After all, many of our best authors started off as our readers, just like you. With up to a 50% royalty, world-class editorial services, and a name you trust, there's nothing to lose. Visit https://pragprog.com/become-an-author/ today to learn more and to get started.

Thank you for your continued support. We hope to hear from you again soon!

The Pragmatic Bookshelf

SAVE 30%!
Use coupon code
BUYANOTHER2024

Functional Programming in Java, Second Edition

Imagine writing Java code that reads like the problem statement, code that's highly expressive, concise, easy to read and modify, and has reduced complexity. With the functional programming capabilities in Java, that's not a fantasy. This book will guide you from the familiar imperative style through the practical aspects of functional programming, using plenty of examples. Apply the techniques you learn to turn highly complex imperative code into elegant and easy-to-understand functional-style code. Updated to the latest version of Java, this edition has four new chapters on error handling, refactoring to functional style, transforming data, and idioms of functional programming.

Venkat Subramaniam
(274 pages) ISBN: 9781680509793. $53.95
https://pragprog.com/book/vsjava2e

Java by Comparison

Improve your coding skills by comparing your code to that of expert programmers so you can write code that's clean, concise, and to the point: code that others will read with pleasure and reuse. Get hands-on advice to level up your coding style through small and understandable examples that compare flawed code to an improved solution. Discover handy tips and tricks, as well as common bugs an experienced Java programmer needs to know. Make your way from a Java novice to a master craftsman.

Simon Harrer, Jörg Lenhard, Linus Dietz
(206 pages) ISBN: 9781680502879. $40.95
https://pragprog.com/book/javacomp

Automate Your Home Using Go

Take control of your home and your data with the power of the Go programming language. Build extraordinary and robust home automation solutions that rival much more expensive, closed commercial alternatives, using the same tools found in high-end enterprise computing environments. Best-selling Pragmatic Bookshelf authors Ricardo Gerardi and Mike Riley show how you can use inexpensive Raspberry Pi hardware and excellent, open source Go-based software tools like Prometheus and Grafana to create your own personal data center. Using the step-by-step examples in the book, build useful home automation projects that you can use as a blueprint for your own custom projects.

Ricardo Gerardi and Mike Riley
(160 pages) ISBN: 9798888650509. $40.95
https://pragprog.com/book/gohome

Small, Sharp Software Tools

The command-line interface is making a comeback. That's because developers know that all the best features of your operating system are hidden behind a user interface designed to help average people use the computer. But you're not the average user, and the CLI is the most efficient way to get work done fast. Turn tedious chores into quick tasks: read and write files, manage complex directory hierarchies, perform network diagnostics, download files, work with APIs, and combine individual programs to create your own workflows. Put down that mouse, open the CLI, and take control of your software development environment.

Brian P. Hogan
(326 pages) ISBN: 9781680502961. $38.95
https://pragprog.com/book/bhcldev

Seven Obscure Languages in Seven Weeks

Explore seven older computer languages and discover new and fresh ideas that will change the way you think about programming. These languages were invented before we settled into our current C-style syntax and OO biases, so language designers were free to imagine what was possible. You'll find their insights thought-provoking, and their ideas will inspire you to try different (and possibly more productive) ways of programming. From a text manipulation language where every line is a potential state machine event, to a concurrent language where everything is done using actors, you're sure to come away from these seven languages inspired and excited.

Dmitry Zinoviev
(270 pages) ISBN: 9798888650639. $55.95
https://pragprog.com/book/dzseven

Test-Driven React, Second Edition

Turn your React project requirements into tests and get the feedback you need faster than ever before. Combine the power of testing, linting, and typechecking directly in your coding environment to iterate on React components quickly and fearlessly!

Trevor Burnham
(172 pages) ISBN: 9798888650653. $45.95
https://pragprog.com/book/tbreact2

Become a Great Engineering Leader

As you step into senior engineering leadership roles, you need to make an impact, and you need to make it fast. This book will uncover the secrets of what it means to be a successful director of engineering, VP of engineering, or CTO. With a hands-on, practical approach, it will help you understand and develop the skills that you need, ranging from how to manage other managers, to how to define and execute strategy, how to manage yourself and your limited time, and how to navigate your own career journey to your desired destination.

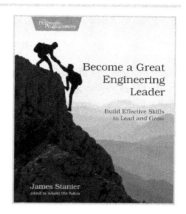

James Stanier
(400 pages) ISBN: 9798888650660. $64.95
https://pragprog.com/book/jsenglb

Machine Learning in Elixir

Stable Diffusion, ChatGPT, Whisper—these are just a few examples of incredible applications powered by developments in machine learning. Despite the ubiquity of machine learning applications running in production, there are only a few viable language choices for data science and machine learning tasks. Elixir's Nx project seeks to change that. With Nx, you can leverage the power of machine learning in your applications, using the battle-tested Erlang VM in a pragmatic language like Elixir. In this book, you'll learn how to leverage Elixir and the Nx ecosystem to solve real-world problems in computer vision, natural language processing, and more.

Sean Moriarity
(372 pages) ISBN: 9798888650349. $61.95
https://pragprog.com/book/smelixir

The Pragmatic Bookshelf

The Pragmatic Bookshelf features books written by professional developers for professional developers. The titles continue the well-known Pragmatic Programmer style and continue to garner awards and rave reviews. As development gets more and more difficult, the Pragmatic Programmers will be there with more titles and products to help you stay on top of your game.

Visit Us Online

This Book's Home Page
https://pragprog.com/book/utj3
Source code from this book, errata, and other resources. Come give us feedback, too!

Keep Up-to-Date
https://pragprog.com
Join our announcement mailing list (low volume) or follow us on Twitter @pragprog for new titles, sales, coupons, hot tips, and more.

New and Noteworthy
https://pragprog.com/news
Check out the latest Pragmatic developments, new titles, and other offerings.

Save on the ebook

Save on the ebook versions of this title. Owning the paper version of this book entitles you to purchase the electronic versions at a terrific discount.

PDFs are great for carrying around on your laptop—they are hyperlinked, have color, and are fully searchable. Most titles are also available for the iPhone and iPod touch, Amazon Kindle, and other popular e-book readers.

Send a copy of your receipt to support@pragprog.com and we'll provide you with a discount coupon.

Contact Us

Online Orders:	*https://pragprog.com/catalog*
Customer Service:	*support@pragprog.com*
International Rights:	*translations@pragprog.com*
Academic Use:	*academic@pragprog.com*
Write for Us:	*http://write-for-us.pragprog.com*

www.ingramcontent.com/pod-product-compliance
Lightning Source LLC
LaVergne TN
LVHW081336050326
832903LV00024B/1168